Bed, Breakfast & Bike Northern California

A Cycling Guide
To Country Inns

by Naomi Bloom

*Bob -
Hope you get to do all
of these miles !
Yours,
Naomi*

White Meadow Press
*P.O. Box 56
Boonton, NJ 07005*

Cover art by Karen Strattner. Illustrations in the book courtesy of the innkeepers.

Maps: Gayle Rembold-Furbert, Dan Goldfischer

CONTENTS

PREFACE

There was a time when I would encounter bicycle tourists on the road and say to myself, "I could never do that." How would I ever figure out which roads to ride? Or camp out in strange surroundings? But then I discovered that I could "camp out" at country inns, and a whole new mode of travel opened up to me.

I'm not alone, either. Cycling vacations based at country inns have become tremendously popular. Witness the success of outfitters like Backroads Bicycle Tours who draw thousands of paying customers to such trips each year. Now, with this book, you can set up your own inn-based bike tour, and discover, as I did, the joys of exercise in the fresh air combined with the relaxed, friendly atmosphere of B&Bs.

Bicycling is an invigorating way to go sightseeing. On a bike you can take in so much more than you ever thought was there to see, touch, taste and feel. Impersonal motels and "rough-it" campgrounds pale by comparison to staying at a B&B; instead of TV, telephone and sterile sameness, you get quiet gardens, beautiful scenery, and fascinating collections of antiques.

This is the third Bed, Breakfast & Bike guide published by White Meadow Press, and the first that I have had the privilege of writing. I was a guest at each inn featured in this book and would not hesitate to recommend each one to cyclists as a "base camp." Northern California has hundreds more bed-and-breakfast inns like these from which cyclists can ride out to interesting destinations. (Suggestions for future editions are indeed welcome.)

When choosing the bike routes, I consulted the innkeepers, local bike shops and clubs, and fellow cyclists who had ridden in the area. Occasionally I was able to adapt a century route that passed by or near the inn.

I greatly enjoyed preparing this book and hope that you will find these rides and inns as rewarding as I have.

Naomi Bloom
Cupertino, California
December 1993

ACKNOWLEDGMENTS

Good bike rides don't leap to the mind in a fit of divine inspiration. They are passed along from rider to rider, club to club, tour leader and century planner to paid customer or guest. The following individuals and organizations introduced me to routes or inns, offered suggestions, and/or accompanied me on rides, and I thank them profusely for their input.

Marcia Ackerman
Almaden Cycle Touring Club
Almanor Wheelpeople
Amador County Bike Club
Backroads Bicycle Tours
Mark Bohrer
Randall Braun
Joan Brohmer
Jean Dresden
Eagle Cycling Club
Chuck Elliot & Lisa Jo Sedlacek
Alan Forkosh
Barrie & Kathy Freeman
Keith Giles
Global Cyclists Exchange
Chuck Guzis
Kay Johnson
Scott Kelly
Frank Klotz
Karl Kneip
Andy Kirk
Richard Krebs
Brad Kurtz
Simon Lowings
Carol Means

Leo Moll
Napa Bicycle Club
Ron Nowell
Carol O'Hare
Sue & Marty Powell
Leif Rasmussen
Kathy Reese
Steve Richardson
Santa Cruz County Cycling Club
Santa Rosa Cycling Club
Skyline Cycling Club
Robert Sottardi
Larry Stafford
Susan Stecklair
Leslie Train
Ken Torbert
Hy Tran
Anne Virtue
Bob Ward
Ken Wells
Western Wheelers Bicycle Club
Fred Westphal
John Wilson

And an enormous thank you to Christine Gebhard for sending me that ad she spotted in *Bicycle USA*.

HOW TO USE THIS BOOK

Bed, *Breakfast & Bike/N orthern California* is divided into seven main sections (plus a section of recipes from the inns). Each section represents a different geographic region of Northern California. (These regions are drawn rather arbitrarily, based on cultural and/or scenic "boundaries," rather than political ones.) The regions appear in the book in alphabetical order, and the inns featured for each region also come in alphabetical order.

Each chapter contains a description of the inn and the experience of staying there as a guest. The chapter headings include basic information that will help you make a decision about staying there yourself and making a reservation to do so: address, phone number, 1993 rates, type of breakfast served, smoking policy, and a short description of the inn's ambience. Here is an example of the first inn that shows how these features are listed.

AMERICAN RIVER INN

Will and Maria Collin
P.O. Box 43
Georgetown, CA 95634
800-245-6566; 916-333-4499
Ambience: Antique Victorian

Rates: $85-$105
Bed & Breakfast Inn
Full breakfast
Smoking outdoors only

Rates Rather than set up arbitrary rate categories that can be misleading when those rates are raised, I have chosen to quote each inn's range of rates, from the least expensive single to the most expensive double or larger. Just remember that these are 1993 rates and adjust your expectations accordingly. You may be pleasantly surprised to find that many rates have not changed at all!

Type of inn "Bed & Breakfast" indicates small establishments, usually with six or fewer rooms, most of which impart the feeling a family home more than a hostelry. "Bed & Breakfast Inn" indicates larger B&Bs where the number of guests necessitates a more organized, systematic way of doing things. "EP" stands for European Plan, where no meals are included but a restaurant serves all meals for additional cost. "Housekeeping" refers to furnished cabins for rent where guests can cook their own meals.

Breakfast The vast majority of the inns in this book provide guests with a full breakfast, more than adequate to fuel a morning of cycling. A few serve an "expanded Continental" breakfast, which is often just as filling as a full breakfast. There is one inn on the European plan, where you pay for all your meals in the dining room separately. Of the two resorts featured, one offers a choice of breakfast included, European plan or housekeeping cabins, while the other, a mountain bike school, includes all meals in the flat weekly fee.

Ambience Some country inns are elaborately decorated with fine antiques and a great deal of Victorian gingerbread, others are more elegantly appointed with simple decor, and still others can be downright funky. While many inn guests relish the more elaborate atmosphere, others prefer something less extreme. Since Northern California offers a broad range to choose from, the "ambience" category attempts to give readers an overall impression of what to expect in this vein.

CYCLING FROM THE INNS

For each inn, the author researched at least two bike routes, creating detailed cue sheets and a map of each. Some of these routes are on rough roads, although when the pavement disappears completely, mountain bikes are recommended. In addition, it was not always possible to avoid heavy traffic. The primary concern was to find scenic vistas, points of interest and fun destinations.

The cycling section for each inn contains information on the **Terrain**, particularly which rides have steep climbs and if they are avoidable. The **Road Conditions** section describes surfaces and whether or not to expect room to ride on the shoulders. **Traffic** warns riders about congested areas and tells them about roads that are so remote, the livestock actually takes interest in a passing bicycle! **Nearest Bike Shop** might be helpful if you left your spare tube at home or suddenly need a repair beyond your capabilities.

Best Time To Ride points out the months that offer the best weather, scenic highlights or events in the area. **Mountain Biking Opportunities** is a short description of local or nearby parks, preserves or forests where offroad cycling is allowed. The **Rides** section describes each ride featured, including points of interest along the way.

CUE SHEETS

Reading these point-to-point directions is relatively straightforward. From left to right, the columns are headed:

Pt.-to-Pt. for distance between turns, towns, summits or points of interest. Note that distances for offroad rides are often approximations, owing to inaccurate or simply nonexistent odometers.

Cume for overall distance accumulated to that point.

Direction, or which way to turn at that point.

Abbreviations in the Direction column represent:

L	Left
R	Right
S	Straight
C	Continue (similar to straight)
BL	Bear Left
BR	Bear Right
IL	Immediate Left
IR	Immediate Right
SL	Sharp Left
SR	Sharp Right
U	U-turn or turnaround point
X	Cross

Street/Landmark gives the name of the street to turn on, or the landmark, town or summit reached, and is printed in **boldface**, while side or cross streets and other useful information, such as the presence of a grocery store or restroom, are in plain type. "At T" in the description indicates an intersection where the road does not continue but forces either a left or right turn; "at Y" indicates a fork intersection that splits one road into two. Important cautions such as an unusually steep hill or busy street are noted in *italic*.

MAPS

Maps are intended to give the reader a general outline of the routes. Many show potential shortcuts as well. As the maps are just a general outline (and not exactly to scale), use the cue sheets to follow each route turn-by-turn.

Most of the maps are based on maps from the California State Automobile Association. Wherever possible, however, maps expressly created for cycling were used. Detail maps of town centers are often provided where space permits. Incline is indicated by triangles pointing uphill (similar to those on Michelin maps). One triangle = 4% to 6% grade, 2 triangles = 7% to 8%, and 3 triangles = 9+%.

It is a good idea to carry a local map with you whenever you ride. The best are the bicycle touring maps from Krebs Cycle Products, available at most local bike shops and limited to the greater Monterey Bay Area and San Francisco Bay Area (including Wine Country). Innkeepers can often provide you with local maps highlighting points of interest and good restaurants.

BEFORE YOU GO

With the ride descriptions, cue sheets and maps collected in this book, any cyclist, or group of cyclists, can set up a self-guided bicycle tour from an inn, or several inns, in any of seven regions in Northern California. The problems of where to ride and which roads to take have already been solved for you.

However, there are other preparations to make before taking off on any bike tour. If you intend to do rides of 40 miles or more on consecutive days, knowing ahead of time that you have built up the strength, stamina and skill to do so goes a long way toward self-assurance on the road.

Training Individuals who do not consider themselves avid cyclists but are in good aerobic shape from running, swimming or working out at the gym need only build a little specialization into their routines to meet the physical readiness requirements of touring. A 20- to 30-mile ride at least once a week (preferably twice) during the month prior to your trip will probably suffice.

However, if you are unaccustomed to vigorous exercise, you should work up to it more gradually. If you are in otherwise good physical health (you may want to consult your doctor on this), start riding regularly two to three months before you go. Begin with short rides of ten miles or less and work your way up to a target distance in increments of 10%. You might choose to join a bike club; the members will be delighted to "show you the ropes" and you'll have plenty of company on your training rides.

The bike Don't neglect the condition of your bicycle, either. Take it in for a safety check: make sure the brakes and derailleurs are adjusted properly, the tires have good tread, and the headset and bottom bracket are in good shape. If you have never fixed a flat tire, now is the time to learn how, before you need to. And never ride anywhere without a pump, at least one spare inner tube, and a patch kit (check the glue to make sure it hasn't dried up).

If you are just starting out in cycling, or just getting back to it after a long break, make sure your bike fits you properly. Since most bicycles are designed for the average man's physique, fit is more likely to be a problem for short women. However, anyone who rides a bike that is too large or too small, too long or too short, risks stress injury.

On the bike Weather can have a debilitating effect on your conditioning. If rain threatens, carry a waterproof jacket. If the temperature drops below 65 degrees (60 degrees when it's sunny), cover your knees or your entire legs with tights or lightweight pants. This is especially important if you suffer from knee stress or pain. Wear UV-screened sunglasses to ward off not only the effects of the sun's rays, but also the drying, tearing effects of the wind.

A major health hazard for cyclists, especially in the hot, dry California summer climate, is dehydration. Carry water at all times and take sips regularly. To avoid the bonk (i.e., complete depletion of fuel) the rule is: "Eat before you're hungry; drink before you're thirsty."

Safety The California Vehicle Code clearly states that bicyclists on the road have the same rights and responsibilities as motorists. This means stopping for red lights and stop signs, yielding right of way, and in general operating your "vehicle" in a safe manner. Ride to the right, within designated bike lanes or the shoulder if feasible. You may leave the shoulder to avoid debris or hazards, to pass a slow or standing vehicle, or to make a left turn. When you do so, signal your intention to others. When riding in a group, call out and/or point to hazards and approaching vehicles.

Off the road, remember that you are sharing the trail with equestrians and hikers. Control your speed on descents, especially when there are blind turns. Announce your presence quietly to horse and rider and ask for permission to pass. Some horses are easily spooked by the sight of a human being on a bicycle. Smile and wish your fellow trail denizens a nice day—we can use the good PR. And for goodness sake, whatever you take in with you, take it back out!

The best piece of advice any bicyclist can get, however, is to wear an ANSI- or SNELL-approved helmet. Beginning in 1994, all cyclists in California under the age of 18 MUST wear a helmet; it's the law. Discussions of head injuries suffered by cyclists who don't wear helmets are simply too frightful to attempt in this book.

Take these precautions and you will find cycling to be a safe, healthy activity. The aerobic and cardiovascular benefits (not to mention the ability to eat like a horse and not gain weight) are legion. And there's nothing quite as invigorating as getting there under your own power!

BICYCLE VACATIONING IN NORTHERN CALIFORNIA

"We live in paradise." I've no idea how often I've repeated that phrase to fellow cyclists in Northern California. There are so many good country roads connecting so many scenic, cultural, historic and downright interesting places to visit on a bicycle, it's hard for newcomers and visitors to grasp at first.

Of course, any traveler is going to encounter congested urban areas in Northern California, just as one would "back East" (which out here means anywhere east of the Great Basin deserts). But Northern California is not all freeways, cable cars, or the tilt-up architecture of Silicon Valley. In spite of a certain amount of suburban sprawl, it's often just a few short cycling miles to bucolic ranchlands, towering redwoods or majestic seacliffs.

All this and a climate that rarely exhibits rainfall between June and October (except for the Alpine climate of the High Sierras, where summer thunderstorms are part of the tourist experience). Even during spring and fall, temperatures rarely fall below the sixties, and many winter days are just as warm and rain-free. Paradise, indeed.

With this book as a guide, vacationing cyclists can select a region in Northern California, lift their bikes onto the car rack, and drive to a bed-and-breakfast inn. Maps and cue sheets for over 70 rides, covering nearly 2600 miles, provide all the information for an enjoyable two to three days of cycling from each of the B&Bs in this book.

I must admit to a few prejudices about this paradise that are reflected in this book. One is that there is precious little of interest where the terrain is flat. Thus there are no rides or inns in the Central Valley, although there are some on coastal plains and in high mountain valleys that offer enjoyable flat terrain. Most of the rides, however, feature uphill climbs. Some of these ascents can offer a real challenge to any rider, while others can be classified as gently rolling. The reward for such effort, lest we forget, is usually a breathtaking view, followed by a sweeping descent.

Another personal prejudice is that it is hardly worth mounting a bike on a rack and driving to these destinations for rides of less than 30 miles. Even if I did not take this attitude, distances between outposts of civilization in the West are often vast compared to those on the Eastern seaboard. As a result, most of the rides in this book cover more than 36 miles, and some exceed 60.

The exceptions are mostly mountain bike rides. Mountain biking was invented in California over 20 years ago (my, how time flies!). Today there is hardly a road cyclist who does not own a fat, knobby-tired bike for exploring dirt roads and single-track trails on which cycling is not only allowed, but often encouraged. Riding these heftier machines on terrain that tends to vary from solid hardpack to slithery mud to shifting sand requires astonishing levels of energy. It is not unusual for a 25-mile off-road ride to be as physically demanding as a full century on pavement.

Looking for more miles and rides in these areas? Consult one of the books listed at the end of the introduction to each region. For more information about Northern California tourist attractions, bed-and-breakfast accommodations, transportation services and route planning, contact:

California Office of Tourism
P.O. Box 9278
Department A1003
Van Nuys, CA 91409
800-862-2543

Redwood Empire Association
785 Market Street. 15th Floor
San Francisco, CA 94103
415-543-8334

California State Parks
P.O. Box 942896
Sacramento, CA 94296
916-445-6477

INN LOCATOR FOR MAP ON PAGE 16

Gold Country
1 American River Inn
2 Chichester-McKee House
3 Cooper House
4 Red Castle Inn
5 Wedgewood Inn
High Sierra Nevada
6 Chaney House
7 High Country Inn
8 Karen's Bed & Breakfast
9 Sorenson's Resort
Monterey Bay Area
10 Bed & Breakfast San Juan
11 Blue Spruce Inn
12 Fairview Manor
13 Gosby House Inn
North Coast
14 Gingerbread Mansion Inn
15 Highland Dell Inn
16 Pudding Creek Inn
17 Tomales Country Inn
San Francisco Bay Area
18 Bear Valley Inn
19 Dancing Coyote Beach
20 Rancho San Gregorio
21 Zaballa House
"Superior" California
22 Benbow Inn
23 The Bidwell House
24 The Feather Bed
25 Mount Shasta Ranch
26 Otter Bar Lodge
Wine Country
27 Hope-Merrill House
28 The Ink House
29 Thistle Dew Inn
30 The Webber Place

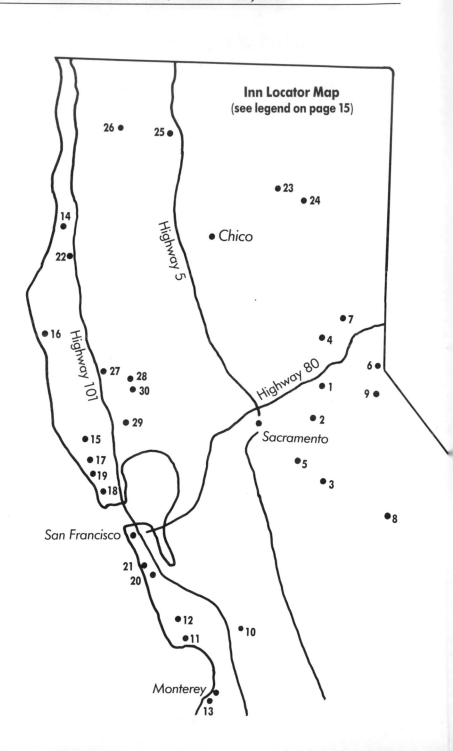

Inn Locator Map
(see legend on page 15)

GOLD COUNTRY INNS AND RIDES

There's hills in them thar hills! The California Gold Country, also frequently referred to as "The Mother Lode," spans nearly 200 miles of the western slope of the Sierra Nevada, from the low foothills to nearly 6,000 feet elevation. It is a region of rolling, grassy hills and big valleys, small ranches, colorful towns and villages, and a history enriched by legends of the Forty-Niners who flocked here for a piece of the wealth generated by the Great California Gold Rush.

A bicyclist can explore much of this history on roads originally built to serve the miners in remote areas where gold was discovered, then played out, often in a matter of months. In towns like Georgetown, Nevada City, Coloma and Columbia many Gold Rush era buildings are still standing, most preserved within state historic parks. State Highway 49 winds through most of these towns. Unfortunately, most of the highway is narrow, twisting and filled with heavy traffic, making it unsuitable for cycling.

Spring is the best time to ride here, when the rains and snows of the past winter have turned the hills bright green, with wildflowers splashing purple, yellow, white, and orange across them. Summer days can be extremely hot. Autumn, especially mid-October, brings fall colors and cool temperatures. During winter snow often falls in towns as low as Georgetown and Jackson.

Cycling at high altitude, such as encountered around Nevada City and Placerville, can easily exhaust "flatland" cyclists who are not accustomed to it. You can take precautions: Drink extra liquids to avoid dehydration in the dryer air. Apply plenty of sunscreen to ward off the stronger ultraviolet rays. And spend at least the first day or two taking it easy to allow your cardiovascular system to acclimate to the lower atmospheric pressure.

One of the most delightful aspects of the Gold Country experience is the character of the bed-and-breakfast inns that dot the landscape. All the innkeepers seem bent on preserving the history and architecture of their respective inns, many of which are prominent landmarks in their communities' heritage.

The **American River Inn** in Georgetown served as a hotel, rooming house, sanitarium and private residence during the Gold Rush. Will and Maria Collin have added their own special touches to the elegant Victorian atmosphere, including a swimming pool, spa, putting green and aviary.

Chichester-McKee House has the honor of being the first house in Placerville built with indoor plumbing! Bill and Doreen Thornhill are only the fourth owners of this handsome Victorian, which looks much as it did over a century ago.

Cooper House in Angels Camp dates to 1911, when Dr. Cooper built it for both his family and his practice. It's just up the hill from the site of the Annual Jumping Frog Jubilee, inspired by Mark Twain's story of mining days in Calaveras County. A stay here combines the recent history of Craftsman design with Forty-Niner lore and fine wineries.

A lovingly restored Gothic Revival Victorian, **The Red Castle Inn** was built in 1860. Perched atop a prominent hilltop, it gives guests an unparalleled view of Nevada City's historic district, not to mention the finish line of the racecourse for the Tour of Nevada City, the criterium Greg Lemond cut his teeth on in the early '80s.

A departure from all this regional history, **Wedgewood Inn** is a Victorian farmhouse built from scratch on 10 wooded acres just east of Jackson by Vic and Jeannine Beltz. It's a perfectly rural jumping-off place for exploring history old and new in the Volcano/Sutter Creek/Jackson area.

FOR MORE INFORMATION ABOUT GOLD COUNTRY BICYCLING:

California Dream Cycling with Bodfish by Chuck Elliot. Bodfish Books, P.O. Box 69, Chester, CA 96020.

Cyclist's Route Atlas, A Guide to The Gold Country & High Sierra/North and *Cyclist's Route Atlas, A Guide to The Gold Country & High Sierra/South* by Randall Gray Braun. Heyday Books, Box 9145, Berkeley, CA 94709.

Mountain Biking in the Northern Sierra, Volume One, The Crystal Basin by Bob Ward. Bobo Productions, P.O. Box 19815, Sacramento, CA 94819

Mountain Biking in the Northern Sierra, Volume Three: The Donner Burn and Points North by Bob and Ann Ward. Bobo Productions, address above.

AMERICAN RIVER INN

Will and Maria Collin
P.O. Box 43
Georgetown, CA 95634
800-245-6566; 916-333-4499
Ambience: Antique Victorian

Rates: $85-$105
Bed & Breakfast Inn
Full breakfast
Smoking outdoors only

Georgetown sits placidly at the top of a prominent ridge—the "Georgetown Divide"—some 2,000 feet above the surrounding countryside. So there's no getting around it: no matter which direction you choose to ride, you must descend on the way out, and climb to return.

Main Street Georgetown consists of the Post Office, Odd Fellows Hall (dating back to 1859), Civil War Armory (1867), general store, and the American River Inn at the corner of Main and Orleans at the east end of town. A sign at the front, placed by Native Daughters Parlor 186, reads:

The American Hotel Built in 1863
Served as - Hotel, Rooming House,
Sanitarium & Private residence during mining era
Burned in 1897 fire, rebuilt in 1899

As B&Bs go, American River Inn is enormous, with eight rooms on three floors, plus the Annex out back with five more, and the Queen Anne Inn next door, a fine old Victorian which inkeepers Will and Maria Collin keep reserved for weddings, corporate meetings and other such private groups.

The grounds are extensive, too, with a swimming pool, spa, croquet court, putting green and dovecote scattered throughout the Victorian gardens. There's even a fleet of vintage coaster brake and old 10-speed bikes waiting for some adventuresome guests to hop on for a ride.

I was delighted to occupy Room #1 at the front of the inn, with windows on a balcony that overlooks Orleans Street. I had a large mirrored armoire to hang my jacket in and my choice of two THICK terry-cloth robes. The brass and porcelain "honeymoon" bed was piled invitingly high with a feather mattress and down comforter.

And when I picked up the handle of the antique telephone at the bedside, the lamp that crowned it turned on!

But the piece de resistance of this Victorian recreation was the bathroom. A huge clawfoot tub with brass feet was the perfect place to retire to after my long ride. There was also an old-fashioned "highboy" commode and a hand-painted dressing table with tiny "cubbyhole" drawers for milady's creams and rouges.

The rest of the rooms in the inn were similarly furnished. Most impressive were the "Library Suites" on the top floor, two magnificently decorated rooms joined by a library.

The public rooms mix the Victorian theme with an eclectic antique collection. An old "honest weight" scale sits in a corner of the downstairs restroom, which is accessible from the back porch. At the foot of the stairs is Maria's Boutique, filled with artifacts like hand-made birdhouses, antique Teddy Bears and more. The wares seem to spill out the door into the front hall and up the stairs, which provide comfortable seating for more Teddy Bears and Raggedy Ann dolls.

Plush Victorian furniture adorns the parlor, where you can choose an old-time radio tape to listen to in your room. "When was the last time you heard 'The Shadow?' " asks the sign above the tape collection. The parlor is also the scene of the 6:00 p.m. cocktail hour, with complimentary wine, cheese and canapes.

Here I met the only other guests during my early spring stay, an elderly couple from Texas accompanied by their two sons, both of whom live in San Francisco. The men of the family had just returned from a river rafting trip on the South Fork of the American River. Whitewater rafting is a popular recreational pursuit. If you'd like to give it a try, expect to spend an entire day off the bike. The nearest put-in place is between Georgetown and Auburn. The Collins will be happy to make reservations for you.

After wine and hors d'oeuvres, we all repaired to the Georgetown Grille, one of the two choices in town for dinner (the other, the Mexican restaurant in the Georgetown Inn, is closed on Wednesdays).

The menu in the American River Inn dining room the next morning included fruit and yogurt, followed by more fresh fruit, 95% fat-free ham (Will drives to Sacramento to procure such healthy ingredients), quiche Lorraine and fresh-baked blueberry muffins. Seconds are established routine and required if you're planning to tackle any ride involving a climb back up to Georgetown.

BIKING FROM AMERICAN RIVER INN

Terrain Like the rest of the Mother Lode Country, the region of the Georgetown Divide is riddled with hills. Georgetown itself sits at 2800 feet elevation, while the surrounding beds of the North Fork and South Fork of the American River are at only 800' and 700' respectively. The result is a great downhill on Marshall Grade and Prospectors Road, a grinding climb back up on Highway 193.

Road Conditions Highway 49 displays its usual lack of amenities for bicyclists, but there is a good shoulder between Pilot Hill and Cool. Highway 193 has a somewhat rough surface with no shoulder at all. All roads, whether state highways or county backroads, are amazingly clean and free of debris. When I remarked on this fact, innkeeper Will Collin responded with, "You throw a bottle out here, you get shot!"

Traffic Heavy traffic is at a premium in the Georgetown Divide region. The most prevalent vehicles I encountered on a spring weekday were school buses. Highway 193 (of the nonexistent shoulder) gets a good deal of use, but the drivers are friendly. Highway

49 between Coloma and Cool, on the other hand, was all but empty.

Nearest Bike Shop
Terry's All-Cycle
Main Street
Georgetown
Right across the street from American River Inn—minor repairs and parts replacements only

Best Time To Ride April through mid-May

Mountain Biking Opportunities Rock Creek Recreational Trails Area is just four miles east of the American River Inn off Wentworth Springs Road. Although it's billed as "multi-use," it's extremely popular with dirt motorbikers. Still, with 85 miles of trails, there's plenty of opportunity to share. The Darling Ridge section, to the south of Georgetown, is closed from November to May 1 to protect the Pacific Deer Herd. Pick up a map from the Ranger Station on Wentworth Springs Road, about 2.5 miles before the Rock Creek trailhead.

GREENWOOD LOOP (19.8 MILES)

This is the ideal leisurely country tour. The settlement of Greenwood is downright idyllic, there's food available at the Garden Valley Store, and there's abundant shade on Marshall Grade Road for the climb back up the divide.

MARSHALL GOLD DISCOVERY PARK (38.2 MILES)

James Marshall was the foreman of Sutter's Mill, the birthplace of the California Gold Rush. Today a replica of the mill is the centerpiece of the Marshall Gold Discovery State Historic Park in Coloma, ten mostly downhill miles from Georgetown. The park surrounds a one-mile section of Highway 49 with restored buildings, streets and, up a side street, Marshall's own cabin. If you're a history buff, you'll want to spend some time here before you head back up the divide.

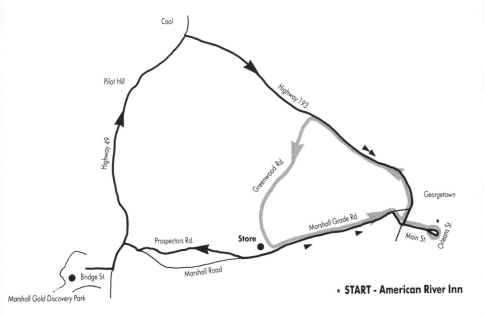

American River Inn

Greenwood Loop — 19.8 Miles

Marshall Gold Discovery Park — 38.2 Miles

GREENWOOD LOOP

PT.-PT.	CUME	DIRECTION	STREET/LANDMARK
			From American River Inn's Historic Sign
0.0	0.0	R	**Main Street**
0.3	0.3	R	**Highway 193**
10.1	10.4	L	**Greenwood Road**. Historic plaque and fire bell on right
5.0	15.4	L	**Marshall Grade Road**. Garden Valley Store on left
4.0	19.4	R	**Main Street**. Georgetown Store on left, market on right
0.3	19.7	U	At American River Inn
0.1	19.8	R	**Orleans Street/American River Inn**

MARSHALL GOLD DISCOVERY PARK

PT.-PT.	CUME	DIRECTION	STREET/LANDMARK
			From American River Inn's Historic Sign
0.0	0.0	R	**Main Street**
0.3	0.3	L	**Marshall Grade Road**. Garden Valley Store on right, just beyond Greenwood Road
6.0	6.3	R	**Prospectors Road**. Sierra views on right
3.0	9.3	R	**Marshall Road**
0.2	9.5	L	**Highway 49**. Deli with outdoor seating across the street
0.5	10.0		Picnic area on left — restrooms
0.5	10.5	R	**Bridge Street** to Visitors Center. Sutter's Mill Replica on left, across Highway 49. Continue down Highway 49 for Beer Garden Picnic Area on right, "Refreshment Saloon" on left
0.0	10.5	L	**Highway 49**
8.0	18.5		**Pilot Hill** — no services Grange Hall landmark on left

MARSHALL GOLD DISCOVERY PARK (CONT.)

PT.-PT.	CUME	DIRECTION	STREET/LANDMARK
3.3	21.8	**R**	**Highway 193**. Deli and general store on left in Cool, 0.2 miles beyond 193 on Highway 49
7.0	28.8	**R**	**Greenwood Road**. Historic plaque and fire bell on right
5.0	33.8	**L**	**Marshall Grade Road**. Garden Valley Store on left
4.0	37.8	**R**	**Main Street**. Georgetown Store on left, market on right
0.3	38.1	**U**	At American River Inn
0.1	38.2	**R**	**Orleans Street/American River Inn**

CHICHESTER-MCKEE HOUSE

Bill and Doreen Thornhill
800 Spring Street   Rates: $75-$85
Placerville, CA 95667   Bed & Breakfast
800-831-4008; 916-626-1882   Full breakfast
Ambience: Unpretentious Victorian   Smoking outdoors only

Placerville began as Dry Diggins, one of the first permanent mining camps of the California Gold Rush. After a couple of lynchings took place in the middle of town, the name changed to Hangtown. But it wasn't long before the local citizens decided to improve their image, and Placerville has been the name since the mid-1850s.

Not a few historical buildings remain in Placerville, including two or three on narrow, twisting Main Street, which has apparently been widened only once, to accommodate those newfangled motor cars early in this century.

Just a short walk from Main Street, across U.S. Highway 50 and up the hill a piece, stands the big yellow Victorian house Daniel Chichester built for his bride 101 years ago. A B&B since 1983, Chichester House was renamed Chichester-McKee in 1992 at its centennial celebration. The present owners, Doreen and Bill Thornhill, wanted to honor the name of the family that occupied the house directly after the Chichesters left and for the next 64 years.

Quite likely the first house in Placerville to have indoor plumbing, Chichester-McKee has undergone surprisingly few changes in its lifetime. Mrs. McKee disliked the boxy Victorian look, so she added an Italianate porch. One of the original chimneys now sits in a corner of the yard, a pedestal for a bird feeder. The fireplace in the front parlor has been replaced with one from the old Barbary Coast Hotel in San Francisco, although the library fireplace still has its original redwood mantel. Mr. McKee's wool gabardine and Italian broadcloth topcoat still hangs on the upstairs landing.

The kitchen is the first room guests get to know. That's where, upon arrival, they are urged to sample Doreen's Special Caramel Brownies with a cold drink or coffee. Doreen showed me where a water tank once stood behind the wood stove, providing the family with running hot water all year long. Although both kitchen and plumbing have been updated, the upstairs bath still has the origi-

nal pedestal sink (refinished) and clawfoot tub (now the home of a friendly rubber ducky).

The library is stacked with games, puzzles and books. In the dining room you can examine an impressive teacup collection, while the parlor holds Doreen's collection of Story Book Dolls and a couple of antique record machines. Then there's the conservatory, complete with the original tin floor, full of growing things and, soon after I visited, a new water fountain.

The walls in the halls and downstairs rooms capture the imagination. Attractions include a "bird's eye view" of Placerville in 1888 (before the house was built), a pre-1900 photo of the house, and several paintings by local artist Thomas Kinkade, best known for his "Victorian Christmas" series. Doreen was quite pleased that Kinkade had recently painted Chichester-McKee House and was displaying it in his gallery.

Upstairs, three guest rooms impart a Victorian atomsphere without the usual "gingerbread" and chintz. The Yellow Rose Room offers the most in romance, with its canopy bed and heart-shaped pillows. Doreen showed me where the chimney flue prevented expansion of the half bath, so the last owners installed a stainless steel pull-down Pullman sink above the toilet!

My room was the Carson Room, named for the last owners. The queen brass bed was covered with a Mennonite Lone Star quilt. "Mrs. Rabbit" lay on the pillows, while an antique nightcap and straw bonnet hung from each side of the headboard. An antique combined washstand/dresser on one wall contained sachets, a flashlight, magazines and—surprise!—a chamber pot (guess that first-generation plumbing failed occasionally).

The wood floor was covered with an oriental rug, the windows with fringed shades and antique lace curtains. Inside the armoire was a robe for trips to the shared bath, and an antique corset for unnamed purposes. A half bath contained a modern toilet and sink with a beveled mirror and magnified shaving mirror. In the shared bath I found a large basket of "goodies", from shampoo and bubble bath in a wine bottle to hair dryer and curling iron.

The unquestioned "lady" of the house is the Thornhills' dachsund, Heidi. She greets nearly each guest, tagging along up and down the indoor and outdoor stairways on house tours. And during breakfast she displays her skills in math, answering such questions as, "What's the square root of 25?"

"We have to teach her a new number to answer 'How old are you?' " Doreen said. "Once she reaches ten this year, that's as far as we're going to go."

Also at breakfast, served by candlelight, my fellow guests Alan and Joan from North Carolina and I sampled oatmeal-chocolate chip coffee cake (see recipe section) with our coffee or tea. We'd started with juice and fresh fruit in a yogurt-cinnamon sauce. Then Doreen brought us individual servings of eggs Benedict. I had to have the apple cider as a fitting introduction to a ride through the Apple Hill region, the best reason for visiting Placerville in autumn.

BIKING FROM CHICHESTER-MCKEE HOUSE

Terrain The first thing you notice about Chichester-McKee is that there's no bike or auto access from Spring Street, which on this block alone is also California Highway 49. To park or ride in, you must climb some steep city blocks off Coloma Street, then plunge down the driveway to the private parking lot.

To be honest, the worst hills I climbed in the Placerville area were city streets. If you want to avoid these little "walls," you may prefer to drive out to Broadway, where you can park in the shopping areas, before you start your rides. You can also skip the little side trip to Gold Bug Mine, the return from which takes riders over some more steep streets.

Road Conditions Carson Road, which leads up into the Apple Hill area, is abominable: narrow and full of bumpy patches and potholes. Surprisingly, descending is easier than climbing it. Once you leave Carson Road, things ease up a bit, although all the Apple Hill roads, and most of the route to Newtown, are narrow with no shoulder. A pleasant break from all this is the paved 1.7-mile Smith Flat Bike Trail connecting Jacquier Road with Main Street and Broadway.

Traffic From early October through Halloween, Apple Hill is jampacked with tourists. Carson Road bears the brunt of this crush; once you leave it for the backroads, things lighten up. Weekends, of course, are the worst; even on Columbus Day Monday I encountered much less traffic than on the previous Sunday. Also, I'm given to understand that during November, traffic thins out appreciably, yet the Apple Hill farms are open until Thanksgiving.

Nearest Bike Shop
Placerville Bike Shop
1307 Broadway
Placerville, CA 95667
916-6220-3015

Best Time To Ride October-November for Apple Hill and fall colors, although the later in the season you ride, the colder and wetter the weather will be.

Mountain Biking Opportunities The Crystal Basin Recreation Area of the Eldorado National Forest begins about 20 miles or so east of Placerville on U.S. Highway 50. Most of the trailheads are on Ice House Road, which connects directly to Highway 50. This area has been extremely well documented for all kinds of mountain bike routes by Bob Ward in his book, *Mountain Biking in the Northern Sierra, Volume 1*. You'll find a copy in the library at Chichester-McKee House.

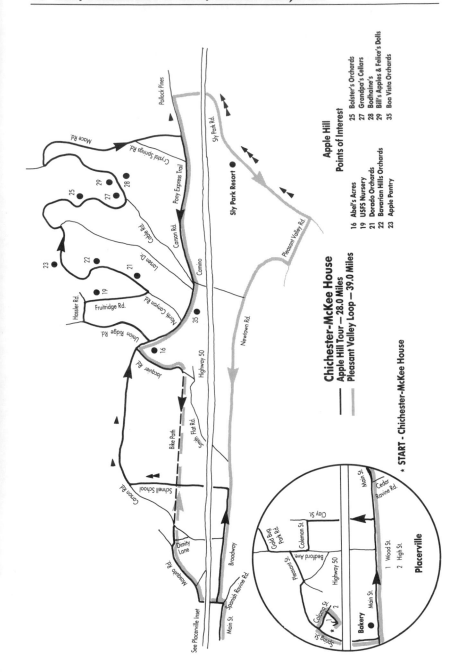

Apple Hill
Points of Interest

16 Abel's Acres	25 Bolster's Orchards
19 USFS Nursery	27 Grandpa's Cellars
21 Dorado Orchards	28 Bodhaine's
22 Bavarian Hills Orchards	29 Bill's Apples & Felice's Dolls
23 Apple Pantry	35 Boa Vista Orchards

Chichester-McKee House
— Apple Hill Tour — 28.0 Miles
— Pleasant Valley Loop — 39.0 Miles

★ START - Chichester-McKee House

APPLE HILL TOUR (28.0 MILES)

In the 1960s the fruit growers in the canyons east of Placerville were losing their shirts after a devastating pear blight. Determined to improve their lot, they put in apple orchards and devised a plan to market the apples directly to the public. The result is Apple Hill, a formal organization of ranches spread along some 20 miles of country roads north of Highway 50 and east of Placerville. Sure, you can buy apples by the bushel at these ranches. But you can also sample freshly pressed apple cider and delicious snacks and desserts. Several of the farms also invite artisans to set up craft booths on the weekends.

There are also pumpkin farms, Christmas tree farms, U-pick orchards and wineries on the Apple Hill tour. I've included only the most compelling apple stops along this route, but you may find you want to make more stops or choose others than I've featured. Bon appetit!

This short tour includes a side trip to Hangtown's Gold Bug Mine about a mile from town. Self-guided tours are available daily in summer and on weekends in spring and fall. It's worth the trip!

PLEASANT VALLEY LOOP (39.0 MILES)

Climb up through Apple Hill orchards all the way to the pine trees on the old route followed by the Pony Express. Then, drop 1600 feet in nine miles on Sly Park Road! The rest of the loop through Pleasant Valley and Newtown is rolling, and the whole thing is a fall fiesta of rural scenery and colors!

APPLE HILL TOUR

PT.-PT.	CUME	DIRECTION	STREET/LANDMARK
			From Chichester-McKee Parking Lot
0.0	0.0	**R**	**Wood Street**
		IL	**High Street**
0.1	0.1	**L**	**Coloma Street**
0.2	0.3	**L**	**Spring Street**
0.1	0.4	**X**	Highway 50
0.1	0.5	**C**	**Main Street**. Hangtown Bakery on left
0.7	1.2	**L**	**Main Street** at Cedar Ravine Road
0.6	1.8	**L**	**Main Street** at Spanish Ravine Road

APPLE HILL TOUR (CONT.)

PT.-PT.	CUME	DIRECTION	STREET/LANDMARK
		IR	**Broadway**
0.6	2.4	L	**Schnell School Road** (short, steep uphill)
0.3	2.7	R	**Carson Road**
2.4	5.1	L	**Union Ridge Road. Abel's Acres** at intersection—pony rides, bake shop
0.5	5.6	R	**Hassler Road**
0.7	6.3	R	**Fruitridge Road**
0.3	6.6		**USFS Nursery** on left — tours at 12:00 and 2:00 p.m.
0.6	7.2	L	**North Canyon Road**
0.2	7.4		**Dorado Orchards** on right — train ride, crafts
0.6	8.0		**Bavarian Hills Orchards** on right
0.9	8.9		**Apple Pantry** on left — tamales, bake shop, gift shop
2.3	11.2	L	**Larsen Drive**
1.1	12.3		**Bolster's Orchards** on left — picnic tables, crafts
0.3	12.6	L	**Cable Road**
0.1	12.7		**Grandpa's Cellars** on left; **Bodhaine's** on right — do not leave without trying the Blackberry-Apple-Sour Cream Pie!
0.2	12.9		**Bill's Apples and Felice's Dolls** on left
0.5	13.4	R	**Mace Road.** Follow the yellow line.
1.0	14.4	R	**Pony Express Trail**
1.4	15.8	R	**Carson Road** at stop sign
0.5	16.3		**Camino**—market, restaurant on left
3.0	19.3		**Boa Vista Orchards** on left — sandwiches, bakery, crafts
2.0	21.3	L	**Jacquier Road**
0.9	22.2	R	**Bike Path** at Smith Flat Road
1.7	23.9	R	**Dimity Lane** at T (no sign)
		IL	**Mosquito Road**
0.2	24.1	R	**Mosquito Road** at stop sign

APPLE HILL TOUR (CONT.)

PT.-PT.	CUME	DIRECTION	STREET/LANDMARK
0.1	24.2	**S**	**Main Street**
0.3	24.5	**R**	**Main Street** at Cedar Ravine Road
0.1	24.6	**R**	**Clay Street**
0.2	24.8	**L**	**Coleman Street** — *steep for one block!*
0.3	25.1	**R**	**Bedford Avenue**
0.1	25.6	**R**	**Bedford Avenue** at stop sign
0.6	26.2	**R**	**Gold Bug Park Road**
0.1	26.3		**Mine entrance** on right
0.0	26.3	**L**	**Gold Bug Park Road**
0.1	26.7	**L**	**Bedford Avenue**
0.6	27.3	**R**	**Pleasant Street**
0.1	27.4	**R**	**Spring Street**
0.3	27.7	**L**	**Coloma Street**
0.2	27.9	**R**	**High Street**
		IR	**Wood Street**
0.1	28.0	**L**	**Chichester-McKee** parking lot

PLEASANT VALLEY LOOP

PT.-PT.	CUME	DIRECTION	STREET/LANDMARK
			From Chichester-McKee parking lot
0.0	0.0	**R**	**Wood Street**
		IL	**High Street**
0.1	0.1	**L**	**Coloma Street**
0.2	0.3	**L**	**Spring Street**
0.1	0.4	**X**	Highway 50
0.1	0.5	**C**	**Main Street**
0.7	1.2	**L**	**Main Street** at Cedar Ravine Road
0.6	1.8	**L**	**Main Street** at Spanish Ravine Road
		S	**Mosquito Road**
0.1	1.9	**L**	**Mosquito Road** at freeway ramp
0.2	2.1	**R**	**Dimity Lane**
		IL	**Bike Path** to Smith Flat
1.7	3.8	**L**	**Jacquier Road**
0.9	4.7	**R**	**Carson Road**—Apple Hill farms
5.0	9.7		**Camino**—market, restaurant on right

PLEASANT VALLEY LOOP (CONT.)

PT.-PT.	CUME	DIRECTION	STREET/LANDMARK
0.7	10.4	L	**Pony Express Trail**
5.0	15.4		**Pollock Pines**—restaurants, delis
0.6	16.0	R	**Sly Park Road**
4.3	20.3		**Sly Park Resort** on right — grocery store, snack bar
7.2	27.5	R	**Pleasant Valley Road.** Market, pizza on left at junction
1.0	28.5	R	**Newtown Road**
6.1	34.6	C	**Broadway**
1.2	35.8		Bakery on left
0.7	36.5		Shopping Area — Togos, deli, McDonald's, markets
0.7	37.2	L	**Main Street**
0.6	37.8	R	**Main Street** at Cedar Ravine Road
0.3	38.1		Hangtown Bakery on right
0.4	38.5	X	Highway 50
0.1	38.6	C	**Spring Street/Highway 49**
0.1	38.7	R	**Coloma Street**
0.2	38.9	R	**High Street**
		IR	**Wood Street**
0.1	39.0	L	**Chichester-McKee** parking lot

COOPER HOUSE

Tom & Kathy Reese
1184 Church Street
Angels Camp, CA 95222
800-225-3764, Ext. 326; 209-736-2145
Ambience: Turn-of-the-Century Arts & Crafts

Rates: $90
Bed & Breakfast
Full Breakfast
No smoking

Angels Camp was the setting for Mark Twain's classic story, "The Celebrated Jumping Frog of Calavaras County." Every third week in May the Annual Jumping Frog Jubilee attempts to recreate the tale, along with the hurly-burly atmosphere of a gold rush mining town. But just a week later everything had returned to normal when I arrived at the top of Church Street for a stay at Cooper House.

Simplicity is the key to life at Cooper House, a refreshing contrast to the elegant Victorians I'd been visiting up and down the Mother Lode. The first bed-and-breakfast inn in Angels Camp, the house was built in 1911 by Dr. George Cooper to serve as both family home and medical clinic. Today it is a showpiece of turn-of-the-century Craftsman design.

The Craftsman, or Arts and Crafts, style gained favor in the first two decades of this century because it was a swing of the fashion pendulum from elaborate Victorian to stark form-follows-function. The style was faithfully restored at Cooper House by the Stevenot family, early settlers in Angels Camp and currently best known for their fine wines.

In 1992 Tom and Kathy Reese of Oakland bought Cooper House from the Stevenots, after first passing muster as proper neighbors for the elderly Stevenot matriarch next door.

The centerpiece of the living room is a mammoth fireplace built of local greenstone with three large quartz keystones under the mantel. The center keystone, Kathy told me, has a vein of gold running through it that can be seen when the sun shines on it through the opposite window. An Indian basket collection and original paintings by local colorful character Jay Booth complement the deep glow of the authentic Craftsman furniture.

I spent the night in the Cabernet Suite, a bedroom and sitting room which were once Dr. Cooper's examining and waiting rooms.

Each has two private entrances, one from a balcony in front of the house, the other from one-lane, one-way Church Street. Not only could I look out the window and see my car and bike on the roof rack, I could reach them in less than six seconds!

The simple decor in the Cabernet Suite carried through the turn-of-the-century ambience. My white cast iron queen-size bed shared space with a small chiffonier and an early American rocker. The sitting room was furnished with a love seat/sofa bed and an early American bench. A private bath with shower rounded out my personal domain.

Coffee and tea were waiting on the dining room sideboard early the next morning for me and the five motorcyclists occupying Zinfandel and Chardonnay (each with private bath) on their way to a Memorial Day rally hundreds of miles north. Kathy then served breakfast family style at Archie Stevenot's old dining table: a gigantic basket filled with bagels, muffins and croissants; home-fried red potatoes; a fruit plate of melons, kiwi, fresh pineapple and huge strawberries; a choice of cranberry or orange juice; and "Parmesan" eggs baked in individual crockery for each of us.

As the names of the suites indicate, Cooper House also reflects the Stevenot family's interest in creating fine wines. Stevenot Winery is the flagship of a plethora of premium winemakers in Calaveras County. Kathy treated me to a personal tasting of reds along with the plentiful complimentary cheeses, crackers, fresh veggies and dip she served in the late afternoon. I was quite impressed with both the warm and mellow Stevenot Merlot (a vintage no longer available, alas!) and the tangy, peppery Black Sheep Zinfandel.

BIKING FROM COOPER HOUSE

Terrain All the streets east of Main Street in Angels Camp are steep uphills! Church Street is one-way in the downhill direction. To reach Cooper House, which sits above the classic New England Congregational Church, climb Raspberry Lane on the south end of town, or take Bret Harte Road to Summit Road on the north.

Once you venture out of town, you'll find the rest of the terrain even more given to ups and downs. Parrots Ferry Road serves up some steep switchbacks climbing out of the Stanislaus River bed. Sheep Ranch Road features brutal grades on some of its more remote sections.

Road Conditions Highway 4/49 in Angels Camp is wide with a broad shoulder and good visibility. Once it turns east from 49, however, 4 drops the shoulder and narrows to two lanes. Parrots Ferry Road to Columbia is smoothly paved with a good shoulder except for a few nasty uphill switchbacks. The rugged backroads between Murphys and Altaville have many sections of rough pavement.

Traffic Traffic is heavy on Highway 49 and Parrots Ferry Road. (In 1992 logging trucks from post-forest fire clear cutting on Sheep Ranch Road were a constant factor on both.) All other roads are subject to tourist traffic in season, especially on weekends, but otherwise are peaceful and quiet.

Nearest Bike Shop
Mountain Pedaler
1219 S. Main Street (between Raspberry and Church)
Angels Camp, CA 95222
209-736-0771

Best Time To Ride Mid-April through May or mid-September through October (for the grape "crush")

Mountain Biking Opportunities Glory Hole Recreation Area, three miles south of Angels Camp on Highway 49, has over 12 miles of trails at the very edge of New Melones Reservoir. According to Rod Olson at the Mountain Pedaler, "It's easy to get lost in Glory Hole, and before you find your way again, you could do 20 miles." For maps (and some great off-road tall tales) visit Rod during business hours.

COLUMBIA TOUR (32.7 MILES)

Columbia enjoys a reputation as the best-preserved of the historic Mother Lode towns. A living history project smack-dab in the middle of a real community, its Main Street buildings house museum displays right alongside present-day banks, stores and restaurants. You can ride a stagecoach, pan for gold, set a spell at the blacksmith shop, or just ride your bike up and down the Main Street (where no cars are allowed), and then on up to the fascinating town cemetery on Schoolhouse Hill.

MOUNTAIN BIKES: MURPHYS WINERY LOOP (19.2 MILES)

Although most road touring cyclists won't mind the well-graded dirt section of Six-Mile Road to Murphys, some may balk at the rather more technical downhill parts of San Domingo Road. All told, it's an ideal ride for mountain bikes, which also provide the low gears you'll need on Sheep Ranch Road.

If you'd like to do some wine sampling, the route passes three excellent opportunities: Kautz Vineyards off Six-Mile Road, Millaire in Murphys, and the venerable Stevenot Winery on San Domingo. It's a good idea to call ahead to confirm that tasting rooms will be open (the Reeses at Cooper House will be happy to do this for you).

SHEEP RANCH ROAD (49.0 MILES)

Some of the most horrifying "war stories" I've heard about pain and suffering on bike tours have been about Sheep Ranch Road. Most of these tales are absolutely true. The grades on Sheep Ranch and Mountain Ranch Roads can be downright brutal, and the country is remote, with only the outposts of Sheep Ranch and Calaveritas

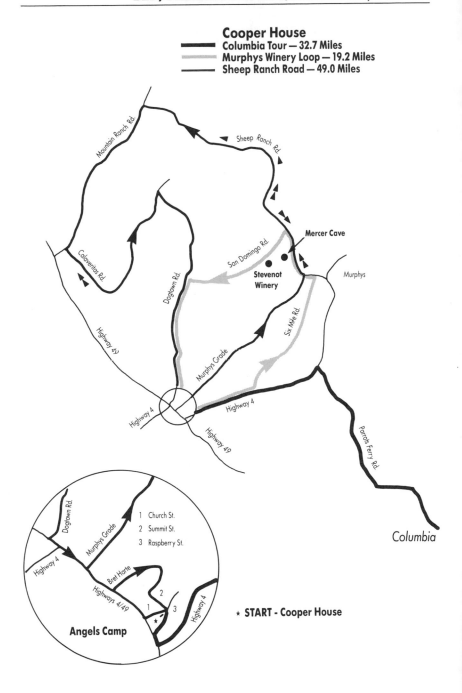

Cooper House
Columbia Tour — 32.7 Miles
Murphys Winery Loop — 19.2 Miles
Sheep Ranch Road — 49.0 Miles

Sheep Ranch Rd.

Mountain Ranch Rd.

Mercer Cave

San Domingo Rd.

Calaveritas Rd.

Stevenot Winery

Murphys

Dogtown Rd.

Six Mile Rd.

Highway 4?

Murphys Grade

Highway 4

Highway 4

Highway 49

Parrots Ferry Rd.

Columbia

Dogtown Rd.

Murphys Grade

1 Church St.
2 Summit St.
3 Raspberry St.

Highway 4

Bret Harte

Highways 4/49

Highway 4

Angels Camp

★ **START - Cooper House**

to give some relief to the torture. If this is your kind of ride, go for it. Just stay away during seasons of hot weather and short daylight!

COLUMBIA TOUR

PT.-PT.	CUME	DIRECTION	STREET/LANDMARK
			From Cooper House
0.0	0.0	L	**Church Street**
0.1	0.1	L	**Main Street/Highway 4/49**. Mountain Pedaler Bike Shop on left
0.2	0.3	L	**Vallecito Road/Highway 4**
5.0	5.3	R	**Parrots Ferry Road**
2.0	7.3		Moaning Cavern turnoff
4.0	11.3		River vista/ferry historical marker
4.0	15.3	L	**Green Street**
0.1	15.4	IR	**Broadway Street**
0.3	15.7	L	**Columbia Street**. Restrooms on left
0.3	16.0	L	**Fulton Street**
0.1	16.1	R	**Main Street**—museum buildings and displays, blacksmith shop, restaurants, stores
0.1	16.2	R	**State Street**
0.1	16.3	L	**Fulton Street**
0.1	16.4	C	**Bigler Street**
0.1	16.5	L	**Pacific Street**
0.2	16.7	R	**Schoolhouse Street**
			Old Schoolhouse on right, cemetery dead ahead
		C	Through cemetery, which loops back to Schoolhouse Street
0.2	16.9	C	**Schoolhouse Street**
0.2	17.1	R	**Pacific Street**
0.1	17.2	L	**Broadway Street**
0.1	17.3	R	**Green Street**
0.1	17.4	R	**Parrots Ferry Road**
1.0	18.4		Columbia Marble Quarry marker on right
9.0	27.4	L	**Vallecito Road/Highway 4**

COLUMBIA TOUR (CONT.)

PT.-PT.	CUME	DIRECTION	STREET/LANDMARK
5.0	32.4	R	**Main Street/Highway 49/4**
0.2	32.6	R	**Raspberry Street**
0.1	32.7	L	**Church Street** to Cooper House

MURPHYS WINERY LOOP

PT.-PT.	CUME	DIRECTION	STREET/LANDMARK
			From Cooper House
0.0	0.0	L	**Church Street**
0.1	0.1	L	**Main Street/Highway4/49**. Mountain Pedaler Bike Shop on left
0.2	0.3	L	**Vallecito Road/Highway 4**
2.5	2.8	L	**Six Mile Road**. Becomes dirt at the turnoff for the Youth Conservation Camp. Dirt continues for 2-3 miles. Becomes Scott Street in **Murphys**
4.4	7.2	L	**Main Street—Millaire** tasting room on right
1.4	8.6	R	**Sheep Ranch Road**
3.8	12.4	L	**San Domingo Road**. No sign except to Stevenot Winery
1.0	13.4		**Stevenot Winery** on left—restrooms San Domingo becomes gravel in about another 0.5 mile, dirt in about 1.0 mile.
4.0	17.4	L	**Dogtown Road**
0.8	18.2	L	**Highway 49/4**
0.7	18.9	L	**Bret Harte Street**
0.2	19.1	L	**Summit Street**
0.1	19.2	R	**Church Street** to Cooper House

SHEEP RANCH ROAD

PT.-PT.	CUME	DIRECTION	STREET/LANDMARK
			From Cooper House
0.0	0.0	R	**Church Street**
0.0	0.1	R	**Main Street/Highway 4/49**
1.2	1.3	R	**Murphys Grade.** Becomes **Main Street** in Murphys
6.5	7.8	L	**Sheep Ranch Road** at Mercer Cave sign
1.0	8.8		**Mercer Cave** entrance on left
8.0	16.8		**Sheep Ranch**
4.5	21.3	L	**Mountain Ranch Road**
8.6	29.9	L	**Calaveritas Road**
4.2	34.1	R	**Dogtown Road**
0.1	35.1	IL	**Dogtown Road**
12.9	48.0	L	**Highway 49**
0.8	48.8	L	**Bret Harte**
0.7	49.5	L	**Summit**
0.2	49.7	R	**Church Street**
0.1	49.8		**Cooper House** on left

RED CASTLE INN

Conley and Mary Louise Weaver
109 Prospect Street
Nevada City, CA 95959
916-265-5135
Ambience: Elegant Victorian

Rates: $95-$105
Bed & Breakfast Inn
Full breakfast
Smoking outside only

The first bicycle race I ever saw was the Tour of Nevada City, a steep, hotly contested criterium that takes place every Father's Day. That year a young newcomer to the national racing scene won the junior competition and was permitted to compete with the seniors (including his father). The youngster, just 17, lapped the pack three times on his way to first place.

That amazing junior was Greg Lemond, and I will always remember the excitement of watching him make mincemeat out of 33 laps of the steep hills in downtown Nevada City. And that is why I chose to stay at the Red Castle Inn. From the top two floors of this fantastic Gothic Revival mansion you can stand on a balcony and look directly up the Broad Street section of the race course on the opposite side of Deer Creek. It's an inspirational view even for non-cyclists. And it is an ideal spot from which to watch the race, if you happen to be lucky enough to reserve a room for Father's Day Weekend far enough in advance.

The best view is from the veranda off the Garret suites at the top of the house. Tucked under the eaves, this three-room suite (two bedrooms, parlor and shared bath) is the one behind those magnificent arched windows you can see from the town below.

Actually, every room in the inn has some outside access just steps away, allowing every guest to relax outdoors in privacy. My room, the Morningstar Suite on the middle level, was adjacent to the balcony just beneath the Garret veranda, with a similar view. I also had a view of the forest-thick surrounding trees from every window, a peaceful sight in the daylight, and an effective screen for the lights in town at night. I felt no need whatsoever to draw the shades.

The Morningstar and the Sunset View Suite across the landing comprised the children's floor in what was once the home of Judge John Williams, a genuine '49er who made his fortune in gold.

Built in 1860, Red Castle Inn is one of only two genuine Gothic Revival brick houses on the entire West Coast. Although it was always a town landmark, it fell into serious disrepair until rescued in 1963 by Jim Schaar, who lovingly restored it. When he retired, the Weavers took over and in 1992 hosted their predecessor for a celebration of 30 years as a bed-and-breakfast inn.

Each of the seven rooms is decorated around a central theme, from the Garden Room's elegant American Empire furnishings and canopy bed to the Bufano sculpture in the Gold Room.

Morningstar featured cabbage roses and rosebuds, complemented by dusky rose-painted walls in the tiny sitting room. The cozy bathroom held a shower and just about every amenity I could have needed, including cotton balls, Q-tips and tissues popping out of a fishing creel on the wall!

The main parlor was the scene of evening tea, served at 5:30, when my fellow guests and I were treated to apple cheesecake and orangeade. Later I made my way on foot into town and up Broad Street for a full Italian dinner at one of the many excellent restaurants in Nevada City.

"Shoeleather express" is the best way to explore the historic district, and getting to town from the Red Castle is a short hike through the terraced gardens and woodland to Sacramento Street and across the bridge. Nevada City is a wonderful place to window shop, plus there are many landmarks, including the National Hotel and Nevada Theater, that you would hardly even notice while descending Broad Street on a bike.

Breakfast at the Red Castle is "lots and lots of very good," as one fellow guest put it. We feasted on a carbohydrate-rich cheese pudding (see the recipe for Faux Cheese Souffle) topped with a chunky tomato and basil sauce, rice pudding, sliced bananas and cherries in plum sauce, juice, coffee and tea. All of this was available to stack on a tray and seek out quiet surroundings in the garden or in one's room or private veranda.

Such good food deserves repeat sampling, and the Weavers are hoping to accommodate their guests with more at dinner, in the form of a price-fixed menu. No date was given for this new venture, so inquire when you make reservations.

BIKING FROM THE RED CASTLE INN

Terrain Higher in the Sierra Nevada than many other old mining towns, Nevada City is built on steep, pine forested inclines. The streets follow old miners' trails that come together and zigzag on uneven terrain. The Red Castle Inn itself is perched on one of the most prominent hills; the Weavers suggest circling around what they call "the back way" via Nile and Clay streets to avoid the steep grades on Prospect. As for the surrounding countryside, expect more of the same. On the Pleasant Valley Loop, you'll drop to the Yuba River, then face the long climb back out.

Road Conditions You'll encounter everything from smooth newly laid pavement to the potholes of Nevada City Highway and Main Street in Grass Valley and an extremely bumpy descent to Bridgeport on the Yuba River in Pleasant Valley. Striped shoulders are unheard of but most roadways are wide enough to share or are otherwise devoid of traffic.

Traffic Construction on Highway 49 about five miles from town made the already heavy traffic even more unnerving, but this long-term bridge replacement project was nearing completion in 1993. Heavy traffic on badly maintained surface on Nevada City Highway and Main Street in Grass Valley can also be a nuisance, but drivers seem used to cyclists and willing to share the road.

Nearest Bike Shop
Tour of Nevada City Bike Shop
457 Sacramento Street
Nevada City, CA 95959
916-265-2187

Best Time To Ride Late April (after snowmelt) to mid-May, or late September to mid-October, for the fall colors

Mountain Biking Opportunities Strong mountain bikers may want to ride the 16 miles to Malakoff Diggins State Historical Park. The first six miles are paved, beginning at North Bloomfield Road just west of the junction of Highways 49 and 20. The rest of the ride is a dirt climb that's open to motor vehicles (although not recommended for trailers).

All hiking trails in the Empire Mine State Historical Park that are open to horses are also open to bikes. Pick up a map for $.50 at Park Headquarters on Empire Street (see cue sheet) and park at the Staging Area where Empire makes a right-angle turn about .20 miles before the park entrance.

If you're hungry for real Sierra singletrack, visit the Fat Tire Samurai bike shop on Joershcke Drive in Grass Valley for advice and excellent maps with topographic markings and directions.

EMPIRE MINE (12.3 MILES)

You can do this ride by road bike, but I found myself wishing I'd chosen my mountain bike instead. That way I'd have been able to negotiate the rough urban pavement on Grass Valley's Main Street more easily, and I would have had access to the park's trails once I got there.

The mine itself is a revelation. Rather than the pan-by-hand or placer mining we ordinarily think of when we paint mind pictures of the Mother Lode, it was a complex operation encompassing the highest technologies of its day and run by captains of industry. It was in almost continuous operation (with the exception of World War II) until 1957, and the park brochure claims that gold is still buried deep in its shafts "awaiting a time when deep hardrock gold mining might again be profitable." Guided tours are available, or you can pick up a walking tour pamphlet at the Visitor Center. Afterwards you can stop in Grass Valley to sample Cornish pasties similar to the ones the miners packed in their tin lunch pails.

Red Castle Inn
Empire Mine — 12.3 Miles
Pleasant Valley Loop — 39.6 Miles

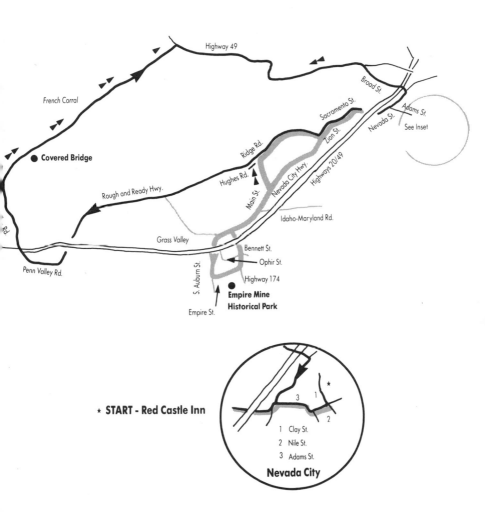

Highway 49

French Corral

Covered Bridge

Rough and Ready Hwy.

Penn Valley Rd.

Rd

Grass Valley

S. Auburn St.

Empire St.

Empire Mine
Historical Park

Bennett St.

Ophir St.

Highway 174

Hughes Rd.

Ridge Rd.

Main St.

Nevada City Hwy.

Sacramento St.

Zion St.

Highways 20/49

Idaho-Maryland Rd.

Broad St.

Adams St.

Nevada St.

See Inset

★ START - Red Castle Inn

3 1 ★

3 1

2

1 Clay St.
2 Nile St.
3 Adams St.

Nevada City

PLEASANT VALLEY LOOP (39.6 MILES)

This is a challenging ride with plenty of scenic and historic opportunities. The first is Rough and Ready, named by Mexican-American War veterans for their commanding officer, "Old Rough and Ready" General Zachary Taylor. Established in 1849, the town is legendary for attempting to secede from the U.S., beginning in 1850. At Bridgeport, if you're sharp-eyed you'll spot the 125-year-old covered bridge across the Yuba River. And at French Corral you'll pass a handsome restoration of an 1853 Wells Fargo building.

EMPIRE MINE

PT.-PT.	CUME	DIRECTION	STREET/LANDMARK
			From Red Castle Inn parking lot
0.0	0.0	L	**Clay Street**
0.0	0.1	R	**Nile Street**
0.1	0.2	R	**Adams Street**
0.1	0.3	L	**Nevada Street**
0.0	0.3	BR	**Sacramento Street** Cross bridge.
0.3	0.6	BR	**Sacramento Street** at Searle. Tour of Nevada City Bike Shop on left
0.3	0.9	BL	**Zion Street**
0.6	1.5	C	**Nevada City Highway** at Ridge Road
1.4	2.9	C	**Main Street**
1.0	3.9	R	**Main Street** at Idaho-Maryland Road
0.3	4.2	R	**Main Street** at Bennett Street
0.1	4.3	L	**S. Auburn Street.** Dubblebees Cornish Pasties on left, about halfway up the hill
0.8	5.1	L	**Empire Street**
1.0	6.1	R	**Empire State Historical Park Visitor Center**; gravel surface, no bike parking facilities
0.0	6.1	R	**Empire Street**
0.2	6.3	L	**Highway 174/Colfax Highway**
0.6	6.9	C	**Ophir Street** where 174 turns left into Colfax Street

EMPIRE MINE (CONT.)

PT.-PT.	CUME	DIRECTION	STREET/LANDMARK
0.4	7.3	L	**Bennett Street**
0.2	7.5	L	**Idaho-Maryland Road**
0.2	7.7	R	**Main Street**
0.3	8.0	L	**Hughes Road** *Gear way down!* To skip the climb, continue on Main and retrace route.
0.7	8.7	R	**Ridge Road**
2.2	10.9	L	**Nevada City Highway**. Becomes **Zion Street**
0.5	11.4	R	**Sacramento Street**
0.5	11.9	L	**Across bridge**
0.1	12.0	R	**Adams Street**
0.1	12.1	L	**Nile Street**
0.1	12.2	L	**Clay Street**
0.1	12.3	R	**Red Castle Inn** parking lot

PLEASANT VALLEY LOOP

PT.-PT.	CUME	DIRECTION	STREET/LANDMARK
			From Red Castle Inn parking lot
0.0	0.0	L	**Clay Street**
0.0	0.1	R	**Nile Street**
0.1	0.2	R	**Adams Street**
0.1	0.3	L	**Nevada Street**
0.0	0.3	BR	**Sacramento Street**. Cross bridge into town
0.2	0.4	BR	**Sacramento** at Searle. Tour of Nevada City Bike Shop on left
0.5	0.9	BL	**Zion Street**
0.5	1.4	R	**Ridge Road**
3.6	5.0	R	**Rough and Ready Highway**
2.5	7.5		**Rough and Ready** — food store on left; historic markers on right
3.2	10.7	C	**Penn Valley Road**
0.6	11.3	R	**Penn Valley Road** at Highway 20

PLEASANT VALLEY LOOP (CONT.)

PT.-PT.	CUME	DIRECTION	STREET/LANDMARK
1.6	12.9	R	**Pleasant Valley Road.** Cross Highway 20. *Extremely rough 2 to 3-mile descent ends just before* **covered bridge** *on right across Yuba River. Steep climb follows.*
10.1	23.0		**French Corral.** 1853 Wells Fargo Building on left
4.7	27.7	R	**Highway 49**; *narrow shoulder, heavy traffic*
10.8	38.4	R	**Broad Street Exit.** Tuck and look fast! You're on the race course! Nevada Theater and National Hotel on left.
0.6	39.0	R	**Sacramento Street**
0.3	39.3	L	**Adams Street**
0.1	39.4	L	**Nile Street**
0.1	39.5	L	**Clay Street**
0.1	39.6	R	**Red Castle Inn** parking lot

WEDGEWOOD INN

Vic and Jeannine Beltz
11941 Narcissus Road
Jackson, CA 95642
800-933-4393; 209-296-4300
Ambience: Family Heirloom

Rates: $85-$130
Bed and Breakfast
Full Breakfast
Smoking outdoors only

Located six miles east of Jackson and three miles west of the tiny settlement of Pine Grove, the Wedgewood Inn sits on 10 secluded acres about a mile off State Highway 88. For Vic and Jeannine Beltz, who built the cozy Victorian farmhouse from scratch in 1987, it is a dream come true.

Nearly every fine detail in every comfortably yet elegantly furnished room has some personal meaning to the Beltz family. The couples' baby clothes and photos reside in Granny's Attic, named for Jeannine's mother, who helped hang the inn's immaculate wallpapers. The couple's bed for 25 years, along with Jeannine's wedding gown, occupy the Heritage Oak Room, while their daughters' gowns are on display in two other rooms.

Jeannine gave me my choice of five rooms. I chose the Country Pine for the greenery both inside and just outside the spacious dormer windows. The secretary desk there, I learned, was used by Jeannine's parents. An heirloom quilt sat at the foot of the bed, and more family baby clothes added to the decor.

There are four other rooms to choose from in the house: The spacious Victorian Rose has a balcony overlooking the garden and oak grove. The Wedgewood Cameo's bay window and balcony look out to the hillsides. Heritage Oak features a view of the gazebo and garden along with that nuptial bed. And Granny's Attic is a suite-like third floor, with vaulted ceiling and skylight.

Then there's the Carriage House, a separate cottage displaying four generations of family heirlooms, right next door to the garage occupied by "Henry," Vic's beloved 1921 Model T. It was here that I parked my Cannondale "mule" in what has got to be the most elegant space she's ever occupied. Yet Wedgewood's location is so remote, behind an electronically controlled gate, you could safely leave your bike outdoors in fine weather.

Each room contains its own library of inspirational and humorous books and magazines for your idle reading pleasure. And be

cause this "Victorian" farmhouse is so new, the plumbing makes for excellent water pressure and a welcome forceful shower after 38 unusually humid miles.

Post-shower, the complimentary iced cran tea, Jeannine's own invention based on a hot herbal tea she serves in winter, was just as welcome. An ideal post-ride rehydrater, the tea was served with a hearty array of cheese and crackers.

When I returned from dinner in Jackson, another complimentary treat lay on the pillow of my turned-down bed: a chocolate truffle accompanied by a printed note: "Sweet Dreams from the Wedgewood Inn Truffle Fairy."

The grounds of the Wedgewood Inn were ideal for stretching my legs in the morning. Walkways surround the rose garden and croquet court, all leading to a spacious gazebo. Hammocks beckon from the shade of the surrounding oaks.

Breakfast at the Wedgewood began with coffee and tea on the upstairs landing long before the meal was served in the dining room (normally at 9:00). We gathered in the parlor with our piping hot cups until Jeannine rang her breakfast bell at the door. Inside, fresh raspberries in a compote with raspberry sherbet, oj, and cranberry muffins waited at our places. These were followed by Swedish pancakes garnished with melon, strawberries and kiwi slices and accompanied by turkey sausage. Seconds on both muffins and pancakes were too tempting to resist.

Wedgewood reflects the love and care Vic and Jeannine have put into their entire lives. No detail is too small for their full attention. When planning your ride or dinner excursion, ask Vic for his "not-even-close-to-scale" map, marked with the locations of landmarks as well as the best restaurants in Sutter Creek and Jackson.

When guests leave, Jeannine offers each their choice of a gift. I took a silk rose, so real looking you can almost smell the fragrance!

BIKING FROM THE WEDGEWOOD INN

Terrain Like all California Gold Country terrain, Amador County is hilly, and most roads slice through water drainages in the traditional, less-than-efficient manner. Be prepared to climb, and to enjoy the downhills.

Road Conditions Conditions run the gamut from wide shoulders and new pavement on Highway 88 to narrow, pothole-pocked Pine Grove-Sutter Creek Road.

Traffic Traffic on State Highways is heavy, especially on 49 in Sutter Creek, where left turns can feel like suicide missions. Backroads are blessedly peaceful and quiet in comparison. However, the later the tourist season gets, the more traffic you'll encounter.

Nearest Bike Shop
Jackson Family Sports
225 East Highway 88
Jackson, CA 95642
209-223-3890

Best Time To Ride April-May

Mountain Biking Opportunities Lake Tabeaud, just over three miles from Wedgewood Inn, has numerous trails to explore. For maps and information, contact Phil Weiss at Jackson Family Sports.

Wedgewood Inn
Volcano Loop — 33.8 Miles
Daffodil Hill — 8.7 or 42.6 Miles

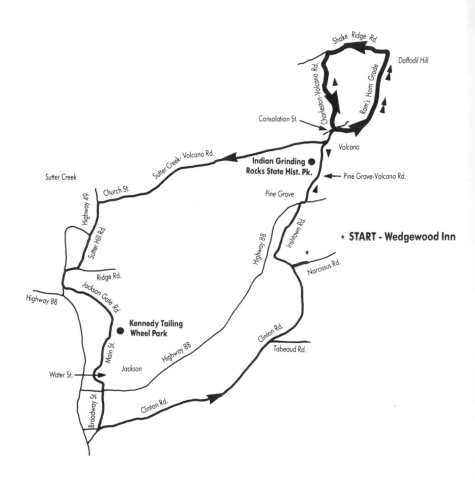

DAFFODIL HILL (42.6 OR 8.7 MILES)

Every spring, more than 4,000 daffodils and 200 varieties of tulips bloom on the McLaughlin Ranch above Volcano. The ranch is open to the public free of charge for four weeks, beginning with the first blossoms (about mid-March to mid-April). You can do this ride as a side option on the Volcano Loop, for 42.6 hilly miles, or drive to Volcano and do the 8.7-mile climb and descent as one excursion, starting from Mile 6.7 of the cue sheet.

VOLCANO LOOP (33.8 MILES)

Billed as the "most picturesque of all Motherlode towns," Volcano (population 85) is a must-see. Take this ride in a clockwise direction and you'll see it after a 3.4 mile creekside descent that reminds you of what backroad cycling is all about! Along the way, stop at Chaw'Se Indian Grinding Rocks State Historic Park for a glimpse into life in the Sierra foothills before the white man arrived.

You can turn this loop into a figure 8 by combining it with the 8.7-mile hop to Daffodil Hill.

On the way back through Jackson, check out the Kennedy Tailing Wheel on Jackson Gate Road, and the downtown Jackson Historic District before your shady climb back up Clinton Road.

DAFFODIL HILL

PT.-PT.	CUME	DIRECTION	STREET/LANDMARK
			From Wedgewood Inn's automatic gate
0.0	0.0	R	**Narcissus Road**
0.3	0.3	R	**Clinton Road**
0.7	1.0	R	**Irishtown Road**
2.0	3.0	R	**Highway 88**
			Pine Grove—store on right
0.2	3.2	L	**Pine Grove-Volcano Road**. Sign: "VOLCANO: Most Picturesque of all Motherlode Towns"
1.6	4.8		Entrance to **Chaw'Se Indian Grinding Rocks State Historic Park** on left
1.9	6.7	R	**Consolation Street** in Volcano
0.3	7.0	R	**Ram's Horn Grade**

DAFFODIL HILL (CONT.)

PT.-PT.	CUME	DIRECTION	STREET/LANDMARK
3.0	10.0		**Daffodil Hill** —Picnic area. McLaughlin Ranch open to public for 4 weeks during spring daffodil bloom.
0.1	10.1	L	**Shake Ridge Road**
2.3	12.4	L	**Charleston-Volcano Road**
2.7	15.1	R	**Consolation Street**
0.3	15.4	L	**Pine Grove-Volcano Road**
0.6	16.0	R	**Sutter Creek-Volcano Road.** *12-mile downhill!* Rough pavement, light traffic. Becomes **Church St.** in Sutter Creek.
12.0	28.0	L	**Highway 49.**
0.3	28.3	L	**Sutter Hill Road.** *Caution, heavy traffic!*
0.8	29.1	BR	**Ridge Road**
0.1	29.2	IL	**Highway 49**; 4-Way Stop, *heavy traffic*
0.9	30.1	L	**Jackson Gate Road** (just before Highway 88 junction); becomes **Main Street** at **Kennedy Tailing Wheel Park** on left.
2.8	32.9	C	**Main Street** into Jackson Historic District
0.3	33.2	L	**Water Street**
0.1	33.3	IR	**Broadway Street**; cross Highway 88
1.0	34.3	L	**Clinton Road**
5.0	39.3	L	**Clinton Road** at Tabeaud Road
3.0	42.3	R	**Narcissus Road**
0.3	42.6	L	**Wedgewood Inn** driveway

VOLCANO LOOP

PT.-PT.	CUME	DIRECTION	STREET/LANDMARK
			From Wedgewood Inn's automatic gate
0.0	0.0	R	**Narcissus Road**
0.3	0.3	R	**Clinton Road**
0.7	1.0	R	**Irishtown Road**

VOLCANO LOOP (CONT.)

PT.-PT.	CUME	DIRECTION	STREET/LANDMARK
2.0	3.0	R	**Highway 88**
			Pine Grove—store on right
0.2	3.2	L	**Pine Grove-Volcano Road.** Sign: "VOLCANO: Most Picturesque of all Motherlode Towns"
1.6	4.8		Entrance to **Chaw'Se Indian Grinding Rocks State Historic Park** on left
1.8	6.6		**Volcano.** Explore on foot or bike. Reverse direction on Volcano-Pine Grove Rd. to
0.6	7.2	R	**Sutter Creek-Volcano Road.** *12-mile downhill!* Rough pavement, light traffic. Becomes **Church St.** in Sutter Creek.
12.0	19.2	L	**Highway 49**
0.3	19.5	L	**Sutter Hill Road.** *Caution, heavy traffic!*
0.8	20.3	BR	**Ridge Road**
0.1	20.4	IR	**Highway 49**; 4-Way Stop, *heavy traffic*
0.9	21.3	L	**Jackson Gate Road** (just before Highway 88 junction); becomes **Main Street** at **Kennedy Tailing Wheel Park** on left.
2.8	24.1	C	**Main Street** into Jackson Historic District
0.3	24.4	L	**Water Street**
0.1	24.5	IR	**Broadway Street**; cross Highway 88
1.0	25.5	L	**Clinton Road**
5.0	30.5	L	**Clinton Road** at Tabeaud Road
3.0	33.5	R	**Narcissus Road**
0.3	33.8	L	**Wedgewood Inn** driveway

HIGH SIERRA NEVADA INNS AND RIDES

Rugged granite outcroppings. Hanging canyons formed by glaciers moving across geological time. Crystal-clear lakes surrounded by towering pines and firs. Air as pure and clean as the driven snow that cools it as it passes over peaks in excess of 10,000 feet in elevation.

This is the High Sierra Nevada, the snowy mountain range named by the early Spanish explorers who caught glimpses of its majesty from the Central Valley as they plied the Mission Trails. Here a bicyclist can experience the challenge of conquering a high pass followed by the exhilaration of the ensuing descent, all the while taking in a vast panorama of scenic wonder.

September is really the best time to ride in the Sierras. The summer tourists have all gone back to the flatlands, and the roads (even state highways) are often empty. But the snow won't fly for at least another month, leaving the late summer sun to warm your back as you pedal in crisp breezes.

The fat-tire cycling up here is unsurpassed nearly anywhere outside of Colorado. Logging roads, jeep tracks, old flumes, cross-country and downhill ski trails combine to make the backcountry experience one an enthusiastic mountain biker will not soon forget.

Cycling at High Sierra altitudes can easily exhaust "flatland" cyclists who are not accustomed to its rigors. There are several precautions to take: Drink extra liquids to avoid dehydration in the dryer air. Apply plenty of sunscreen to ward off the stronger ultraviolet rays. Dress in or carry extra layers of clothing for sudden changes in weather. And give yourself a day or two to acclimate your cardiovascular system to the lower atmospheric pressure before taking off on a really strenuous ride.

Exploring the Sierras can extend well beyond pedal power. Try sailing or motorboating on Lake Tahoe, backpacking in the Desolation or John Muir Wilderness (no bikes allowed!), fly fishing in the Carson River and its tributaries, angling at Bass Lake, taking a ranger-led nature walk in Yosemite, or kicking back in the relaxing vapors of Grover Hot Springs.

All of these activities can be enjoyed during your stay at an inn or resort in the high country. On Lake Tahoe, Lori and Gary Chaney at **Chaney House** give guests a perk only the privileged enjoy — lake access via their own private pier.

At **High Country Inn**, Marlene and Calvin Cartwright provide an idyllic spot for viewing the Sierra Buttes. (You may want to take binoculars along on this one.)

From **Karen's Bed & Breakfast** in Fish Camp it's just a jaunt up the road to Yosemite National Park's southern entrance, beyond which are the wonders of the giant Sequoias and the vistas from Glacier Point.

And **Sorenson's Resort** lies in the heart of Hope Valley, at the base of one of the five passes featured on the Markleeville Death Ride, and within biking distance of Grover Hot Springs. Ahhh!

FOR MORE INFORMATION ON HIGH SIERRA BICYCLING:

California Dream Cycling with Bodfish by Chuck Elliot. Bodfish Books, P.O. Box 69, Chester, CA 96020.

Cyclist's Route Atlas, A Guide to The Gold Country & High Sierra/North and *Cyclist's Route Atlas, A Guide to The Gold Country & High Sierra/South* by Randall Gray Braun. Heyday Books, Box 9145, Berkeley, CA 94709.

Mountain Biking in the Northern Sierra, three volumes by Bob Ward. Bobo Productions, P.O. Box 19815, Sacramento, CA 94819.

Mountain Biking The High Sierra, Guide 3A, Lake Tahoe-South by Carol Bonser. Fine Edge Productions, Route 2, Box 303, Bishop, CA 93514.

Mountain Biking The High Sierra Recreation Maps for North Lake Tahoe Basin and South Lake Tahoe Basin. Fine Edge Productions, Route 2, Box 303, Bishop, CA 93514.

CHANEY HOUSE

Gary and Lori Chaney
4725 West Lake Blvd., P.O. Box 7852
Tahoe City, CA 96145
916-525-7333
Ambience: Lakeside Estate

Rates: $95-$110
Bed & Breakfast
Full Breakfast
Smoking outside only

If you have never been to Lake Tahoe, nothing can quite prepare you for the impact of those towering mountain ranges reflected in that sparkling water. Even those of us who return time after time are blown away by the scenery. Happily, one of the best vantage points is from the front porch of Chaney House — or better yet, from the Chaneys' private pier just across the street.

Built by Italian stonemasons as a summer home in the Roaring '20s, Chaney House is a massive edifice that sits on the west side of the Lake, just one mile north of the downhill ski slopes at Homewood. You can stand on the porch and survey the activity on the beach, piers and water through a telescope (an heirloom from Gary Chaney's father's seafaring days). Or just drink in the glory of the mountains in Nevada, on the opposite side of the lake.

Inside Chaney House, 18-inch-thick stone walls, Gothic arches, and a massive stone fireplace that reaches to the top of the cathedral ceiling were all just plain home to Gary and Lori Chaney for 20 years, while they raised the last two of five kids. Four years ago, when daughter Jeannine left home, Gary and Lori turned the house over to B&B guests, and they have never regretted it.

The family is still very much in evidence, in photos lining the walls, especially along the spiral back stairway that led to my room. Son Russell lives just doors away, and his black Labrador, Ben, is a frequent visitor.

Russell's Suite where I spent the night, is a knotty-pine-paneled retreat with a lake view through the Ponderosa pines. The bookshelves above the dormer windows still hold National Geographic and Landmark Books as well as a few classics. In the corner a beautiful red leather easy chair equipped with ottoman and a lamp positioned at the reader's elbow made reading a serious temptation. And the queen bed beckoned invitingly beneath the pine shutters.

Chaney House

The bath was private, except for the glass-enclosed shower, which I shared with the Master Suite, a retreat set at the end of a hall of mirrors.

Jeannine's Room, on the first floor, has a brass queen bed, stone walls and a fully private bath. And the Honeymoon Hideaway is a separate one-bedroom apartment above the garage, with living room, bath, futon alcove and full kitchen.

Outside, besides lake viewing from pier or porch, you can play horseshoes in the backyard or borrow a mountain bike from the small fleet of Lori's old rejects. (She finally settled on a Rockhopper, which she loves to ride on the local bike paths or up into Blackwood Canyon.) Or you can rent the Chaneys' paddleboat for a bit of extra exercise on the water.

Boats, by the way, are Gary Chaney's thing. He owns Tahoe Yacht Sales, and nautical themes are prevalent in the house decor.

After riding around the lake, plus all this other activity, you'll be ready for a big appetite-appeasing dinner. There are enough good restaurants up and down the lake to please every palate and pocketbook. Take a look through the menu collection at Chaney House, and if you still can't decide, Lori will be happy to make suggestions, as well as your reservations.

After dinner, pick out a VCR from the small tape library in the living room. Or retire early so you can rise early for another gorgeous day, starting with Lori's special breakfast. I gorged on "Swahili Pie," a custard-like concoction in a crust and smothered in a rich apple-raisin sauce (see recipe section). The recipe, Lori told me, came from guests who had once lived in Africa.

This feast began with raspberry parfait — nonfat yogurt and nonfat granola swirled with fresh raspberries. There were also plenty of rich blueberry coffee cake, juice, coffee and fresh fruit.

A suggestion: Rise even earlier than the 8:00 breakfast hour so you can watch the sun rise over the eastern peaks and highlighting the early morning water skiers as they skim by on the lake.

BIKING FROM CHANEY HOUSE

Terrain Circling the lake, you will climb at least one mountain pass, 7,140-foot Spooner Summit, and scale the cliffs above Emerald Bay. Otherwise, it's a surprisingly rolling course. Another pass, 7,199-foot Brockway Summit, leads you to a magnificent descent into Truckee.

Road Conditions It's all state highway or city streets in this territory, so the roads for the most part are good. In addition, on the west, or California, side of the lake, you have the option of riding the paved bike path that parallels Highways 89 and 28. There are two problems with this option, however: 1) the path disappears on the Emerald Bay ascent, where the road is narrow, there is no shoulder, the switchbacks are treacherous, and the tourists are out in force; 2) the path frequently crosses the highway, forcing you to stop for traffic rather than be a part of it.

Traffic Stateline, with its bustling casinos, is awash with heavy traffic all day, as is neighboring South Lake Tahoe, where the road is lined with restaurants, hotels and shops, shops, shops. Also on the Nevada side, but at the northern end of the lake, the strip of Highway 28 between Crystal Bay and Incline Village is narrow, yet traffic maintains high speeds practically all the way from the California border.

Nearest Bike Shop
Tahoe Gear/Mike Shaughnessy, owner
5095 West Lake Blvd.
Homewood, CA
916-525-5233

Best Time To Ride September
All the tourists and summer people have gone home, and ski season is still two to three months away, so there are no crowds and traffic is minimal. Yet the weather is nearly perfect for cycling.

Mountain Biking Opportunities The mind boggles! Next to western Colorado, there is arguably no better high-altitude off-road riding in the continental U.S. That's why you won't find a Tahoe area off-road ride in this chapter: it's just too hard to choose.

Lori Chaney likes to send novices up the paved road into Blackwood Canyon, then back down on the logging road, an easy, nontechnical route with plenty of typical Tahoe scenery. Also within easy riding from Chaney House are the trailhead for the McKinney-Rubicon off-highway vehicle area south of Homewood and the Ward Creek-Paige Meadows trailhead at Pineland on the way to Tahoe City.

For more advanced riders, there's the Tahoe-to-Truckee route over Mt. Watson, which begins at North Lake Tahoe High School, and, on the Nevada side, the world-famous Flume Trail, which you can pick up by riding to Marlette Lake from Spooner Lake State Park just off Highway 50.

Or shuttle up to Brockway Summit and climb the dirt road to the lookout on Martis Peak for one of the most spectacular vistas of Lake Tahoe. Then descend to and cross Highway 267 to play among the ski trails at Northstar, or ride dirt all the way back to Tahoe City. And lots, lots more! Maps and ride guides are available at any bike shop in the area.

BROCKWAY SUMMIT LOOP (51.0 MILES)

Yahoo! This ride features eight miles of almost straight-as-an-arrow downhill! I've had reports of tandems exceeding the speed limit on this stretch, back before it was reduced from 65 mph to the nationally standard 55 mph! Yet the climb up to Brockway Summit from Kings Beach is a relatively short 3 miles, and the return up the Truckee River canyon on Highway 89 is a gradual gain punctuated by a highly recommended lunch stop at River Ranch.

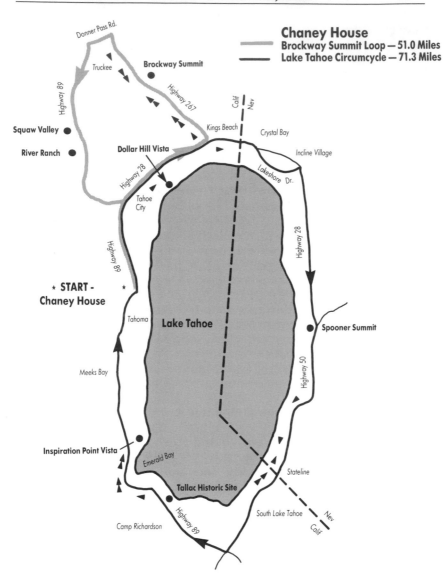

Chaney House
Brockway Summit Loop — 51.0 Miles
Lake Tahoe Circumcycle — 71.3 Miles

Donner Pass Rd.

Truckee

Brockway Summit

Highway 89

Highway 267

Squaw Valley

River Ranch

Kings Beach

Crystal Bay

Calif

Nev

Dollar Hill Vista

Incline Village

Highway 28

Lakeshore Dr.

Tahoe City

★ START -
Chaney House

Highway 89

Highway 28

Tahoma

Lake Tahoe

Spooner Summit

Meeks Bay

Highway 50

Inspiration Point Vista

Emerald Bay

Stateline

Tallac Historic Site

South Lake Tahoe

Nev

Calif

Camp Richardson

Highway 89

LAKE TAHOE CIRCUMCYCLE (71.3 MILES)

The ride around Lake Tahoe is a traditional autumn outing for many Northern California bike clubs. Some opt to ride it counterclockwise (on the inside lane, rather than next to the water), but I prefer the clockwise direction, which offers better views of the lake as well as slightly gentler climbs up the Emerald Bay cliffs and to Spooner Summit. The trade-off is that you're on the cliff edge on the narrow, twisty part of Emerald Bay Road.

For refueling along the way, I'd suggest having lunch in Kings Beach; there are plentiful restaurants and markets, not to mention a dynamite bakery! (There's food as well in Incline Village, but you'll have to deviate from scenic Lakeshore Drive to find it.) Once you strike out for Highway 50 on the Nevada side, there are no services and you'll be plugging your way up to Spooner Summit, a climb you need to tank up for ahead of time. Once you descend and pass through the congestion in Stateline, you can stop for a snack almost anywhere in South Lake.

Another stop you might enjoy is the Tallac Historic Estates just west of South Lake. This nationally registered Historic Place preserves some of the most lavish vacation homes of the rich and famous of yesteryear. Tallac is open from 10:00 a.m. to 4:00 p.m. in the summer, 11:00 a.m. to 3:00 p.m. in September, with tours available on Friday, Saturday and Sunday at 1:00 and 2:30 for $1.50 per person.

BROCKWAY SUMMIT LOOP

PT.-PT.	CUME	DIRECTION	STREET/LANDMARK
			From Chaney House
0.0	0.0	L	**Highway 89/West Lake Blvd.**
5.4	5.4		Fanny Bridge — restaurants, deli
0.1	5.5	R	**Highway 28/North Lake Tahoe Blvd.**
0.2	5.7		**Tahoe City** — Safeway, Olympic Bike Shop on right
2.9	8.6		**Dollar Hill** scenic vista

BROCKWAY SUMMIT LOOP (CONT.)

PT.-PT.	CUME	DIRECTION	STREET/LANDMARK
5.2	13.8	L	**Highway 267/Northshore Blvd.** Continue on 28 for Kings Beach shops, restaurants, bakery.
3.2	17.0		**Brockway Summit** 7199'. *Begin 8-mile downhill!*
8.6	25.6	L	**Donner Pass Road** **Truckee** — all services
1.4	27.0	L	**Highway 89/Lake Tahoe Blvd.** (sign may be missing)
8.6	35.6		**Squaw Valley** entrance on right
1.3	36.9		**River Ranch** on right
8.7	45.6	R	**Highway 89/West Lake Blvd.** Fanny Bridge pit stops
5.4	51.0	R	**Chaney House**

LAKE TAHOE CIRCUMCYCLE

PT.-PT.	CUME	DIRECTION	STREET/LANDMARK
			From Chaney House
0.0	0.0	L	**Highway 89/West Lake Blvd.**
5.4	5.4		Fanny Bridge (named for the tourists leaning over to watch the Truckee River pass beneath) — restaurants, deli
0.1	5.5	R	**Highway 28/North Lake Tahoe Blvd.**
0.2	5.7		**Tahoe City** — Safeway, Olympic Bike Shop on right
2.9	8.6		**Dollar Hill** scenic vista
5.3	13.9		**Kings Beach** — Bakery, restaurants, market, bike shop
1.5	15.4	X	Nevada State Line **Crystal Bay** — *casinos, heavy traffic!*
2.3	17.7	R	**Lakeshore Drive** For shops in Incline Village stay on Highway 28.

LAKE TAHOE CIRCUMCYCLE (CONT.)

PT.-PT.	CUME	DIRECTION	STREET/LANDMARK
3.1	20.8	**R**	**Highway 28/Tahoe Blvd.**
10.0	30.8	**R**	**Highway 50**
			Spooner Summit 7140′
12.0	42.8		**Stateline** — *casinos, heavy traffic!*
2.5	45.3		**South Lake Tahoe** — all services
3.5	48.8	**R**	**Highway 89/Emerald Bay Road**
3.6	52.4		**Camp Richardson** — grocery, bike shop
0.5	52.9		**Tallac Historic Site** on right
4.4	57.3		**Inspiration Point Vista** on right
8.3	65.6		**Meeks Bay** — resort on right
2.8	68.4		**Tahoma** — markets on right
2.9	71.3	**L**	**Chaney House**

HIGH COUNTRY INN

Calvin and Marlene Cartrwright
100 Greene Road, HCR2, Box 7
Sierra City, CA 96125
800-862-1530; 916-862-1530
Ambience: Alpine Retreat

Rates: $85-$110
Bed & Breakfast
Full Breakfast
Smoking outside only

"I think this area is as close to perfect for cycling as you will find anywhere," Randall Braun enthused about the Sierra Buttes/Lake Basin region in his 1987 *Cyclists' Route Atlas, A Guide to The Gold Country & High Sierra/North.* If alpine lakes, meandering rivers, granite peaks and (mostly) gentle grades are your thing, you too will fall in love with this little corner of the Sierra Nevada.

Traveling west on Highway 49, descending from Yuba Pass, there are only a few outposts of civilization. One of them is Bassetts, little more than a store and cafe by the side of the road. But just across the highway is a very civilized stopping place, Calvin and Marlene Cartwright's High Country Inn.

Sitting on the bank of the North Fork of the Yuba River, the inn looks out on a golly-gee-whiz view of the 8600-foot Sierra Buttes. Come back in a few hours and the sunlight will have changed enough to give you an entirely different perpsective of those stark promontories.

The inn itself is a welcome place to relax. Sink into the double-occupancy hammock suspended over the thick grass in the backyard. Or enjoy the view of the Buttes from the rear deck or alongside the pond.

In the Sierra Buttes Suite on the top floor, cathedral windows frame the Buttes and the pond like a nature photograph, and the huge dressing room looks out over the aspens and pines to the river.

The Howard Creek Room, on the pond side of the house, also gives you a view of the Buttes. There are two double beds and, like the suite above, a private bath.

The Golden Pond Room, with its duck-and-dog hunting motif, has private access to the deck, yard and view.

The view from Grandma's Quilt Room, where I stayed, was of the yard and river through the quaking leaves of two aspen trees.

Two showpieces anchored the decor — an authentic spinet desk with hideaway drawers and writing surface, and the quilt on the bed, created in perfect symmetry by Marlene's mother, whose photo graces the desk.

In the roomy closet were two thick terry robes and a selection of personal towels for trips to the shared bath, which was well set up for multiple use. A row of giant hooks held robes and towels, and stacks of shelves flanked the sink for toiletries.

Best of all, turning on the tap produced a glass of water more refreshing and flavorful than any you'd get from a plastic bottle. High Country Inn's water comes directly from a private spring. Cold and pure the year round, it's a treat to drink unadorned and makes coffee and tea taste like nectar of the gods.

In the gigantic living room I found a large selection of books to explore, including Marlene's own collections of both classic and unique children's books, as well as cookbooks and biking/hiking/fishing guides. Plush couches arranged around the stone fireplace invited a long evening's read after a sumptuous dinner at the Gray Eagle Lodge, just over the pass on the Gold Lake Highway.

Before I retired, Marlene took my "order" for coffee, decaf, herbal or regular tea for the morning. Entering my room, I found she had also turned down the bed and left a bedtime mint in a tiny glass dish.

Morning revealed a carafe of hot water and a choice of teas on a tray outside my door. This was followed by breakfast, starting with honeydew melon, unlimited quantities of juice and even more tea or coffee. But the piece de resistance was Marlene's Pumpkin Spice Pancakes (see recipe section) made with yellow corn meal and real pumpkin, with a side of crisp country sausage. Just the ticket for starting out on the Gold Lakes Loop, or a series of bike-and-hike trips to a selection of lakes, or an off-road bike exploration.

BIKING FROM HIGH COUNTRY INN

If you want to do the 50-mile Gold Lakes Loop to Graeagle, then down Highway 89 to Sattley and over Yuba Pass back to Bassetts, consult either *California Dream Cycling with Bodfish* by Chuck Elliot or Randall Braun's *High Sierra North Route Atlas*, a copy of which can be found in High Country Inn's library.

Terrain Here there be mountains, yet both Yuba Pass and Gold Lakes Highway offer relatively gentle grades. Off pavement, you'll find that dirt roads are also quite manageable, while singletracks dish out ever increasing challenges. And Sierra Valley, believe it or not, is flat as a pancake!

Road Conditions Good to excellent. Gold Lake Highway rivals the quality of the state highways. There's no shoulder on 89, 49 or 70, but it's rarely needed.

Traffic The further north you travel in the Sierras, the more logging trucks you will encounter. Yes, they're big and they make a lot of noise, especially when the air brakes are applied. But the drivers are pros who are used to bikes on the road. They actually represent far less threat than RVs piloted by rank amateurs. On the other hand, you'll encounter little other traffic along Gold Lake Highway except for the occasional fishing enthusiast or golf fanatic heading for the links at Graeagle.

Nearest Bike Shop Forget it. The closest is BaseCamp, 45 miles away in Truckee. Carry your own replacement parts!

Best time to ride Late summer through September
The later in the season you visit, the fewer RVs and campers you will meet. On the other hand, as autumn advances, it can be darned cold in the morning!

Mountain Biking Opportunities If you want the real dirt on technical trail riding, check with Brett and Rick Smith, the mountain biking operators of Gray Eagle Lodge, who claim to have ridden every singletrack known to man or beast in the Lakes Basin area.

Otherwise, armed with a Lakes Basin Recreation Area Map (available at High Country Inn), you can explore dirt roads, jeep tracks and hiking trails from Packer Lake and from the Forest Service parking lot at Gold Lake. If you'd like to put in some distance, try the dirt road loop around Haskell Peak, which starts from Howard Creek Road, about half a mile beyond the turnoff to Mills Peak from Church Meadows Road off Gold Lake Highway.

GOLD LAKE HIGHWAY BIKE-AND-HIKE (MAX. 18.0 MILES OUT AND BACK, PLUS UNKNOWN FOOT MILES)

Exploring the lakes east of Gold Lake Highway takes shoe leather rather than knobby tires. The trail to Upper Sardine Lake, for instance, is strewn with cobbles and bigger rocks, most uncomfortable for riding, while the walk into Salmon Lake is beyond all but the most advanced technical trails experts. The cue sheet and map give directions and distances to the trailhead; ride as far as you like, lock your bike and hike as far as you like. Pack your swimsuit and you may be tempted to go no further than the Sand Pond swimming hole on the road to Lower Sardine Lake. In any case, don't miss the fascinating beaver pond nature trail right next to Sand Pond.

MOUNTAIN BIKES: MILLS PEAK (APPROX. 21.6 MILES OUT AND BACK)

Ride your fat tires up Gold Lake Highway to the dirt roadhead just opposite the Gold Lake picnic area entrance and head up to Mills Peak for a look-see at the surrounding peaks and lakes. Along the way you'll get to tackle the singletrack around an approximately one-mile nature trail that features red firs and what's left of an old mine pit.

SIERRA VALLEY (55.4 MILES)

A flat ride in the Sierra Nevada! Sierra Valley looks like a piece of Nebraska plunked down in the midst of Northern California's highest mountain range. Of course, if you absolutely must get some climbing in, you can ride from High Country Inn over Yuba Pass to Sattley before heading out on this no-relief loop. If you drive over, you may want to keep driving to Sierraville, since the cash store in Sattley is closed and there will be no food to buy there at the end your ride.

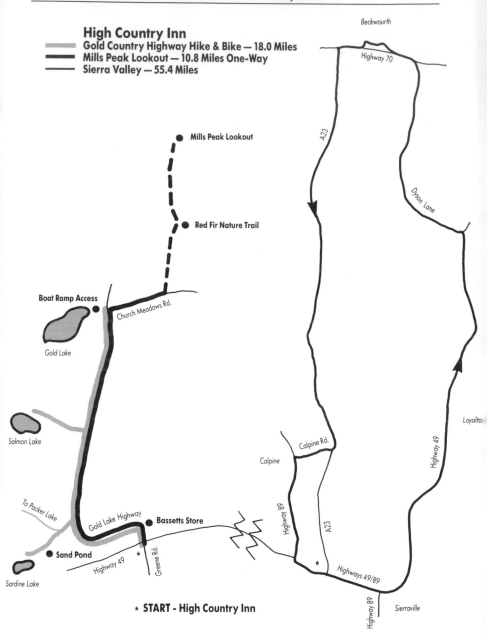

High Country Inn
Gold Country Highway Hike & Bike — 18.0 Miles
Mills Peak Lookout — 10.8 Miles One-Way
Sierra Valley — 55.4 Miles

Beckwourth

Highway 70

A23

Dyson Lane

Mills Peak Lookout

Red Fir Nature Trail

Boat Ramp Access

Church Meadows Rd.

Gold Lake

Loyalto

Calpine Rd.

Calpine

Salmon Lake

Highway 89

A23

Highway 49

To Packer Lake

Gold Lake Highway

Bassetts Store

Sand Pond

Highway 49

Greene Rd.

Sardine Lake

Highways 49/89

★ **START - High Country Inn**

Highway 89   Sierraville

★ **START - Sattley Cash Store**

Another warning: The Highway 49 route signs between Sattley and Sierraville say "north" when you know for a fact you're riding south; the road does eventually swing around back to the north. Last warning: Road signs are virtually nonexistent in Plumas County; check your mileage and be ready to ask locals what road you are on.

GOLD LAKE HIGHWAY BIKE-AND-HIKE

PT.-PT.	CUME	DIRECTION	STREET/LANDMARK
			From High Country Inn
0.0	0.0	L	**Greene Road**
		X	Highway 49
0.1	0.1	C	**Gold Lake Highway** (no sign). Bassetts cafe and store on right
0.1	0.2	BL	**Gold Lake Highway**
1.3	1.5	L	**To Sardine/Packer Lakes**
0.3	1.8	BL	**To Lower Sardine Lake**
0.2	2.0		Bear right for Packer Lake
0.2	2.2		**Sand Pond** on left — swimming hole and beaver pond nature trail
0.6	2.8		**Sardine Lake Lodge**. Trail to Upper Sardine Lake on right
0.0	2.8	U	Reverse to Gold Lake Highway
1.3	4.1	L	**Gold Lake Highway**
2.7	6.8	L	**To Salmon Lake**
1.1	7.9		**Salmon Lake** parking lot. Hiking trail 200 yds. before lot on left
0.0	7.9	U	Reverse to Gold Lake Highway
1.1	9.0	L	**Gold Lake Highway**
2.4	11.4	L	**Gold Lake Boat Ramp Access**. Access to hiking and mountain bike trails
0.0	11.4	R	**Gold Lake Highway**
6.5	17.9	BR	At Bassetts store
		X	**Highway 49**
0.1	18.0	C	**Greene Road**
0.0	18.0	R	**High Country Inn**

MOUNTAIN BIKES: MILLS PEAK LOOKOUT

PT.-PT.	CUME	DIRECTION	STREET/LANDMARK
			From High Country Inn
0.0	0.0	L	**Greene Road**
		X	Highway 49
0.1	0.1	C	**Gold Lake Highway** (no sign); Bassetts cafe and store on right
0.1	0.2	C/BL	**Gold Lake Highway**
6.8	7.0	R	**Church Meadows Road** (dirt — no sign; opposite Forest Service boat ramp; access road for Gold Lake)
1.2	8.2	L	**Toward Mills Peak**
1.4	9.6		**Red Fir Nature Trail** on right (singletrack)
1.2	10.8		**Mills Peak Lookout** 7342'

SIERRA VALLEY

PT.-PT.	CUME	DIRECTION	STREET/LANDMARK
			From Sattley Cash Store at the corner of Highway 49 and Road A23
0.0	0.0	L	**Highway 49/89**
4.0	4.0		**Sierraville** — Cafe, coffee shop, general store
0.2	4.2	BL	**Highway 49** to Loyalton
13.0	17.2		**Loyalton** — General store, restaurant, saloon
7.6	24.8	L	**Dyson Lane**
11.4	36.2	L	**Highway 70**
1.7	37.9	R	**Beckwourth-Genessee Road** (no sign)
0.2	38.1	L	**Main Street**; Beckwourth Store — no food (beer and water only)
0.1	38.2	L	**New Street**
0.1	38.3	R	**Highway 70**
1.2	39.5	L	**A23** (no road sign, just directional sign on 70)
8.5	48.0	C	**A23** at Sierra County line

SIERRA VALLEY (CONT.)

PT.-PT.	CUME	DIRECTION	STREET/LANDMARK
3.1	51.1	**R**	**Calpine Road**

To bail out directly to Sattley:

		C	**A23** for approx. 4.0 miles
0.4	51.5	**L**	**Highway 89**; Water, restrooms in **Calpine**
3.0	54.5	**L**	**Highway 49**
0.9	55.4		**Sattley Cash Store**

KAREN'S BED & BREAKFAST

Karen Bergh
1144 Railroad Avenue, P.O. Box 8   Rates: $85
Fish Camp, CA 93623   Bed & Breakfast
800-346-1433; 209-683-4550   Full breakfast
Ambience: Contemporary Country   Smoking on outside deck only

Ahhh! Mmmm! There's something in the air in the Sierra Nevada foothills around Yosemite National Park that prompts deep breaths, followed by appreciative exclamations. It's a sweet, not-quite-piney, not-quite-floral aroma you won't find anywhere else in the world, according to Karen Bergh of Karen's Bed & Breakfast in Fish Camp.

"It occurs between 4,000 and 6,000 feet in the Sierra Nevada, and there is no other like it," she told me. "It's a mixture of sugar pine, red fir and 'mountain misery,' the bear brush that grows all over the place. You'll know why it's called 'misery' if you walk through it — the sap will stick to anything!"

But it sure smells great when you're struggling up Sierra grades on your way to some of the world's most scenic overlooks, or charging back down to the comforts of home at Karen's rambling, cozy homestead nestled among oaks, pines and cedars less than three miles from the remote south entrance to Yosemite National Park.

So renowned and so well loved for its scenic wonders, Yosemite Valley is the focal point for millions of visitors a year. That's why I prefer to visit the southern part of the park. There are fewer to no crowds, especially in the fall, after the real tourist season is over. And once I hit Glacier Point and Mariposa Grove, I feel I've missed absolutely nothing in the scenery department, either.

I often stay with friends in Wawona, one of the last bastions of private property within the park boundaries. But for B&B comforts, I sought out Karen's, based on her fine reputation for down-home hospitality. And she certainly lived up to that reputation. No sooner had I brought in my bags than she had iced lemonade and cookies ready for my refreshment. And continued to ply the goodies, popping up a huge bowl of popcorn to share with guests after dinner.

A native of San Jose, Karen spent her childhood summers at Camp Wawona, where her father was the director, and her winter

holidays skiing at Badger Pass. It just seemed natural for her to end up in the same "neck of the woods" where she had grown up considering the most important part of her life. She and her husband Lee built their B&B retreat from scratch, adding three guest rooms on a second floor over their own living quarters.

The rooms are small but not cramped, with utilitarian rather than elaborate decor. The Peach Room is the most spacious, with lots of brass and seclusion. The Blue Room is the most romantic. Both have queen beds and private baths.

Mine was the Rose Room, awash with light reflected by the white walls, white and brass twin daybeds and white wicker furniture. The effect is enhanced even further by high-wattage lamps in just the right places. This was one B&B room I stayed in where I could see what I was doing!

The window looked out on Railroad Avenue, a quiet lane lined with trees, trees, and more trees. You'd never know the state highway was only steps away on the other side of the house. The private bath was as small, proportionately, as the room, but everything necessary was quickly at hand. Lots of light emanated from the row of bulbs above the sink. And the rose theme was carried through with refreshing subtlety.

Downstairs, guests have the run of the house, including the library in the dining room, the TV and VCR in the living room, and the inviting lounge chairs spread around the deck, which circles the entire house.

Don't blink when you're traveling through Fish Camp; you might miss the turnoff to Karen's. It's just off Summit Road on the south side of town. Then, says Karen, "it's just 30 feet to a right on Forest Drive, and another 30 feet to a right on Railroad Avenue." Miss either right turn and you could find yourself in near-wilderness!

Evenings descend rapidly in Fish Camp, enhanced by the trees and the presence of Yosemite's higher ranges just a few miles above you. On clear nights, you can spend hours on the deck star-gazing.

Don't forget to eat, though. Fish Camp is not exactly a center of gourmet delights, but if you prefer to walk to dinner, you can simply cross the highway to the dining room in the huge Marriott Tenaya Lodge. A better bet, though, would be to hop in the car and head into the park to the Wawona Hotel or down the hill to the Mountain House at the turnoff for Bass Lake.

If you choose the Wawona Hotel, ask to be seated at one of their eight-person Captain's Tables. It's a great way to meet visitors from other states, countries or persuasions (you may even encounter some hiking their way through!).

Mornings at Karen's are devoted to eating too. Breakfast is served from 7:30 to 8:30, ideal times for cyclists who want to get out and pedaling. And the carbos for the task are part of the menu. I was treated to several helpings of pecan pancakes, served with three syrups: brown sugar, boysenberry and chocolate. Yes, chocolate, which Karen recommended combining with peanut butter; "it's like having a Reese's for breakfast," she said!

Accompanying this sybaritic feast were cranberry juice, stewed apricots, low-fat sausage and coffee or tea. Not to mention that delicious aroma permeating everywhere from the trees and shrubs just beyond the door! Mmmm! Ahhh!

BIKING FROM KAREN'S

Cycling along Highway 41 and in the Yosemite high country is not for beginners. It takes good bike-handling skills, traffic savvy and high-altitude fortitude to enjoy touring in this area. But anyone who puts in some basic training on hills and aerobics can find true enjoyment here.

Terrain From Fish Camp, it's either up or down the mountain on Highway 41 to any destination. To tour the sights in southern

Yosemite, it's up to the park entrance and Mariposa Grove, then down to Wawona, then up to Badger Pass, then down to Glacier Point. To Bass Lake, it's all down, flat around the lake, then all back up again.

Road Conditions Highway 41 twists and turns its way up the mountain, and there is no shoulder. Yet the road was in excellent condition when I visited, since it had just been resurfaced less than two weeks previously. Yosemite Park roads are older but also well maintained. Road 222 into Bass Lake starts out wide, smooth and generously shouldered, but all that ends in just about a mile!

Traffic Fast-moving traffic on Highway 41 can be extremely hazardous. That's why I recommend visiting southern Yosemite in the fall, after most of the tourists have headed for warmer climes, but before the rain and snow begin in earnest. At this time of year the roads should be relatively traffic free.

One note about Yosemite: road signs declare no commercial trucking within the park, but while I was there I counted three loaded logging trucks making their way south towards Highway 41.

Nearest Bike Shop
Miller's Mountain Sports
40015 Highway 49
(in the Raley's shopping center)
Oakhurst, CA 93644
209-683-7946

Best Time To Ride September-October
You may even get away with early November in a dry year. But keep in mind that it gets darned cold in the mountains, and the rains could be snows any time they feel like it!

Mountain Biking Opportunities Best bet: Jackson Road, beginning at the Big Sandy exit from Highway 41, just south of Fish Camp and Sugar Pine. It climbs 3,000 feet at a reasonable grade, with views of Fresno Dome and Iron Mountain. And the return descent is highly recommended!

For singletrack toreros, there's Goat Mountain Trail, about five miles in to a fine lookout atop Goat Mountain. Trailheads are easy to spot along Road 222 around Bass Lake. Lots of climbing and technical terrain.

More information and maps are available at Miller's Mountain Sports in Oakhurst.

ROAD OR MOUNTAIN BIKES: BASS LAKE (44.7 ROAD OUT-AND BACK; 47.4 MOUNTAIN BIKE LOOP)

Bass Lake is a pretty little mountain resort area with a slightly rolling road skirting the southern shore. If you want to completely circle the lake, you need knobby tires...and more. More, as in front suspension (at least in your stem and preferably on your forks). The washboard on the Old Central Camp Road descent is truly impressive!

On a road bike you can easily make a tour of the southern shore, turning around when you most feel like it. Just keep in mind that you will need to climb all the way back up Highway 41, regardless of what kind of bike you're riding.

One last note of caution: The later in the season you ride here, the more likely the resorts on the south side of Bass Lake will be closed.

MARIPOSA GROVE AND WAWONA (23.0 MILES OUT AND BACK)

The climbing on this tourist excursion will give you plenty of workout for your 23 miles, with lots of breaks for sightseeing. If you still want more, combine it with the extended ride to Glacier Point.

Along the way you'll visit the giant Sequoias in Mariposa Grove. Several of the 250 or so big trees are over 200 feet tall and 15 feet in diameter. The 2,800-year-old Grizzly Giant, the oldest known giant Sequoia, is more than 100 feet around! No bikes (or cars) are permitted on the six miles of paved pathways through the Grove, so you can relax and hike or take a motor tram tour.

A stop in my favorite Wawona is essential. First, there's the Wawona Hotel, a National Historic Landmark dating back to 1876. A personal friend who is descended from the original developers has wonderful tales to tell about the area, some of which are illustrated in the Pioneer Yosemite History Center, right next door. But to get the real flavor of what it's like to live in this old-time mountain community, take a ride along the narrow, twisting road to the bridge over Chilnualna Creek.

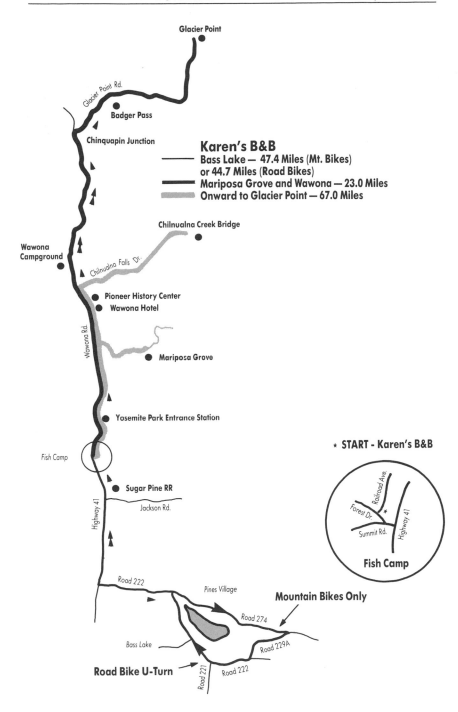

Glacier Point

Glacier Point Rd.

Badger Pass

Chinquapin Junction

Karen's B&B
Bass Lake — 47.4 Miles (Mt. Bikes)
or 44.7 Miles (Road Bikes)
Mariposa Grove and Wawona — 23.0 Miles
Onward to Glacier Point — 67.0 Miles

Chilnualna Creek Bridge

Wawona
Campground

Chilnualna Falls Dr.

Pioneer History Center
Wawona Hotel

Wawona Rd.

Mariposa Grove

Yosemite Park Entrance Station

Fish Camp

★ START - Karen's B&B

Sugar Pine RR

Jackson Rd.

Highway 41

Railroad Ave.

Forest Dr.

Highway 41

Summit Rd.

Fish Camp

Road 222

Pines Village

Mountain Bikes Only

Road 274

Bass Lake

Road 229A

Road Bike U-Turn

Road 221

Road 222

ONWARD TO GLACIER POINT (67.0 MILES OUT AND BACK)

Keep riding beyond Wawona and you begin climbing almost immediately. It's worth the long haul out to the point for the views of the granite cliffs and domes that tower above Yosemite Valley. You'll be able to pick out Yosemite Village, the Ahwahnee Hotel, and more in the Valley. Even better, you'll get a bird's eye view of Half Dome, El Capitan, Cloud's Rest, Vernal Falls, even Little Yosemite Valley.

To make this ride a bit shorter, drive to the Park Entrance and park in the limited lot just outside the gate. Or pay the $5.00 entry fee ($3.00 for bikes, both good for a week) and drive to Wawona, cutting some 14 miles from the total distance.

BASS LAKE

PT.-PT.	CUME	DIRECTION	STREET/LANDMARK
			From Karen's B&B
Mountain and Road Bikes:			
0.0	0.0	**L**	**Railroad Avenue**
0.1	0.1	**L**	**Forest Drive**
		IL	**Summit Road**
0.1	0.2	**IR**	**Highway 41**
9.9	10.1	**L**	**Road 222** to Bass Lake. Mountain House Restaurant on corner
1.4	11.5		Grocery on right
Mountain Bikes:			
2.2	13.7	**BL**	**Road 274**
2.3	16.0		**Pines Village** — Food
6.3	22.3	**R**	**Road 229A/Old Central Camp Road** — dirt descent on much washboard
1.5	23.8	**R**	**Road 222** at stop sign; rugged pavement
1.2	25.0	**R**	**Road 222/Bass Lake Road** at Road 221
3.3	28.3		Miller's Landing Resort
3.2	31.5		The Forks Resort
2.0	33.5	**L**	**Road 222** at Pines Village

BASS LAKE (CONT.)

PT.-PT.	CUME	DIRECTION	STREET/LANDMARK
0.2	33.7	L	**Road 222** at Road 274
3.6	37.3	R	**Highway 41**. Mountain House on right.
7.7	45.0		Sugar Pine RR on right
2.2	47.2	L	**Summit Road**
		IR	**Forest Drive**
		IR	**Railroad Avenue**
0.1	47.4	R	**Karen's B&B**

Road Bikes:

PT.-PT.	CUME	DIRECTION	STREET/LANDMARK
2.2	13.7	BR	**Road 222/Bass Lake Road** at Road 274
0.2	13.9	R	**Road 222** at Pines Village
2.0	15.9		The Forks Resort
3.2	19.1		Miller's Landing Resort
3.3	22.4	U	**Road 222** at Road 221 Junction
8.5	30.9	L	**Road 222** at Pines Village
0.2	31.1	L	**Road 222** at Road 274
3.6	34.7	R	**Highway 41**. Mountain House on corner
7.7	42.4		Sugar Pine RR on right
2.2	44.6	L	**Summit Road**
		IR	**Forest Drive**
		IR	**Railroad Avenue**
0.1	44.7	R	**Karen's B&B**

MARIPOSA GROVE AND WAWONA

PT.-PT.	CUME	DIRECTION	STREET/LANDMARK
			From Karen's B&B
0.0	0.0	L	**Railroad Avenue**
0.1	0.1	L	**Forest Drive**
	0.1	IL	**Summit Road**
0.1	0.2	IL	**Highway 41**
0.3	0.5		Market on left
2.3	2.8	X	**Yosemite Park Entrance Station**. $3.00 entrance fee (good for 1 week)

MARIPOSA GROVE AND WAWONA (CONT.)

PT.-PT.	CUME	DIRECTION	STREET/LANDMARK
0.1	2.9	R	**To Mariposa Grove** at stop sign
2.0	4.9		**Mariposa Grove** — Rest rooms, snack bar, gift shop, tram tours
0.0	4.9	U	**To Wawona**
2.0	6.9	C	**Wawona Road** at stop sign/entrance station
4.2	11.1		**Wawona Hotel** on right
0.3	11.4		**Pioneer History Center** on right
0.5	11.9	R	**Chilnualna Falls Drive**
0.3	12.2		Ranger Station on right
0.9	13.1		Market on left
0.8	13.9		**Chilnualna Creek Bridge**; last 0.2 miles on dirt
0.0	13.9	U	**Chilnualna Falls Road**
2.0	15.9	L	**Wawona Road** to Highway 41
4.7	20.6	R	**Entrance Station**
2.0	22.6		**Fish Camp** — Market on right at 22.9 miles
0.2	22.8	R	**Summit Road**
	22.8	R	**Forest Drive**
	22.9	R	**Railroad Avenue**
0.1	23.0	R	**Karen's B&B**

ONWARD TO GLACIER POINT

PT.-PT.	CUME	DIRECTION	STREET/LANDMARK
			From Karen's B&B
0.0	0.0	L	**Railroad Avenue**
0.1	0.1	L	**Forest Drive**
	0.1	IL	**Summit Road**
	0.2	IL	**Highway 41**
0.3	0.5		Market on left
2.3	2.8	X	**Entrance Station;** $3.00 fee, good for 1 week
			Mariposa Grove to right, 2.0 miles
0.1	2.9	L	**Wawona Road**

ONWARD TO GLACIER POINT (CONT.)

PT.-PT.	CUME	DIRECTION	STREET/LANDMARK
4.2	7.1		**Wawona**. **Wawona Hotel** on right
0.4	7.5		**Pioneer History Center** to right
0.5	8.0		**Ranger Station** to right on Chilnualna Falls Road
0.8	8.8		**Wawona Campground** on left (restrooms)
8.3	17.1	R	**Glacier Point Road** at **Chinquapin Junction** (restrooms on right)
5.0	22.1	C	**Glacier Point Road** at Badger Pass turnoff (7300′)
11.0	33.1	R	**Glacier Point**, upper parking lot. Stop for the views!
0.7	33.8	C	**To lower vista point** — Snack bar, gift shop (both closed after first snow), and more, better views!
0.0	33.8	U	**Glacier Point Road**
16.0	49.8	L	**Wawona Road** to Highway 41 at **Chinquapin Junction** (restrooms on left)
8.3	58.1		**Wawona Campground** on right (restrooms)
1.7	59.8		**Wawona**
4.5	64.3	R	**Entrance Station**
2.0	66.3		**Fish Camp** — Market on right at 66.6 miles
0.5	66.8	R	**Summit Road**
	66.8	IR	**Forest Drive**
	66.9	IR	**Railroad Avenue**
0.1	67.0	R	**Karen's B&B**

SORENSON'S RESORT

John and Patty Brissenden
14255 Highway 88   Rates: $60-$250
Hope Valley, CA 96120   Bed & Breakfast/EP/Housekeeping
800-423-9949; 916-694-2203   Full-service restaurant
Ambience: Backcountry Rustic   No Smoking

Cycling season is off-season at Sorenson's Resort. Snuggled
in Hope Valley, roughly halfway between South Lake Tahoe and
Kirkwood Ski Resort, the place bustles with hyperactivity during
the snowy months. There's even a small cross-country ski area on
the premises.

But for cyclists, it's the second weekend of July that reaches a
fever pitch of activity. That's when nearby Markleeville hosts the
Tour of the California Alps, more familiarly known as the Death
Ride, and the biggest annual event in Alpine County (population a
mere 1100). Sorenson's is the base camp of choice for hard-riding
participants who like their creature comforts after facing the rigors of conquering Monitor, Luther, Ebbets and Carson passes, the
last of which is just a few miles above the resort.

Sorenson's began in 1890 as a sheepherder's outpost. It became so prominent a stopping point for travelers on the Emigrant
Trail that founder Martin Sorenson's name ended up on the map
(it's still there, thanks to AAA). Twenty years ago the place fell on
hard times while developers were attempting to turn it into a
Scandianavian-style resort. In 1982 John and Patty Brissenden took
over and began the task of turning around 12 years of deterioration.

They've done a smashing job! Although you can nearly always
find evidence of razing and rebuilding, the cabins themselves are
immaculate and comfortable. There's something for everyone
here, from two small B&B cabins, with complimentary breakfast
served at the Country Cafe just steps away, to housekeeping cabins and even family-style homes for up to eight persons.

Of the B&B cabins, Lupine is the more spartan. It has two bedrooms, which Sorenson's will rent to one group of four or to two
couples willing to share the one bathroom.

I stayed in Pinon, the one-bedroom B&B unit. Small but cozy
and charming, it was packed with little details that let you know

you're in a B&B. A queen bed shares the small single room with two comfortable rockers. In the bath, an antique tub invites a good soak, before or after a trip to the sauna next door.

The ambience here may be "rustic," but every cabin offers full electricity, including heaters, hot water, a refrigerator in the B&B units, and full kitchens in the housekeeping cabins.

I was invited to take a peek at one of the housekeeping cabins, St. Nick's, a little further up the hill. Moved intact from Santa's Village in Scotts Valley, it represents an imaginary North Pole home for Mr. and Mrs. Claus. A spiral staircase leads from the kitchen/dining/sitting room to the sleeping area above. Open log rafters are suspended below the eaves. The bath is equipped with a Jacuzzi. A woodburning stove turns away winter's chill, and a private deck in back invites nighttime stargazing.

At the Country Cafe you can fuel up on hearty soups, fresh seafood, appealing vegetarian dishes, pasta, and great desserts. The wine list is impressively thorough, and the portions are extremely generous. My apple pie at dinner was at least 8 inches high, chock full of walnuts and cinnamon. Breakfast was the kind of stuff Death Riders need for carbo loading: granola, oatmeal, waffles.

Hope Valley is indeed backcountry. Over 97% of the land in Alpine County is public land, including the Carson Iceberg and Mokelumne Wilderness Areas. Lakes, streams, peaks and meadows abound. At night, when you step out of your cabin, the stars demand all your attention. In September, the Big Dipper hangs just above the ridge across the highway, looking close enough to touch.

Not to be missed day or night is a trip to Grover Hot Springs State Park in Markleeville. For $4.00 you can soak all you want in steaming mineral-rich water up to 125° F, jump in the Olympic-size cold pool, then head back to the hot. The pools are open from 11:00 a.m. to 9:00 p.m. Markleeville also offers a few restaurants, a fascinating little museum, and just about the only gas or groceries for miles around.

BIKING FROM SORENSON'S

Terrain In a word, mountainous. But then, what else would one expect in the High Sierra Nevada? If you want to replicate the Markleeville Death Ride, just head for every major pass in a 30-mile radius (with the exception of Daggett Pass, between Highway 395 and Heavenly Valley). However, if you stick to the rides featured here, you'll only have to scale Luther Pass, the mildest of the five. Don't despair, though; you'll still have plenty of climbing to do, especially on the way to Fallen Leaf Lake and Burnside Lake.

Road Conditions Sorenson's sits by the side of State Highway 88, just east of the junction with State Highway 89, which connects to U.S. Highway 50 and State Highway 4. All these major highways are a delight to ride, even though double lanes and wide shoulders are scarce. The roads into Fallen Leaf Lake are generally narrow, winding and potholed, calling for extreme caution in many cases. If you're mountain biking, you'll have no problems with Burnside Lake Road, which is nicely graded all the way to the campground.

Traffic Depending on the time of year, recreational traffic can be a bit heavy on the state highways, but the later in the season you ride, the less traffic you will encounter. Fallen Leaf Lake is a popular family resort, and since the road in is a narrow one-laner, you need to keep a sharp eye out for opposing traffic. Burnside Lake Road, on the other hand, may be a well-known hunters' and anglers' route, but, according to mountain bike guide author Carol Bonser, "hardly anyone goes out this road..."

Nearest Bike Shop
Tahoe Bike Shop
2277 Lake Tahoe Blvd.
South Lake Tahoe, CA
916-544-8060

Best Time To Ride Late summer: August-September
Any earlier in the season and you're a sitting duck for the mosquitoes!

Mountain Biking Opportunities In spite of Hope Valley's location between two designated wilderness areas, you'll find more bike-legal jeep trails, logging roads and singletracks than you can cover in one visit. Sorenson's has copies of Carol Bonser's excellent map, *Mountain Biking the High Sierra/Lake Tahoe Basin*, on sale. Or come prepared with a copy of Bob Ward's newest guide book — featuring trails out of Hope Valley — to be published in 1994. You can also stop by the Forest Service Service Station on Highway 89 just south of Markleeville for a map and advice.

BURNSIDE LAKE (13.6 MILES OUT AND BACK)

This six-mile dirt road is just one of many great trails within easy reach of Hope Valley, but since the trailhead is a mere mile from Sorenson's, it gets my vote for most convenient. Although there are a few steep pitches, it's basically a "beginner" ride all the way to the lake. If you're looking for something a little more challenging, try the side trip around Pickett Peak and to the lookout on Hawkins Peak.

There's another hard-core option: a singletrack trail from the south end of the lake down to Grover Hot Springs. It's extremely technical riding, especially late in the season when most of the surface is covered with thick dust and sand. It is definitely NOT for beginners, or even intermediate riders! However, it's easy to ride about half a mile beyond the lake to an overlook for a view of the state park below; the only problem is I've never been able to find that overlook myself!

FALLEN LEAF LAKE (41.9 MILES)

To reach Fallen Leaf Lake, you'll cross 7,740-foot Luther Pass with its broad vista on Big Meadow, a typically pleasing alpine set-

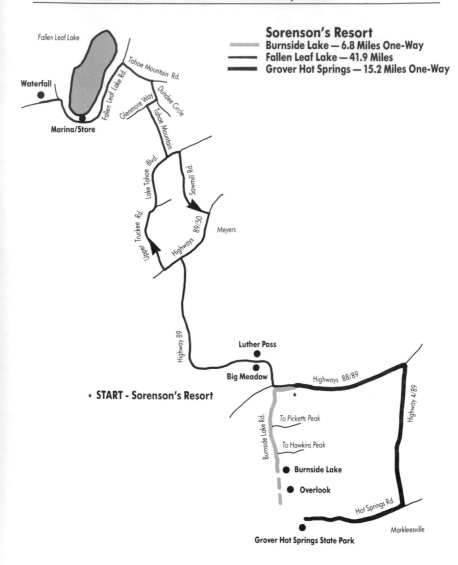

Sorenson's Resort

- Burnside Lake — 6.8 Miles One-Way
- Fallen Leaf Lake — 41.9 Miles
- Grover Hot Springs — 15.2 Miles One-Way

★ START - Sorenson's Resort

ting. Set in a cozy glacier-carved valley east of South Lake Tahoe, Fallen Leaf Lake itself is pretty as a picture, as is the delightful waterfall that feeds the lake, just a third of a mile from the marina snack bar. You can ride right up to it, or lock your bike at the marina and hike the beach/falls trail up.

GROVER HOT SPRINGS (30.4 MILES OUT AND BACK)

The hot springs at this State Park are first rate, with showers, changing rooms (remember to pack your bathing suit!), a cold pool and plenty of mountain air and sunshine. There's just one hitch: Once you've taken the waters, you'll have to climb back on your bike and retrace your route back over hill and dale to Highway 88, then climb back to Sorenson's at some 7,000 feet elevation — all of which will make you hot and sweaty again. So if you're visiting Sorenson's in the company of non-cyclists, you might want to meet them at the hot springs and return in the comfort of a motor vehicle.

BURNSIDE LAKE

PT.-PT.	CUME	DIRECTION	STREET/LANDMARK
			From Sorenson's Resort
0.0	0.0	L	**Highway 88/89**
0.9	0.9	L	**Burnside Lake Road**; at Highway 89 junction (no sign)
3.2	4.1		**Pickett Peak** turnoff on left
1.6	5.7		**Hawkins Peak** turnoff on left
0.5	6.2		**Burnside Lake**
0.1	6.3	C	On singletrack trail
0.5	6.8		**Grover Hot Springs Overlook**

FALLEN LEAF LAKE

PT.-PT.	CUME	DIRECTION	STREET/LANDMARK
			From Sorenson's Resort
0.0	0.0	L	**Highway 88/89**
0.9	0.9	R	**Highway 89**
2.7	3.6		**Luther Pass** 7740'
8.5	12.1	L	**Highway 89/50/Emerald Bay Road**

FALLEN LEAF LAKE (CONT.)

PT.-PT.	CUME	DIRECTION	STREET/LANDMARK
0.5	12.6	R	**Upper Truckee Road**
2.3	14.9	L	**Lake Tahoe Blvd.**
1.3	16.2	L	**Tahoe Mountain Road**
1.0	17.2	R	**Glenmore Way** at Dundee Circle
0.2	17.4	IL	**Tahoe Mountain Road** (no sign — follow sign to Fallen Leaf Lake). *Caution: one-lane road!*
0.7	18.1	L	**Fallen Leaf Lake Road** at T (no sign)
2.5	20.6		**Fallen Leaf Lake Marina and Store** — open through the weekend following Labor Day, good deli sandwiches
0.0	20.6	C	**Fallen Leaf Lake Road**
0.3	20.9		**Waterfall** on right
0.0	20.9	L	**Fallen Leaf Lake Road**
2.8	23.7	R	**Tahoe Mountain Road**
0.7	24.4	R	**Dundee Circle**
0.1	24.5	R	**Glenmore Way**
0.1	24.6	L	**Tahoe Mountain Road**
1.0	25.6	L	**Lake Tahoe Blvd.**
0.3	25.9	R	**Sawmill Road**; market on left
1.8	27.7	R	**Highway 50** **Meyers** — Ranger station, grocery Bear right around Agricultural Inspection Station.
2.1	29.8	L	**Highway 89/Luther Pass Road**
11.2	41.0	L	**Highway 88/89**
0.9	41.9	R	**Sorenson's**

GROVER HOT SPRINGS

PT.-PT.	CUME	DIRECTION	STREET/LANDMARK
			From Sorenson's Resort
0.0	0.0	**R**	**Highway 88/89**
4.9	4.9	**R**	**Highway 4/89**
6.2	11.1		**Markleeville** —Restaurants, grocery, general store
0.1	11.2	**R**	**Hot Springs Road**
3.6	14.8	**S**	**Park Entrance**; follow Hot Springs sign
0.4	15.2		**Hot Springs** parking lot

MONTEREY BAY AREA INNS AND RIDES

Northern California's other "Bay Area" hovers around Monterey Bay, from the north end where the San Lorenzo River empties into the Pacific, to Point Pinos south of Monterey.

Blessed with a climate that allows cycling the year round, this region offers significant climbs in the Santa Cruz Mountains, surf gazing in Santa Cruz, Pacific Grove and Pebble Beach, and long, nearly empty stretches of country roads in the Aromas Hills and Cienega Valley.

Long a tourist mecca drawing vacationers over the hill from the Santa Clara Valley, Santa Cruz County has come of age in the last 20 years, with a sprawling campus of the University of California, a thriving artisan community, and a New Age lifestyle. Surfers have always flocked here, enticed by the legendary waves of Steamer Lane. And genuine 1960s hippies still populate the remote redwood forests of the San Lorenzo Valley.

On the Monterey Peninsula to the south, the demise of Fort Ord may spell economic disaster for several communities, but that's not likely to be felt much in Pebble Beach, haven of the world's wealthiest golfers. Neighboring Carmel still displays the work of local artists at extravagant prices. The Monterey Bay Aquarium still draws thousands of tourists eager to learn about the marine life of the Monterey Bay Submarine Canyon and environs. And Point Lobos State Reserve offers the same educational benefits about the coastal plant and animal population.

For the century lover there are several rides that support roaming from the coast to the mountains and back. Among these are the Pajaro Valley Century in July, and the Monterey Loop/Steinbeck Century, variously held in early spring and mid-autumn.

Food and drink in both Monterey and Santa Cruz counties are of outstanding quality. Local wineries produce fine vintages and excellent restaurants offer culinary delights, often at surprisingly low prices. Along with these establishments you'll find a small but growing selection of fine country inns, each possessing its own intriguing personality, and each just steps from local scenic or historic attractions.

Bed & Breakfast San Juan is the only B&B to be found in rural San Benito County. Its slightly funky, outgoing character is rooted in the friendly quirkiness of owners Todd and Jeanne Cleave.

This 1850s farmhouse is just a few pedal strokes away from a first-class mission restoration and state historical park, not to mention outstanding Mexican cuisine.

Spanning two late 19th century farmhouses on Main Steet in Soquel, **Blue Spruce Inn** features warm Irish hospitality practiced by Pat and Tom O'Brien. Within walking distance of some of Santa Cruz County's best restaurants, this charming B&B gives guests private entrances through which they can dash for the patio hot tub.

High in the Santa Cruz Mountains in the hamlet of Ben Lomond, **Fairview Manor** recreates more relaxing times when San Francisco gentility rode the "Sunshine Special" to vacation homes tucked away in the redwoods. Hostess Nancy Glasson treats guests like family come home to relax by the river, a few paces from her backyard deck.

In Pacific Grove, **Gosby House Inn** rambles over two historic blocks less than a quarter of a mile from scenic Lover's Point and the Monterey Bay Recreational Trail. One of six "Four Sisters Inns" owned and operated by cycling enthusiasts Roger and Sally Post, the inn is a friendly spot where guests mingle freely in spite of private entrances and diverse interests.

FOR MORE INFORMATION ON BICYCLING IN THE MONTEREY BAY AREA:

Favorite Pedal Tours of Northern California by Naomi Bloom. Fine Edge Productions, Route 2, Box 303, Bishop, CA 93514.

Mountain Biking in the Bay Area, Volume One: South from San Francisco Bay by Michael Hodgson and Mark Lord. Western Tanager Press, 111 Pacific Avenue, Santa Cruz, CA 95060.

South San Francisco Bay and Monterey Bay Area Bicycle Touring Map. Krebs Cycle Products, P.O. Box 7337, Santa Cruz, CA 95061.

Roads to Ride South, A Bicyclist's Topographic Guide to San Mateo, Santa Clara and Santa Cruz Counties by Grant Petersen and John Kluge. Heyday Books, Box 9145, Berkeley, CA 94709.

BED & BREAKFAST SAN JUAN

Todd and Jeanne Cleave
P.O. Box 613   Rates: $65-$75
San Juan Bautista, CA 95045-0613   Bed & Breakfast
408-623-4101   Full breakfast
Ambience: Collector's Repository   Smoking on front porch only

If you can't resist the lure of wide-open country roads, the romance of Spanish Colonial history, or discovering forgotten treasures and collections of antiques and memorabilia, then San Juan Bautista is for you.

History buffs will want to explore the 1797 Mission, and the State Historic Park that commemorates the colorful colonial life and the California rebellions against Mexico. Lovers of country roads will get a chance to pedal miles through the open ranges of Cienega Valley, not to mention the strawberry fields of Aromas and the wetlands of Elkhorn Slough.

And treasure hunters will discover the delightful antique shops in town...and the unique collections of Todd and Jeannie Cleave at Bed & Breakfast San Juan. "I'm a pack rat married to a pack rat," Todd told me, and the proof is in the combined parlor/dining room in their tiny 1850s Victorian farmhouse just across the highway from town. The room is crammed with all sorts of goodies, from Todd's expansive LP record collection (bluegrass to jazz to classical) spilling out from an 1890s hotel ice box, to Jeannie's children's books overflowing the built-in shelves.

Just inside the hallway door stands an antique crib filled with Teddy bears and lifesize animal puppets. A doll house built by a local gardener is filled with "stuff we had on hand," said Todd. The wall above holds a framed 42-star American flag commemorating California's statehood. On the opposite wall hangs a Girandole mirror created between 1812 and 1815. At its crest an eagle faces left; according to Todd that means it's an American mirror, since the British had their eagles facing right. The bird holds a ball and chain in its beak, but "I have no idea what that means," Todd confessed.

Express the slightest interest in any of these items and it's "show and tell" time. Todd brought out his 1,000-year-old Tibetan lama carvings, a Spanish law book for the colonies published in 1681, and several of his musical instruments, including two rainmakers,

African instruments that sound like rain falling and rushing along the ground.

None of this treasure trove is for sale. "I love to buy, but I'm not very good at selling," is the way Todd put it.

There's more to see upstairs, starting with the icons of saints from the Mission's Posada festivals of Christmases past, each saint occupying a doorway to one of the five guest rooms. I stayed in the room guarded by San Antonio de Padua and furnished with an oak spindle queen bed made with a flowered quilt, an old oak table and bookcase. A marble-topped sewing machine table, flywheel and foot treadle intact, served as a unique vanity, thanks to the gilt-frame mirror above it.

Two oak spindle-back chairs and a child's straw chair holding a polar stuffed bear completed the decor. Four prints of tall ships graced the walls, as well as two more oil paintings of sailing ships.

I got a glimpse at two other rooms: San Francisco, a cozy nook at the back of the house, and San Carlos at the front, with two double beds, an ideal setup for families.

All the rooms share one upstairs bath, with a six-foot-long tub (bubble bath supplied) opposite a six-foot-long mirror on the wall.

Conversation is one of the best diversions at B&B San Juan. Jeannie bubbles with ideas about her preschool classes, and Todd spins ghost stories, along with a wealth of history about San Juan Bautista.

For more local culture, head across the highway to The Alameda and Third Street. Crafts shops abound. You might also get to attend a performance of El Teatro Campesino, the oldest ethnic Hispanic theater group in the country and the source of such classics as *Zoot Suit* and Linda Ronstadt's *Los Corridos*.

Culinary culture abounds as well. Take your choice of Mexican restaurants in town. The Cleaves especially recommend Felipe's, which also serves a few Salvadorean specialties. The Donkey Deli has a make-your-own sandwich bar. And don't miss the Portugese breads and pastries at the San Juan Bakery, which claims to be the oldest continuously operating establishment of its kind in California.

BIKING FROM B&B SAN JUAN

Terrain San Benito and northern Monterey counties are dotted with rolling hills that look gentle, but the roads through them often take the line of most resistance, resulting in short, steep ascents that reward the rider with short, steep descents.

Road Conditions The further from town, the rougher the roads can be. Tidal conditions can sometimes make Elkhorn Road past the slough wet and muddy.

Traffic The San Juan Highway often bears much traffic, but other country roads are virtually deserted. Hollister is bustling along Highway 156 and on Sunnyslope by the shopping malls, but otherwise it's a quiet little country town.

Nearest Bike Shop
Muenzer's Cyclery
221 Fifth Street
Hollister, CA 95
408-637-8332

Best Time To Ride April through early June

B&B San Juan
Sweet-Scented Hills — 54.3 Miles
Who Knows The Long Way To Cienega Valley? — 55.6 Miles

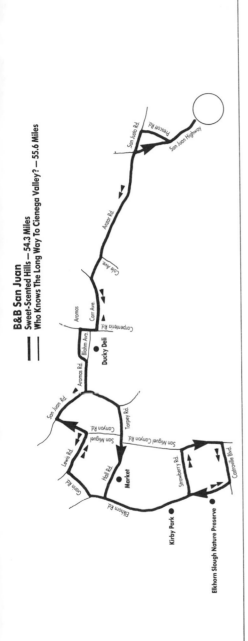

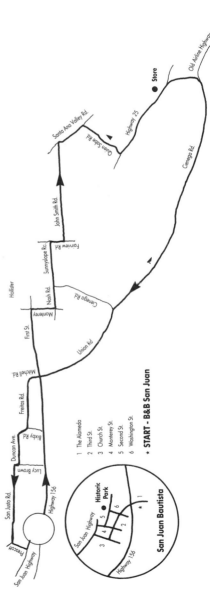

1 The Alameda
2 Third St.
3 Church St.
4 Monterey St.
5 Second St.
6 Washington St.

★ **START - B&B San Juan**

Mountain Biking Opportunities Sad to say, all this backcountry in San Benito County is unavailable to the off-road cyclist. The nearest "official" mountain biking can be found at Henry Coe State Park, 13 miles east of Morgan Hill, which is some 40 miles north of San Juan Bautista on Highway 101.

Don't attempt any trail at Henry Coe, however, unless you are used to long, arduous, steep climbs, technical terrain and generally advanced riding conditions. This place is definitely not for beginners.

SWEET-SCENTED HILLS (54.3 MILES)

The Aromas Hills were named for the sweet, fresh air the early Spanish explorers experienced while camping there. Nowadays the aromas are even more intoxicating in the springtime, when the strawberries are ripening in the fields. The aromas at Elkhorn Slough are of the sea; once the mouth of the Salinas River, the slough is now an estuary of Monterey Bay and is preserved in its natural state, an ideal one for birdwatching.

If you're looking for a short ride, why not just pedal the 23 or so miles out to Aromas and back? That way you'll still get to feast on the great sandwiches and homemade pies and muffins at the Ducky Deli!

WHO KNOWS THE LONG WAY TO CIENEGA VALLEY? (55.6 MILES)

In spring, the open ranges and ranches along Quien Sabe and Cienega roads turn brilliant green, a feast for cyclists' eyes as they make this big loop through San Benito County. To shorten the distance by some 18 miles, eliminate the ride out and back from San Juan by driving to Hollister and starting from the shopping malls at Sunnyslope and Nash roads.

SWEET-SCENTED HILLS

PT.-PT.	CUME	DIRECTION	STREET/LANDMARK
			From B&B San Juan
0.0	0.0	**L**	**The Alameda**
0.1	0.1	**X**	Highway 156; Windmill Market on left; The Alameda becomes **Third Street** — Plaza Market, cafes, bakery

SWEET-SCENTED HILLS (CONT.)

PT.-PT.	CUME	DIRECTION	STREET/LANDMARK
0.7	0.8	R	**Church Street**
0.1	0.9	L	**First Street**
0.2	1.1	C	**San Juan Highway**
0.4	1.5	R	**Prescott Road**
0.5	2.0	L	**San Justo Road** at T
1.3	3.3	L	To cross San Juan Highway
0.1	3.4	C	**Anzar Road**
1.9	5.3	R	**Anzar Road**
3.1	8.4	R	**Anzar Road** at Cole Avenue
0.4	8.8	L	**Carr Avenue**
1.6	10.4	R	**Carpenteria Road** in Aromas
0.4	10.8	L	**Aromas Road**
1.4	12.2	L	**San Juan Road**
1.1	13.3	R	**Tarpey Road**
1.3	14.6	C	**San Miguel Canyon Road**
0.4	15.0	S	**Hall Road**
2.2	17.2		Las Lomas Market on left
0.6	17.8	L	**Elkhorn Road**
2.3	20.1		**Kirby Park** on right — access to Elkhorn Slough — portapotties
1.3	21.4	L	**Strawberry Road**
3.3	24.7	R	**San Miguel Canyon Road**
0.6	25.3	R	**Castroville Blvd.**
3.5	28.8	R	**Elkhorn Road**
0.8	29.6		Elkhorn Superette on right
1.2	30.8		**Elkhorn Slough Nature Preserve** on left
5.2	36.0	L	**Elkhorn Road** at Hall Road
0.3	36.3	R	**Garin Road**
1.4	37.7	R	**Lewis Road**
2.8	40.5	L	**San Miguel Canyon Road**
1.7	42.2	R	**San Juan Road**
2.1	44.3	L	**Aromas Road** (just over top of hill)
0.7	45.0	R	**Blohm Avenue**
0.4	45.4		**Ducky Deli** on right (closed Sundays)
0.1	45.5	R	**Carpenteria Road**
0.2	45.7	L	**Carr Avenue**

SWEET-SCENTED HILLS (CONT.)

PT.-PT.	CUME	DIRECTION	STREET/LANDMARK
1.6	47.3	R	**Anzar Road**
0.4	47.7	L	**Anzar Road** at Cole Avenue
3.9	51.6	R	**San Juan Highway**; becomes **First Street**
2.1	53.7	R	**Monterey Street**
0.1	53.8	L	**Third Street**
0.2	54.0		Cafes, bakery
0.2	54.2	C	**The Alameda**
0.1	54.3	X	Highway 156
		IR	**B&B San Juan**

WHO KNOWS THE LONG WAY TO CIENEGA VALLEY?

PT.-PT.	CUME	DIRECTION	STREET/LANDMARK
			From B&B San Juan
0.0	0.0	L	**The Alameda**
		IR	**Highway 156/San Juan Road.** Becomes **First Street** in Hollister
7.7	7.7	R	**Monterey Street**
0.9	8.6	L	**Nash Road.** Markets/delis in shopping malls on both sides at Sunnyslope Road
1.0	9.6	C	**Sunnyslope Road**
1.1	10.7	R	**Fairview Road** at T (no sign)
0.5	11.2	L	**John Smith Road**
4.9	16.1	R	**Santa Ana Valley Road**
1.8	17.9	R	**Quien Sabe Road**
3.4	21.3	L	**Highway 25** (no sign)
4.6	25.9		Paicines General Store on left
1.4	27.3	R	**Cienega Road**
		IL	**Cienega Road**
1.7	29.0	R	**Cienega Road** at Old Airline Highway
15.0	44.0	L	**Cienega-Union Road**; becomes **Union Road**
3.6	47.6	X	Highway 156/San Juan Hollister Road
0.1	47.7	IR	**Mitchell Road**

WHO KNOWS THE LONG WAY TO CIENEGA VALLEY? (CONT.)

PT.-PT.	CUME	DIRECTION	STREET/LANDMARK
0.6	48.3	L	**Freitas Road**
1.9	50.2	R	**Bixby Road** at T
0.5	50.7	L	**Duncan Avenue**
1.0	51.7	R	**Lucy Brown Road**
0.1	51.8	IL	**San Justo Road**
1.8	53.6	L	**Prescott Road**
0.5	54.1	L	**San Juan Highway**
0.7	54.8	R	**Monterey Street**
0.1	54.9	IL	**Second Street**
0.3	55.2		**Mission San Juan Bautista and State Historic Park** on left
0.1	55.3	R	**Washington Street**
0.1	55.4	L	**Third Street**; Plaza Market on right Third Street becomes **The Alameda** — Windmill Market on right
0.2	55.6	X	Highway 156
		IR	**B&B San Juan**

BLUE SPRUCE INN

Pat and Tom O'Brien
2815 Main Street
Soquel, CA 95073-2412
800-559-1137; 408-464-1137
Ambience: Unpretentious Early American

Rates: $80-$125
Bed & Breakfast
Full breakfast
Smoking outdoors only

"**Where the hell**," the old bumper sticker used to read, "is Soquel?" It's right here, nestled between the Santa Cruz Mountains and Monterey Bay beaches, once a blink of an eye along the road to Watsonville, and now a tony adjunct to the tourist mini-mecca of Capitola.

Soquelites are determined to retain their independence and laid-back country atmosphere. There may be a string of traffic lights going in along Soquel Drive, but the rest of the little village area hovering around Porter Street reflects a gentler time when Soquel (pronounced So-Kell) was considered way, way out in the country.

It's an ideal spot for heading out on a bike tour of picturesque Santa Cruz County. Capitola Beach is less than three miles south, the redwoods are about five miles up, and the lushly fertile fields and orchards of the Pajaro Valley are just down the road a piece.

Smack dab in the middle of all this lovely touring country is the Blue Spruce Inn, B&B hospitality practiced to perfection by Pat and Tom O'Brien (occasionally assisted on weekends by black lab puppy Samantha, who is restricted to the parking lot). In operation only four years, the inn has already won recognition as one of "The Best Places to Kiss in Northern California."

Blue Spruce is actually two side-by-side farmhouses, one built in 1875 and the other in 1893. Pat and Tom worked together to remodel both, and the result is a delightful blend of privacy and social fun.

A maze of gravel walkways between the two houses leads to private patios or garden areas for each of five rooms (a sixth is the only guest room on the second floor of the main house). Yet each of these private areas has direct access to a deck equipped with a hot tub and a tile patio. The gardens themselves were completely redesigned around the old grape arbor and very old rose bushes that still dominate the scene.

Inside, Pat's decorating ideas add a special feeling of lightheartedness. There are skylights in nearly all the rooms as well as the parlor and kitchen. And the picket fence in front of the house keeps reappearing at the most unlikely places!

The cozy parlor has a marble fireplace with an oak mantle, above which hangs a colorful painting of the inn surrounded by summer flowers. A comfortable settee nestles below the bay windows overlooking the gardens. Breakfast is served at the other end of the parlor on a massive oak table.

Each guest room at Blue Spruce is named for the work of a local artist hanging in that room. Amish quilts on the queen beds complement the colors of the artwork. All the rooms have private baths and efficient gas heaters that look like fireplaces.

Hard by the patio fountain, the open, airy Carriage House offers the most privacy. Skylights over the carved oak bed are perfectly aligned to let you view the stars from your pillow. Pat has turned an antique steel-and-ceramic stove with hand-painted tiles into a truly unusual table. And the huge bathroom is dominated by a sunken shower with its own stained glass window.

Summer Afternoon is tucked away in the far corner of the garden, where it catches the late-day sun. Pat and Tom filled the tiny nooks inside with large pieces, and somehow it works! One nook is a sitting area right in the sunshine, while another holds the bed, where an oversize Teddy bear perches on the Log Cabin quilt.

That Bloomin' Farm is based on a painting of The Farm, once a Soquel institution incorporating organic produce grown on the premises and a greenhouse-enclosed restaurant. Countless Sunday morning bike rides would stop there for brunch in the days before the land was developed into low-income housing. Flowers proliferate here, and the bathroom holds a whirlpool tub, should the hot tub outside be too crowded.

The Gazebo is the newest of the guest rooms, where one of Tom's original picket fences serves as the bed frame. French doors lead to the garden. The house's original clawfoot tub (with brass claws) graces the bathroom.

Two Hearts, upstairs under the eaves, is devoted exclusively to romance. A red and white Irish Chain quilt and filmy canopy decorate the bed, and a full-body shower makes keeping clean a whole new experience (one guest dubbed it "the human car wash").

My room was Seascape, on the first floor of the main house, with a private brick patio entrance. Ocean blues and greens dominate the room, including the Lone Star quilt on the wrought iron and brass bed. The whirlpool bath/shower boasts two rubber duckies, a mommy and a baby, plus a dish of bubble bath and a votive candle. Two thick terry robes hang handy to the door for trips to the hot tub.

Just down the street in either direction from the Blue Spruce Inn, you'll find 16 or more restaurants. There's Indian food, pizza, Szechuan, Mexican, pasta, and more. Looking for a good deli? Two excellent choices: Soqueli's Deli on Soquel Drive at Porter, or Gayle's across the freeway on Bay Avenue in Capitola. Bakery? No one can pass Maddock's on Soquel Drive without going in. Try the bucket bread.

For dinner, three recommendations: Like seafood? Head for the Salmon Poacher on Main Street across Soquel Drive. French? Choose Theo's next door. California cuisine? Ranjeet's on Porter Drive just north of Soquel Drive.

When you return from dinner, you'll find next to your turned-down bed a small carafe of fruit wine from Bargetto's Winery up the street, along with a mini-chocolate truffle from Mackenzies candy factory in Santa Cruz. Such decadence!

But save room for Pat's generous breakfast, served buffet style on weekends, or to a "full house," from 8:30 to 9:30. When only one or two rooms are occupied weekdays, breakfast appears sit-down fashion at the hour you choose.

I got a piping hot baked pear (with a "surprise" — cranberries and walnuts — in the center), followed by poached eggs on an English muffin topped with feta cheese, spinach, yogurt, and grated Swiss cheese. All this was accompanied by cranberry coffee cake, tea and juice, a roaring fire and fine music.

BIKING FROM BLUE SPRUCE INN

Terrain The roads in Santa Cruz County run the gamut from dead flat to rolling to seriously steep. These rides will introduce you to some in every category.

Road Conditions Good: Soquel Drive, wide and well-shouldered for most of its length (the exception being the tight squeeze entering Aptos Village). Not so good: the sections of Old San Jose-Soquel Road, Summit Road, Highland Way and Eureka Canyon Road that tend to get washed out each winter. Bottom line: expect just about anything.

Traffic The village areas in Capitola and Aptos are normally heavily congested, as is the Highway 1 freeway interchange spanning Soquel's Porter Street and Capitola's Bay Avenue (this should lighten up some when the new on- and off-ramps are completed). There's also an interchange — from the freeway to Mission Street in downtown Santa Cruz — that can be thoroughly intimidating to novices, even if it is well regulated by traffic lights.

Nearest Bike Shop
The Bicycle Inn
6195 Soquel Drive
Aptos, CA 95003
408-476-0928

Best Time To Ride March through October

Mountain Biking Opportunities Just about the most scenic mountain biking in Northern California (and that's saying quite a bit) can be had at Wilder Ranch State Park, only a mile or so north of Santa Cruz on Highway 1. There's plenty of challenging singletrack as well as old ranch roads, all of which bring you out again and again to high meadows that overlook the seacliffs and the Pacific Ocean.

If you're heading up Aptos Creek Trail in Nisene Marks State Park, you may want to check out some of the old logging roads in the Soquel Demonstration Forest. Access is directly from Nisene Marks, and although it's easy to get lost, you should eventually wind up somewhere above Eureka Canyon. At least I've never heard of anyone disappearing permanently...yet!

EUREKA CANYON LOOP (39.4 MILES)

A favorite with bike clubs from all over both Bay Areas, this route is the first leg of Santa Cruz County Cycling Club's Pajaro Valley Century. The redwoods are first-rate and the ocean views from high up on Highland Way and Summit Road are fantastic. Then there's that terrific 11-mile descent down Old Soquel-San Jose Road!

Best bet for a fuel stop: Summit Store, about a quarter of a mile west of Old Soquel-San Jose on Summit. There is usually cool water flowing freely from a couple of springs on Highland, perfect for a quick dip on a hot summer day.

MOUNTAIN BIKES: THE FOREST OF NISENE MARKS STATE PARK (APPROX. 38.9 MILES, APPROX. 20 MILES ON DIRT)

Gear way, way down for a challenging climb to the crest of Mount Santa Rosalia, followed by a super-scenic descent on Buzzard Lagoon Road, which during winter is closed to cars on its upper, dirt section. If you're finding the climb a bit too much for you, you can bail out via the left fork at Sand Point, which will take you out on a rather hair-raising descent to Olive Springs Road, which connects to Old Soquel-San Jose Road. And if you'd rather not pedal the paved miles between Blue Spruce Inn and Aptos Village, you can drive them and park near the Aptos Station shops on Aptos Creek Road, returning to your car on the route back from Corralitos.

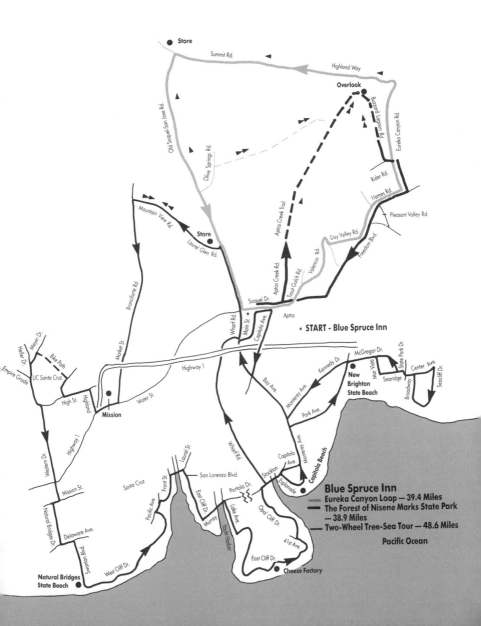

Store

Summit Rd.

Highland Way

Overlook

Old Soquel-San Jose Rd.

Buzzard Lagoon Rd.

Eureka Canyon Rd.

Olive Springs Rd.

Rider Rd.

Mountain View Rd.

Aptos Creek Trail

Hames Rd.

Pleasant Valley Rd.

Store

Day Valley Rd.

Laurel/Glen Rd.

Valencia Rd.

Freedom Blvd.

Branciforte Rd.

Aptos Creek Rd.

Trout Gulch Rd.

Soquel Dr.

Aptos

Wharf Rd.

Main St.

Capitola Ave.

★ START - Blue Spruce Inn

Meyer Dr.

Heller Dr.

Bike Path

McGregor Dr.

State Park Dr.

Empire Grade

UC Santa Cruz

Market St.

Highway 1

Bay Ave.

Monterey Ave.

Kennedy Dr.

New Brighton State Beach

Mar Vista

Searidge

Center Ave.

Broadway

Seacliff Dr.

High St.

Highland

Water St.

Park Ave.

Monterey Ave.

Mission

Highway 1

Wharf Rd.

Capitola Ave.

Monterey Ave.

Western Dr.

Laurel St.

Capitola Beach

Mission St.

Santa Cruz

Front St.

San Lorenzo Blvd.

Stockton

Esplanade

Blue Spruce Inn

Natural Bridges Dr.

Pacific Ave.

East Cliff Dr.

Portola Dr.

Eureka Canyon Loop — 39.4 Miles

Murray

Lake Ave.

Opal Cliff Dr.

The Forest of Nisene Marks State Park — 38.9 Miles

Yacht Harbor

41st Ave.

Two-Wheel Tree-Sea Tour — 48.6 Miles

Delaware Ave.

Swanton Blvd.

West Cliff Dr.

East Cliff Dr.

Cheese Factory

Pacific Ocean

Natural Bridges State Beach

TWO-WHEEL TREE-SEA TOUR (48.6 MILES)

The Santa Cruz Chamber of Commerce promotes a scenic motor route they call the "Tree-Sea Tour." This is my cycling version, which takes you to such spots as the University of California, Santa Cruz campus, the redwood groves on Laurel Glen, Mountain View and upper Branciforte Roads, and old standbys like Seacliff State Beach, Capitola Village, Natural Bridges State Beach, the Santa Cruz Yacht Harbor, and the Cliff Drives. The downtown Pacific Avenue Mall, virtually destroyed by the Loma Prieta earthquake in 1989, is flourishing once again. This is the best place to buy a lunch to eat at Natural Bridges Beach. The O'Briens recommend Zoccoli's, a sidewalk cafe with takeout food on Pacific just off Mission, and Zenato's Market on Front Street.

If you're on this ride between October and April, be sure to allow time to view the Monarch butterflies wintering over at Natural Bridges.

EUREKA CANYON LOOP

PT.-PT.	CUME	DIRECTION	STREET/LANDMARK
			From Blue Spruce Inn
0.0	0.0	L	**Main Street**
0.1	0.1	R	**Soquel Drive**
2.8	2.9		Cafe, deli on right in Aptos Center
0.3	3.2		Bakery on right
0.3	3.5	L	**Trout Gulch Road**
0.4	3.9	BR	**Valencia Road** at Y
2.6	6.5	L	**Day Valley Road**
2.0	8.5	L	**Freedom Blvd.**
0.1	8.6	IL	**Hames Road**
0.6	9.2	R	**Pleasant Valley Road**
0.0	9.2	IL	**Hames Road**
1.5	10.7	L	**Eureka Canyon Road**. Corralitos Market on right before intersection
9.0	19.7	C	**Highland Way**
4.8	25.5	C	**Summit Road** at Spanish Ranch
2.7	28.2	L	**Old Soquel-San Jose Road** Continue on Summit Road for 0.2 miles for Summit Store.
7.0	35.2		Casalegnos Store on right

EUREKA CANYON LOOP (CONT.)

PT.-PT.	CUME	DIRECTION	STREET/LANDMARK
4.0	39.2	L	**Soquel Drive** Soqueli's Deli across Soquel Drive on right
0.1	39.3	R	**Main Street**
0.1	39.4		**Blue Spruce Inn** on right

THE FOREST OF NISENE MARKS STATE PARK

PT.-PT.	CUME	DIRECTION	STREET/LANDMARK
			From Blue Spruce Inn
0.0	0.0	L	**Main Street**
0.1	0.1	R	**Soquel Drive**
2.8	2.9		Cafe, deli on right in Aptos Center
0.3	3.2		Bakery on right
0.2	3.4	L	**Aptos Creek Road** at Aptos Station shops
1.0	4.4	C	**Aptos Creek Trail** when pavement ends
9.0	13.4	BR	**Aptos Creek Trail** at Sand Point Bear left to bail out down to Olive Springs Road.
5.0	18.4		**Mt. Santa Rosalia Overlook**
1.5	19.9	R	**Buzzard Lagoon Road** (closed to motor traffic in winter)
4.3	24.2		Pavement begins
2.4	26.6	L	**Rider Road**
0.4	27.0	R	**Eureka Canyon Road**
2.1	29.1	R	**Hames Road**; Corralitos Market on left
1.5	30.6	R	**Pleasant Valley Road**
		IL	**Hames Road**
0.6	31.2	BR	**Freedom Blvd.**
2.4	33.6	R	**Soquel Drive**
0.8	34.4	L	**Soquel Drive** at Monroe Avenue
1.2	35.6		Aptos Station on right
3.2	38.8	L	**Main Street**
0.1	38.9		**Blue Spruce Inn** on right

TWO-WHEEL TREE-SEA TOUR

PT.-PT.	CUME	DIRECTION	STREET/LANDMARK
			From Blue Spruce Inn
0.0	0.0	**L**	**Main Street**
0.1	0.1	**R**	**Soquel Drive**
0.2	0.3	**R**	**Capitola Avenue**
0.6	0.9	**L**	**Bay Avenue**; Market on right, Gayle's Deli on left
0.2	1.1	**L**	**Park Avenue**
0.9	2.0	**R**	**McGregor Drive; New Brighton State Beach** on right — restrooms
1.2	3.2	**R**	**Mar Vista**
0.2	3.4	**L**	**Searidge Rd.**
0.3	3.7	**R**	**State Park Drive**
0.1	3.8	**L**	**Center Avenue**
0.3	4.1	**R**	**Seacliff Drive**
0.6	4.7	**R**	**Broadway**
		IL	**Center Avenue**
		IR	**State Park Drive**
0.1	4.8	**L**	**Searidge Rd.**
		IR	**McGregor Drive**
1.7	6.5	**C**	**Kennedy Drive** at Park Avenue
0.3	6.8	**C**	**Monterey Avenue**
0.6	7.4	**L**	**Monterey Avenue** at Bay Avenue
0.3	7.7	**R**	**Capitola Avenue. Capitola Village** — restaurants, delis
0.1	7.8	**L**	**Stockton**
		X	Soquel Creek Bridge
0.1	7.9	**IR**	**Wharf Road**
1.5	9.4	**R**	**Wharf Road** at Robertson Street
0.2	9.6	**L**	**Porter Street** Soqueli's Deli on left at Soquel Drive
0.4	10.0	**S**	**Old San Jose Road**
4.0	14.0	**L**	**Laurel Glen Road**; Casalegnos Store on right
2.8	16.8	**C**	**Mountain View Road**
1.0	17.8	**BL**	**Branciforte Road**
6.8	24.6	**C**	**Market Street**
1.0	25.6	**R**	**Water Street**

TWO-WHEEL TREE-SEA TOUR (CONT.)

PT.-PT.	CUME	DIRECTION	STREET/LANDMARK
0.8	27.4	C	**Mission Street**
0.4	27.8	L	**Front Street/Pacific Avenue** Keep right for Pacific Avenue and Zocolli's Cafe, left for Front Street and Zenato's Market.
		IR	**Church Street**
0.1	27.9	R	**Cedar Street**
		IR	**Center Street**; bakery on right
0.1	28.0	IL	**Mission Street**
0.2	28.2		**Santa Cruz Mission** on right
0.1	28.3	X	Chestnut Street/Highway 1 Interchange
		IR	**Highland Avenue**
0.2	28.5	L	**High Street**
1.4	29.9	R	**UC Santa Cruz Gate**
0.3	30.2	L	**Bike Path** (just beyond Carriage House)
1.5	31.7	L	**At end**
0.1	31.8	L	**Meyer Drive**
0.2	32.0	L	**Heller Drive**
0.8	32.8	L	**Empire Grade**
1.0	33.8	R	**Western Drive**; *steep descent!*
1.6	35.4	X	Highway 1
0.1	35.5	R	**Mission Street**
0.1	35.6	L	**Natural Bridges Drive**
0.5	36.1	L	**Delaware Avenue**
0.2	36.3	R	**Swanton Blvd.**
0.2	36.5	R	**Natural Bridges State Beach**; restrooms, picnic areas, butterflies in season, but no longer any natural bridges! After visiting park, return to entrance and
		S	**West Cliff Drive**; (optional parallel bike path)
3.5	40.0	R	**Pacific Avenue**
0.1	40.1	SR	**Front Street**
0.2	40.3	R	**Laurel Street**

TWO-WHEEL TREE-SEA TOUR (CONT.)

PT.-PT.	CUME	DIRECTION	STREET/LANDMARK
0.2	40.5	X	San Lorenzo River Bridge
0.2	40.7	R	**San Lorenzo Blvd.**
0.4	41.1	C	**East Cliff Drive**
0.5	41.6	L	**Murray Street**
0.5	42.1	X	Yacht Harbor Bridge
0.2	42.3	R	**Lake Avenue**
0.5	42.8	L	**East Cliff Drive.** Yacht Harbor restaurants, etc. on right
0.8	43.6	R	**East Cliff Drive** at 17th Avenue Cheese Factory on right
		IL	**East Cliff Drive**
2.3	45.9	L	**41st Avenue**
		IR	**Opal Cliff Drive**
0.8	46.7	R	**Portola Drive**
0.5	47.2	R	**Esplanade. Capitola Beach** — restaurants, delis — restrooms at end of Esplanade
0.1	47.3	L	**Monterey Avenue**
0.3	47.6	C	**Bay Avenue** at Monterey Avenue
0.2	47.8		Gayle's Deli on right
0.3	48.1	X	Highway 1
0.2	48.3	R	**Main Street**
0.3	48.6	L	**Blue Spruce Inn**

FAIRVIEW MANOR

Nancy Glasson
245 Fairview Avenue
Ben Lomond, CA 95005
800-894-3055; 408-336-3355
Ambience: Redwood Lodge

Rates: $99-$109
Bed & Breakfast
Full breakfast
Smoking outdoors only

Deep in the Santa Cruz Mountains, between Monterey Bay and the Santa Clara Valley, there's a string of quiet little communities known collectively as the San Lorenzo Valley.

"Valley" is a misnomer, actually, since the San Lorenzo River has barely cut a pathway down the mountainsides toward the bay. More or less paralleling the river, California State Highway 9 serves a growing number of people eager to get away from the Silicon Valley rat race.

Smack in the middle of this meandering redwood retreat is the town of Ben Lomond, named by Scotch settlers for the mountain in their homeland. Just up a shallow hill from the highway, a short walk from the center of the village, Fairview Manor sits on two and a half acres of land that once was the site of the bustling Ben Lomond Hotel, which burned down in the aftermath of the 1906 earthquake.

Built in 1924, the present house was for nearly 60 years the summer home of a prominent San Francisco family. It became a bed-and-breakfast in 1981, when Nancy Glasson "just walked in and made my decision right there; I knew the feeling was right."

Indeed, Fairview Manor imparts an instant feeling of warmth to all who enter. The entire house is paneled in richly finished redwood which somehow sends a message through the eyes to the brain that here is a place of comfort.

When I arrived, Nancy was laying a fire in the Franklin stove in the parlor's giant stone fireplace. A chintz-covered sofa and easy chair, along with two wing-back chairs, form a conversation group around the fire, where guests can mingle with ease. A watercolor painting of Fairview Manor in high summer hangs above the mantel, which holds a small collection of Bavarian beer steins.

Opposite the sitting area is a library of built-in shelves next to a Conn organ holding a collection of stuffed and ceramic elephants

and rabbits. An antique chess table holding brass and pewter pieces and a copy of *Winning Chess* stands in front of the shelves.

The far wall of the dining area is all windows looking out over the redwoods.

The redwood deck offers plenty of seating for fair weather relaxing and munching. Nancy puts out an array of cheeses and crackers with white wine at 5:00 p.m., and a small refrigerator in the corner is stocked with soft drinks.

Fairview Manor has five guest rooms, four with private attached baths, two of which have clawfoot tubs. The back room, overlooking the yard and river, has a king-size brass bed, a small oak hotel dresser, a hand-painted converted oil lamp and a marbletop vanity with beveled mirror.

The room behind the fireplace is the only one without redwood paneling; instead the walls are covered with a lovely floral wallpaper. The queen bed has a slatted oak headboard, and there is another oak hotel dresser with beveled mirror.

The room opposite mine, overlooking the garden and redwood trees in front of the house, is furnished with a white wrought iron double bed, a marbletop sideboard with a gilt-framed mirror on the paneling above, and a huge built-in armoire-style closet with drawers below.

Redwood paneling covers not only the walls in my room, but the ceiling as well. Furniture includes an oak slatted headboard on the queen bed, a fine old secretary desk, and a bentwood and cane rocker. Dimity lace curtains frame the windows, and a redwood walk-in closet occupies part of one wall.

As warm and inviting as the rooms are, a good part of Fairview Manor's charm is in the grounds — redwood groves, a rose garden, lawns, a gazebo, and pathways down to river, where you can see new redwood groves forming.

You can take a short walk down Fillmore Street to the Tyrolean Inn for German and Austrian food — schnitzels, spaetzle, potato pancakes. Or try the pasta at the new Ciao Bella Restaurant down the street.

If you're exploring off the bike, be sure to ride the narrow-gauge train at Roaring Camp in Felton. Or take a hike through the Fall Creek sector of Henry Cowell Redwoods State Park (alas, no mountain bikes allowed!).

Whatever you plan for the day, from hiking to pedaling your bike up the steep Santa Cruz Mountain grades, Nancy will send you off with a hearty breakfast. During my stay she served a full house of guests omelets, fruit, juice, hash browns and muffins, all dished out individually around the huge dining room table overlooking those eternally peaceful redwoods.

BIKING FROM FAIRVIEW MANOR

Terrain You'll be doing a lot of climbing in these mountains, but don't consider it a burden. Take it at a slow pace, so you don't miss a bit of the majestic forest scenery. When you finally descend Jamison Creek Road, you'll be hanging on for dear life!

Road Conditions Side roads like Ice Cream Grade, Smith Grade and Felton-Empire Road suffer from annual deterioration, so you may encounter rough spots. Lodge Road, the super-scenic back route into Big Basin State Park, is rough and only one lane wide for most of its distance; signs instructing motorists to "sound horn" appear at blind turns.

Traffic Highway 9 through the San Lorenzo Valley has become a busy major artery best handled by experienced cyclists. Off the highway, however, bikes may be as frequent as cars; in fact, signs at either end of Felton-Empire Road inform motorists that "bicycles share roadway." Still, many long-time residents resent the presence of bicycles on "their" roads; a low-key attitude helps alleviate much of their resentment.

Nearest Bike Shop
The Bike Rack
221 Mount Hermon Road
Scotts Valley, CA 95065
408-438-2530

Best Time To Ride August-September

Mountain Biking Opportunities Within Big Basin State Park are miles of old logging roads that are a gas to ride. Most popular is the downhill run on Gazos Creek Road from just beyond park headquarters to the coast. Be prepared for a challenging climb back up! You can also connect with the Butano Fire Road through Gazos Creek Tree Farm by climbing to the top of China Grade. From there it's a scenic ride all the way to Butano State Park just south of Pescadero.

There's also a challenging loop ride through Henry Cowell Redwoods State Park, beginning at the main parking lot a mile south of Felton on Highway 9 and climbing to an observation deck above the Roaring Camp railroad. According to Michael Hodgson and Mark Lord in *Mountain Biking in the Bay Area/South*, the swimming holes along the river make this ride a must-do in summer.

BIG BASIN LOOP (51.7 MILES)

This loop is based on the Big Basin Mini-Challenge, a popular annual ride of the early '80s. It will take you up and down steep grades through the redwoods and along a seldom-traveled back route into Big Basin State Park, the first state park in California.

BONNY DOON (31.9 MILES)

More a state of mind than a town or village, Bonny Doon is a loosely knit community spread out along Bonny Doon and Pine Flat roads. Robert Heinlein spent his last years here, and the redwoods are rumored to shelter other obscure celebrities. You can easily combine this ride with the Big Basin Loop for a metric century (or longer). But take extra food and water for Smith Grade, which dishes up a much tougher climb than the one on Ice Cream Grade.

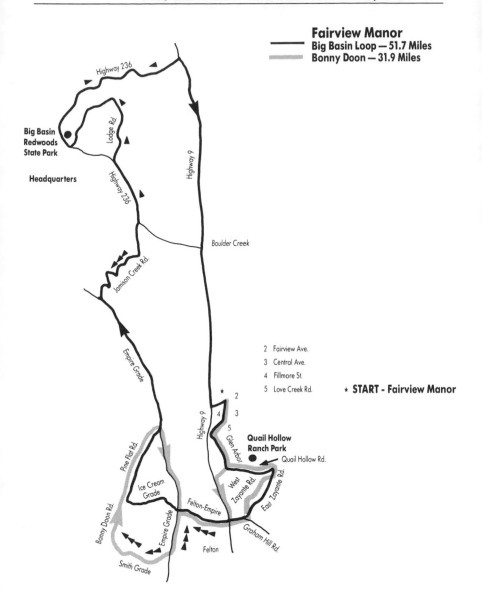

Fairview Manor
Big Basin Loop — 51.7 Miles
Bonny Doon — 31.9 Miles

Highway 236

Big Basin
Redwoods
State Park

Headquarters

Lodge Rd.

Highway 236

Highway 9

Jamison Creek Rd.

Boulder Creek

Empire Grade

2 Fairview Ave.
3 Central Ave.
4 Fillmore St.
5 Love Creek Rd.

★ **START - Fairview Manor**

Highway 9

Glen Arbor

2
4 3
5

**Quail Hollow
Ranch Park**
Quail Hollow Rd.

Pine Flat Rd.

Ice Cream
Grade

Bonny Doon Rd.

Empire Grade

West Zayante Rd.

East Zayante Rd.

Felton-Empire

Graham Hill Rd.

Smith Grade

Felton

BIG BASIN LOOP

PT.-PT.	CUME	DIRECTION	STREET/LANDMARK
			From Fairview Manor
0.0	0.0	R	**Fairview Avenue**
0.1	0.1	C	**Central Avenue** at Fillmore
0.2	0.3	R	**Love Creek Road** at T
0.1	0.4	SL	**Highway 9** around stop sign — *caution!*
		IL	**Glen Arbor Road**
1.0	1.4	L	**Quail Hollow Road** at Y (no sign)
1.0	2.4		**Quail Hollow Ranch Park** on left (open weekends and holidays May through October) — restrooms, picnic area
1.1	3.5	R	**East Zayante Road**
1.9	5.4	R	**Graham Hill Road**
0.4	5.8		**Felton** — market on left, also delis, grocery
		X	Highway 9
0.1	5.9	C	**Felton-Empire Road**
3.8	9.7	C	**Ice Cream Grade** at Empire Grade
2.5	12.2	R	**Pine Flat Road**
2.1	14.3	L	**Empire Grade**
6.0	20.3	R	**Jamison Creek Road**; *steep, winding descent for 2 miles*
3.0	23.3	L	**Highway 236**
3.3	26.6	R	**Lodge Road**; *one-lane road with blind turns*
5.0	31.6	R	**Highway 236** at T; Blooms Creek Campground dead ahead — restrooms
0.5	32.1		**Park Headquarters** — snack bar, restrooms on right
8.3	40.4	R	**Highway 9**
7.7	48.1		**Boulder Creek** — market on right, natural foods bakery and cafe on left
3.3	51.4	L	**Fillmore Street**
0.2	51.6	L	**Fairview Avenue** at Central Avenue
0.1	51.7	L	**Fairview Manor**

BONNY DOON

PT.-PT.	CUME	DIRECTION	STREET/LANDMARK
			From Fairview Manor
0.0	0.0	R	**Fairview Avenue**
0.1	0.1	C	**Central Avenue** at Fillmore
0.2	0.3	R	**Love Creek Road** at T
0.1	0.4	L	**Highway 9** around stop sign — *caution!*
		IL	**Glen Arbor Road**
1.7	2.1	L	**Highway 9**
1.5	3.6		**Felton** — market, delis, grocery
		R	**Felton-Empire Road**
3.8	7.4	L	**Empire Grade**
3.4	10.8	R	**Smith Grade**
5.3	16.1	R	**Bonny Doon Road**
2.0	18.1	C	**Pine Flat Road** at Ice Cream Grade
2.1	20.2	BR	**Empire Grade** at end of Pine Flat Road
1.8	22.0	L	**Felton-Empire Road**
3.8	25.8		**Felton** — market on right, also delis, grocery
		X	Highway 9
0.1	25.9	C	**Graham Hill Road**
0.4	26.3	L	**East Zayante Road**
0.8	27.1	L	**West Zayante Road**
1.2	28.3	L	**Quail Hollow Road**
1.1	29.4		**Quail Hollow Ranch Park** on right (open weekends and holidays May through October) — restrooms, picnic area
1.0	30.4	R	**Glen Arbor Road**
1.1	31.5	R	**Highway 9**
		IR	**Love Creek Road**
0.2	31.7	L	**Central Avenue**
0.1	31.8	C	**Fairview Avenue** at Fillmore Street
0.1	31.9	L	**Fairview Manor**

GOSBY HOUSE INN

Roger and Sally Post/Shirley Butts
643 Lighthouse Avenue
Pacific Grove, CA 93950
800-527-8828; 408-375-1287
Ambience: Elegant Victorian

Rates: $85-$150
Bed & Breakfast Inn
Full breakfast
No Smoking

The **Monterey Peninsula** is a motor tourist mecca that cyclists rarely consider for long-distance excursions. Although backroads are few, the scenic rewards far outshadow any slight inconvenience that comes from sharing some roads with autos. Besides, the recently completed Monterey Bay Recreational Trail, which runs from north of Fort Ord all the way down to Pacific Grove, gives bicyclists an exclusive close-up view of such sights as Fisherman's Wharf, Cannery Row, Hopkins Marine Station, the Monterey Bay Aquarium and Lover's Point.

Less than a quarter of a mile from the trail's terminus at Lover's Point is the Gosby House Inn, a rambling series of add-ons to an 1887 Queen Anne Victorian that stretches up the hill from Lighthouse Avenue between Eighteenth and Nineteenth Avenues.

One of six "Four Sisters Inns" owned by cycling enthusiasts Roger and Sally Post, Gosby House boasts 22 tastefully decorated rooms, most of which offer queen beds and private baths. (Four have double beds, two share a bath, and 12 have gas fireplaces.)

The name "Four Sisters," by the way, does not refer to the inns, but to the Posts' four daughters, two of whom have joined their parents in running this small B&B empire. Of the other inns in the group, one, Green Gables, is half a mile away, just off the Recreational Trail in Pacific Grove, one is in neighboring Carmel, two are in San Francisco, and one is down south near San Diego.

The Gosby House seems to be constantly buzzing with activity, most of it social. Guests congregate in the parlor and dining room after 4:30 p.m. for an elaborate spread of hors d'oeuvres and for conversation with fellow travelers from other parts of the country — and the world. "What we did today," "what we're planning to do tomorrow," and "where we're going to have dinner" are favorite topics.

There's a minimum of clutter in these common rooms, facilitating conversation even more. Of special note is the dining room's

antique doll collection, including a boy and girl pair of cloth dolls and an authentic 1874 French Jumeau doll, reputed to be one of the finest ever made.

I fell in love with my room in the Julia Pratt House, with its private entrance on Eighteenth Avenue. It was just a step from the sidewalk to the small porch and into the last century. The room was all nooks and crannies, like the one next to the door, which held a handsome oak desk with an inlaid leather surface.

In the nook next to the fireplace sat a gigantic armoire of highly polished cherry wood. Inside were two thick terry robes, extra pillows and blankets. The fireplace itself, as well as the hearth, was covered with hand-painted tiles, and the white mantel had hand-painted details. The gas fire came on by flicking a wall switch, instantly filling the room with warmth and inviting me to curl up on the facing settee, which was upholstered with a large floral print on a black background (a dead match for the wallpaper).

Above the mantel a mirror framed in rich walnut and two lights added to the sensation of warmth. Two wing-back chairs upholstered in pink and green brocade accented the pink and green floral theme of the room. The queen bed had a walnut headboard carved in the shape of a throne. The wall next to the bed held a painting of a medieval feast, while on the opposite wall I was de-lighted to find a framed fragment of hand-tatted lace of amazing intricacy.

On the white brocade bedspread sprawled an upside-down Teddy bear with his legs spread as if he were turning a cartwheel in joy at greeting me. When I returned from dinner, the spread had been turned down, Teddy was upright and was sharing the bed with chocolates, a pink rose and a card with a poetic senti-ment printed on it.

The last nook beyond the armoire held the bathroom sink with its oval beveled mirror and oversized brass and ceramic fixtures. Further inside the bath was a shower with a fantastic "whirling massage" action. A plumply lined basket on the toilet tank held a batch of goodies, from bubble bath to French milled soap.

Outside, brick walkways wended their way around the house and through the many annexes, creating more nooks and cran-nies. Two cats prowled the premises, one indoors, one outdoors.

Special Gosby House services include telephones in the rooms, a newspaper delivered to your door in the morning, and compli-mentary soft drinks from a refrigerator near the back of the main house stairs. You can order a picnic lunch for the next day, or breakfast in bed for the next morning.

I passed on breakfast in bed in favor of more socializing. With new-found friends I circled the buffet table in the dining room, helping myself to granola and a choice of toppings, an omelet souffle, sliced fresh fruit, bagels (with a toaster handy) and bran muffins. From the sideboard we added our choice of orange or cranberry juice and cocoa, tea or coffee.

Pacific Grove is not the countryside, nor is it the bustle of Monterey or Carmel. Founded in 1875 as a Methodist Church re-treat, the town soon added the first Chautauqua Assembly in the West. Blue laws remained in effect into the 1960s, and the ensu-ing years have changed little about the quiet aspect of life here.

Spacious Victorians nestle next to seaside cottages all along the three-mile stretch of beach and up the side streets to Light-house Avenue. Like the Gosby House, many of the homes are historic landmarks, each labeled with its builder's name and the date of origin. Many of the fine local restaurants are housed in old Victorians, where you dine in one of two or three small rooms with two or three tables in each.

The Monterey Bay Aquarium, built into an old cannery building with new wings to match, is within walking distance, as is Cannery Row and Lover's Point Beach.

Pacific Grove is also an ideal place to visit with a golfing fanatic. While you pedal to scenic spots, your companion can get in 18 holes within sight of the beach at Pebble Beach (for which you must reserve over a year in advance, and pay enormous greens fees!), Spyglass Hill, or the municipal course in Pacific Grove, which is much less expensive and has views that are almost as fantastic.

BIKING FROM GOSBY HOUSE INN

Terrain Lots of little ups and downs, especially in Pebble Beach and Carmel. Aguajito Road into Monterey offers a relatively gentle climb with a sweeping descent as reward.

Road Conditions Good road almost everywhere in Pebble Beach and Monterey, but the winding back streets of Carmel leave a great deal to be desired. Sand often encroaches on the shoulder anywhere near the beach, including on Highway 1 past San Jose (aka Monastery) State Beach. Fog can also be a road hazard, particularly during the early summer months.

Traffic Highway 1 is almost always full of fast-moving motor traffic, and Ocean Avenue in Carmel is always congested. The worst traffic, however, is on Del Monte Avenue in Monterey.

Nearest Bike Shop
Winning Wheels
223 15th Avenue
Pacific Grove, CA 93950
408-375-4322

The Posts also recommend:
Joselyn's Bicycles
638 Lighthouse Avenue
Monterey, CA
408-649-8520

Best Time To Ride March through November

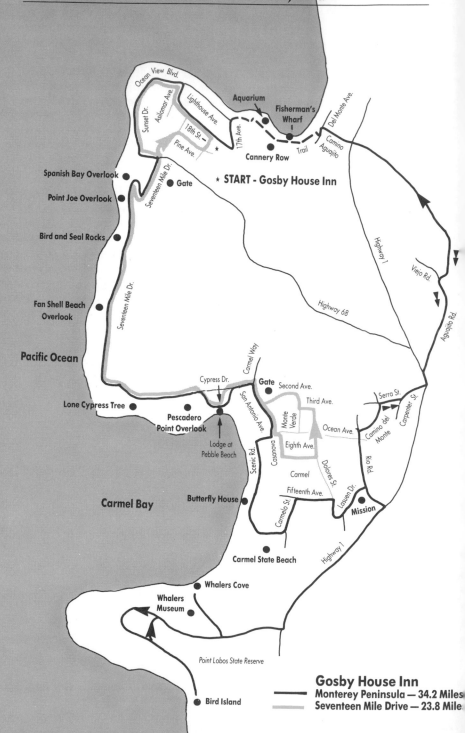

Ocean View Blvd.

Lighthouse Ave.

Asilomar Ave.

Sunset Dr.

18th St.

Pine Ave.

17th Ave.

Aquarium

Fisherman's Wharf

Del Monte Ave.

Camino Aguajito

Cannery Row

Trail

Spanish Bay Overlook

Point Joe Overlook

Bird and Seal Rocks

Seventeen Mile Dr.

Gate

★ **START - Gosby House Inn**

Highway 1

Viejo Rd.

Aguajito Rd.

Fan Shell Beach Overlook

Seventeen Mile Dr.

Highway 68

Pacific Ocean

Carmel Way

Cypress Dr.

Gate Second Ave.

Third Ave.

Serra St.

Carpenter St.

Lone Cypress Tree

Pescadero Point Overlook

Lodge at Pebble Beach

San Antonio Ave.

Monte Verde

Ocean Ave.

Camino del Monte

Rio Rd.

Eighth Ave.

Scenic Rd.

Casanova

Carmel

Carmel Bay

Butterfly House

Carmelo St.

Fifteenth Ave.

Dolores St.

Lasuen Dr.

Mission

Carmel State Beach

Highway 1

Whalers Cove

Whalers Museum

Point Lobos State Reserve

Bird Island

Gosby House Inn
Monterey Peninsula — 34.2 Miles
Seventeen Mile Drive — 23.8 Mile

Mountain Biking Opportunities Although much of the Los Padres National Forest in the Big Sur area is within the Ventana Wilderness, you can find dirt trails and roads where fat tires are legal. One opportunity is the Coast Road from the Bixby Bridge (of such photographic fame) to Andrew Molera State Park. Ride it from north to south for the easier climb and steeper descents.

Just south of Lucia, which is 26 miles south of Big Sur, Plaskett Creek Campground makes an excellent starting point for exploring old coastal ranch roads. (While you're there, ditch the bikes in favor of a walk through the cow pastures on the coast side to scale the cliff down to Jade Cove. Visit the cove just after a storm and you're likely to find scraps of jade among the shale on the beach.)

MONTEREY PENINSULA TOUR (34.2 MILES)

Instead of backtracking from Carmel on the Seventeen Mile Drive, this ride goes on down the coast to Point Lobos State Reserve, then back up to the hills behind Monterey before descending to the Monterey Bay Recreational Trail. Be sure to take a lock and allow plenty of time to explore the Carmel Mission, Fisherman's Wharf, the Aquarium and Cannery Row in addition to Carmel and Point Lobos.

SEVENTEEN MILE DRIVE (23.8 MILES)

It costs automobiles $4.00 each to tour this private road through Pebble Beach, but bicycles enter free of charge. You will have to sign a waiver at the entry gate, however. Access is limited to daylight hours only, and on weekends bicyclists may not enter through the gates at Carmel or Highway One, so that part of this ride must be covered on the Monterey Peninsula Tour. There's a "designated bike lane" which unfortunately ends long before the scenic vistas do, but experienced cyclists should have no problem handling the hills and turns all the way to the culinary delights of Carmel.

MONTEREY PENINSULA TOUR

PT.-PT.	CUME	DIRECTION	STREET/LANDMARK
			From Gosby House Inn
0.0	0.0	**L**	**Lighthouse Avenue**
1.0	1.0	**R**	**Asilomar Avenue** at T
0.3	1.3	**L**	**Ocean View Blvd.** at T

MONTEREY PENINSULA TOUR (CONT.)

PT.-PT.	CUME	DIRECTION	STREET/LANDMARK
0.7	2.0	C	**Sunset Drive** at Lighthouse Avenue
1.6	3.6	R	**Seventeen Mile Drive**
0.1	3.7	X	**Pacific Grove Gate.** Bikes are free. Must sign waiver. No entry after half-hour before sunset. Follow "17" signs and red-and-yellow dotted lines.
0.9	4.6	R	**Seventeen Mile Drive** to Spanish Bay
0.3	4.9		**Spanish Bay Overlook**
0.5	5.4		**Point Joe Overlook**
0.8	6.2		**Bird and Seal Rocks**
1.0	7.2		**Fan Shell Beach Overlook**
1.3	8.5		**Lone Cypress Tree** on right
0.8	9.3		**Pescadero Point Overlook**
0.4	9.7	R	**Cypress Drive** to The Lodge at Pebble Beach
0.3	10.0		Market on left
0.2	10.2		Restaurant on right
1.0	11.2	R	**Carmel Way**
0.3	11.5	X	**Carmel Gate**
0.4	11.9	C	**San Antonio Avenue**
0.3	12.2	R	**Ocean Avenue**
0.1	12.3	L	**Scenic Road**
1.2	13.5		**Frank Lloyd Wright Butterfly House** on left
0.4	13.9	L	**Carmelo Street. Carmel State Beach** on right — restrooms. *Caution: Speed Bump!*
0.3	14.2	R	**Fifteenth Avenue**
0.3	14.5	R	**Dolores Street**
		IL	**Lasuen Drive**
0.3	14.8	R	**Rio Road. Mission San Carlos Borremeo Del Rio Carmelo** on right before intersection
0.6	15.4	R	**Highway 1**. Market and deli in The Barnyard, on Rio across Highway 1
2.2	17.6	R	**Point Lobos State Reserve**

MONTEREY PENINSULA TOUR (CONT.)

PT.-PT.	CUME	DIRECTION	STREET/LANDMARK
0.1	17.7	**X**	Entry Kiosk; $2.00 entry fee for bicycles ($6.00 for cars). Pick up map for 50 cents.
0.1	17.8	**R**	**To Whalers Cove**
0.3	18.1		**Whalers Museum** on left
0.1	18.2	**U**	**At Whalers Cove**
0.4	18.6	**R**	At intersection
0.4	19.0	**BR**	**To Cypress Grove and Bird Island**
0.9	19.9	**U**	**At end**
0.7	20.6	**R**	**To park exit**
0.5	21.1	**L**	**Highway 1**
2.3	23.4	**L**	**Rio Road**
0.7	24.1	**R**	**Junipero** at Y after Mission
0.7	24.8		Market on right
0.4	25.2	**R**	**Camino del Monte**
0.8	26.0	**R**	**Serra Street**
0.6	26.6	**S**	**Carpenter Street**
0.1	26.7	**L**	**Highway 1**
0.2	26.9	**R**	**Highway 68/Aguajito Road Exit**
0.1	27.0	**R**	**Aguajito Road** *Steep descent in 1.2 miles*
1.4	28.4	**R**	**Aguajito Road** at Viejo Road
2.4	30.8	**X**	Highway 1 Freeway
		C	**Camino Aguajito**
0.3	31.1	**L**	**Del Monte Avenue** at T
0.2	31.3	**R**	**Monterey Bay Recreational Trail** (parallels Del Monte)
0.3	31.6	**R**	**At Fisherman's Wharf Parking Lot**
		IL	On Trail
0.9	32.5		**Cannery Row** on left
0.5	33.0		**Monterey Bay Aquarium** on right
0.9	33.9	**R**	**Ocean View Blvd.** at end of trail
0.1	34.0	**C**	**17th Avenue**
0.2	34.2	**R**	**Lighthouse Avenue** **Gosby House Inn** on left at 18th Avenue

SEVENTEEN MILE DRIVE

PT.-PT.	CUME	DIRECTION	STREET/LANDMARK
			From Gosby House Inn
0.0	0.0	L	**Lighthouse Avenue**
1.0	1.0	R	**Asilomar Avenue** at T
0.3	1.3	L	**Ocean View Blvd.** at T
0.7	2.0	C	**Sunset Drive** at Lighthouse Avenue
1.6	3.6	R	**Seventeen Mile Drive**
0.1	3.7	X	**Pacific Grove Gate.** Bikes are free. Must sign waiver. No entry after half-hour before sunset. Follow "17" signs and red-and-yellow dotted lines.
0.9	4.6	R	**Seventeen Mile Drive** to Spanish Bay
0.3	4.9		**Spanish Bay Overlook**
0.5	5.4		**Point Joe Overlook**
0.8	6.2		**Bird and Seal Rocks**
1.0	7.2		**Fan Shell Beach Overlook**
1.3	8.5		**Lone Cypress Tree** on right
0.8	9.3		**Pescadero Point Overlook**
0.4	9.7	R	**Cypress Drive** to The Lodge at Pebble Beach
0.3	10.0		Market on left
0.2	10.2		Restaurant on right
1.0	11.2	R	**Carmel Way**
0.3	11.5	X	**Carmel Gate.** Turnaround point on weekends
0.4	11.9	C	**San Antonio Avenue**
0.3	12.2	L	**Ocean Avenue**
0.1	12.3	R	**Casanova Avenue**
0.1	12.4	L	**Eighth Avenue**
0.1	12.5	L	**Dolores Street.** Village Market on right, as well as an English tearoom and several other restaurants on Dolores and Ocean
0.4	12.9	L	**Third Avenue**
0.2	13.1	R	**Monte Verde Street**
0.1	13.2	L	**Second Avenue.** *One-lane twisting descent*

SEVENTEEN MILE DRIVE (CONT.)

PT.-PT.	CUME	DIRECTION	STREET/LANDMARK
0.3	13.5	R	**San Antonio Avenue**
0.0	13.5	X	**Carmel Gate**
0.3	13.8	L	**Seventeen Mile Drive.** (It's easy to wander off the Drive on turns, keep following red-and-yellow dotted line.)
7.8	21.6	L	**Seventeen Mile Drive** at T
0.9	22.5	X	**Pacific Grove Gate**
0.1	22.6	C	**Seventeen Mile Drive** at Sunset
0.5	23.1	R	**Pine Avenue**
0.5	23.6	L	**Eighteenth Street**
0.2	23.8		**Gosby House Inn** on right at Lighthouse Avenue

NORTH COAST INNS AND RIDES

The California coast north of the San Francisco Bay Area has a reputation — and a well deserved one — for ruggedness. Bicyclists who explore coastal State Highway 1 and its byways will discover this fact in short order as they tackle hills shaped like giant sand dunes between Bodega Bay and Fort Bragg. This is the venue of The Terrible Two, a sparsely supported double century featuring climbs that have defeated many an otherwise strong rider.

Up north, I hasten to add, there's some flat land to be enjoyed near the mouth of the Eel River, one of the enticements of Ferndale. It is even possible to avoid the most taxing of climbs further south, as many of the rides in this section do.

Of course, the climbs reward cyclists with fine descents, not to mention views of the Pacific Ocean, uninterrupted all the way to Japan (if one could see that far). Add the tendrils of fog that sneak over the coast, the giant redwood trees the fog nourishes, and side roads that leave the Highway 1 traffic behind, and the result is a fine cycle touring experience.

This is especially true during what the locals call "secret summer," the post-tourist season after Labor Day when the marine fog layer normally remains well offshore, allowing the sun to reign supreme without blasting riders with extreme heat.

Seafood lovers will be in their glory on the North Coast as they sample the fruits of the Pacific, from salmon caught on long lines by the Noyo Harbor fleet at Fort Bragg, to oysters taken directly from Tomales Bay.

Tucked away in towns and villages up and down the coast are inns that add another dimension to the experience. This is especially true on the Mendocino coast, from Fort Bragg south to Gualala, where it sometimes seems that every other house is a bed-and-breakfast inn. The ambience at these establishments ranges from down-home country to truly decadent, but all display a hospitality that will make any cycling vacation extra-special.

You've probably seen photos of the **Gingerbread Mansion Inn** in the picturesque Victorian town of Ferndale, just south of Eureka. The mansion's wine and peach exterior, graced by a matching bicycle in the topiaried front garden, has been featured on the cover of many a B&B guide. There's even a jigsaw puzzle of the famous photo. Host Ken Torbert spares no effort to ensure that each and every guest's visit is also picture perfect.

Perched on a high bank along the Russian River, **Highland Dell Inn** in Monte Rio recalls the reckless abandon of earlier times, from the Roaring Twenties into the anything-goes Sixties. The elegant old resort hotel is now a well-run B&B with easy access to the redwoods and the coastal cliffs.

Pudding Creek Inn in Fort Bragg is just far enough away from Mendocino to avoid the tourist crush in that artist-colony-turned-shopping-mecca, while providing an enjoyable tool down Highway 1 to see the phenomenon for yourself. The atmosphere here is decidedly casual, amidst all the Victorian elegance and redwood paneling of an earlier California.

Hugging a strip of Highway 1 just south of the Sonoma-Marin county line, tiny Tomales is where B&B hospitality at the **Tomales Country Inn** meets carboloading heaven at the Tomales Bakery. All this and the hills and seacliffs of northwest Marin dairy country to boot.

FOR MORE INFORMATION ON BICYCLING ON THE NORTH COAST:

California Dream Cycling with Bodfish and *Cycling The California Outback with Bodfish* by Chuck Elliot. Bodfish Books, P.O. Box 69, Chester, CA 96020.

GINGERBREAD MANSION INN

Ken Torbert
400 Berding Street, P.O. Box 40
Ferndale, CA 95536
707-786-4000
Ambience: Deluxe Elegant Victorian

Rates: $110-$185
Bed & Breakfast Inn
Full Breakfast
No smoking

"**Oh, Toto, I don't think** we're in California anymore!" That was my reaction while riding through the delta dairylands that surround the village of Ferndale, just south of Eureka. I felt as though some maelstrom must have picked me up, bicycle and all, and deposited me somewhere in Wisconsin.

Where else would I be rolling endlessly over miles and miles of flat roads through green pastures populated with just about every breed of dairy cow known to humanity?

According to Ken Torbert, the affable innkeeper at the Gingerbread Mansion Inn, it's the delta formed by the Eel River that makes this such a fertile dairy farming area. The river floods with reliable regularity, enriching the soil (and toppling many a house and barn).

In fact, the land is so rich it made the dairy farmers rich. Shipping their milk, cream and butter directly to San Francisco proved so profitable at the end of the last century, many found they could afford to build fine Victorian homes in the village. Dubbed "butterfat palaces," many of these old mansions survive today as private homes and, happily, as bed-and-breakfast inns.

Certainly the best known is the Gingerbread Mansion, one of the most photographed buildings in all of Northern California. Small wonder. This combination Queen Anne/Eastlake Victorian packs all the "gingerbread" you can imagine onto one tiny corner lot, and it's all done to perfection. The color scheme of the house — yellow, wine and peach — is carried through even to the one-speed bikes and giant umbrellas guests can borrow to explore the village.

The garden carries the theme even further. Although there's not much land to work with, the landscape design successfully emulates the mazes of English country estates, right down to the charming topiaries.

Built in 1899 for a local physician, the house later served as a hospital, a rest home and an American Legion Hall. In the '50s it became an apartment building, but a decade later it was ready for

Gingerbread Mansion Inn
An Extraordinary Northern California Inn

condemnation. Two landscape designers bought and refurbished it, creating the clever garden at the same time. In 1981 Torbert and partner Wendy Hatfield purchased the mansion and opened the B&B in 1983.

A stay at the Gingerbread Mansion is a totally deluxe experience. Arrive at tea time and you are offered a dazzling choice of fresh-baked pastries, sweet breads, coffee and tea. This "high tea" tea is served in one of four parlors, ranging from highly social to quietly solitary ("a good place to curl up with a book," as Ken puts it).

Climb the broad staircase and your feet spring back from the plush cabbage rose carpeting. Enter your room and relish the spaciousness, the high ceilings and the thick walls that virtually block out any potentially disturbing sound.

There are nine such rooms, each with a unique decor and special features. Mine was the Strawberry Hill Room, bathed in light from a row of huge windows framed by soft peach curtains and peach and green wallpaper. Mauve and green paisley wallpaper covered the ceiling, and two chandeliers (one in the foyer, the other above the bed and controlled by a dimmer) hung from an elaborate frieze that looked like sugar cake frosting.

The nineteenth century wooden bed was so high, a plush stepping stool was provided. The magnificent fireplace was surrounded by the original redwood mantel and custom-designed peach and green tiles. In the foyer was a marble-topped sideboard with a panel of green glass and hand-painted tiles. The walls were hung with gilt-edged mirrors.

The bathroom was fully half the size of the huge bedroom, with a new pedestal sink, a marble-top dresser, a shower-tub combination and more mirrors. (Other bathrooms have antique clawfoot tubs, one with matching "his and her" tubs next to a fireplace!)

Old-fashioned rod radiators heated the bathroom and bedroom. And then there was the brass bar underneath the windows. What was that for, I asked myself. When I returned from dinner I learned its purpose when I discovered the Battenburg lace comforter from the bed hanging over it.

That's just one example of the service at the Gingerbread Mansion. Another: the staff will ask you to let someone know when you leave for dinner so they can turn down your bed without disturbing you. And of course, they leave a locally made chocolate cream on your pillow.

Breakfast in Gingerbread Mansion's dining room is a family-style, social affair. I shared a table, and plenty of lively conversation, with a business couple from Atlanta, a mother-and-daughter team from the Sacramento area and two vacationing couples from the United Kingdom.

We helped ourselves to coffee from carafes and juice from pitchers and passed around plates or baskets piled with fresh fruit, coffee cake and pumpkin muffins. The staff took orders for eggs Benedict served casserole style in individual ramekins. Who could resist?

Warning: Ferndale is dairy country, so there's plenty of cheese, butter and real cream on the table, all extremely fresh and dangerously delicious!

Exploring Ferndale is a must, whether you tool around on your own bike, one of the inn's one-speeds, or on foot. Rescued by locals from the wrecking ball in the 1960s, the entire village of vintage Victorian buildings is a Registered California Historical Landmark within walking distance from the inn. Art galleries, live theater, a hand-dipped candy factory and good restaurants keep the town bustling.

For dinner, Ken recommends Bibo and Bear on Main Street. If you'd rather have more traditional fare than their "California nouveau" cuisine, head for the Victorian Village Inn. For lunch, try Diane's, or if you come back from a ride hungry in the late afternoon, the Stage Door deli next to the theater serves up "blue plate specials" all day long.

BIKING FROM GINGERBREAD MANSION INN

Terrain Flat as a buttermilk pancake. There are a few climbs available if you look for them, particularly if you're on a mountain bike seeking dirt.

Road Conditions Okay, here's the bad news. These are down-and-dirty country roads featuring irrigation sprayers and territorial dogs, not to mention enough potholes, patches and loose gravel to convince you that the cows must trample them twice a day. The exceptions are the state highway into Ferndale (old U.S. 101) and the roads crisscrossing Table Bluff to and from the state beach.

Traffic You might see an occasional car, even a logging truck, on the country roads, but rarely. The one bottleneck you will have to negotiate is the bridge connecting Ferndale to the outside world. It's narrow and has fast-moving traffic but no shoulder; the best way to cross it is to take the lane and scoot!

Nearest Bike Shop
Sport and Cycle
475 Fortuna Blvd.
Fortuna, CA
707-725-9405

Best Time To Ride Spring through autumn
Supposedly the sunniest weather occurs in September, but when I was there two weeks after Labor Day, it was gray and overcast. Conclusion: the weather is unpredictable and fog may push in from the coast at any time of year.

Mountain Biking Opportunities There are dirt roads along the ridge and bluffs southwest of town. Access is up Poole Road, on the left a little over four miles out Centerville Road. Die-hard dirt lovers may not be satisfied, however, unless they trek north of Eureka to the state parks beyond Trinidad and Orick.

LOLETA-TABLE BLUFF LOOP (29.0, 37.0 OR 45.2 MILES)

After stops at the grocery and Cheese Factory in Loleta, you'll have all the picnic fixings you need to accompany your view of Humboldt Bay from atop Table Bluff. You can ride down to the

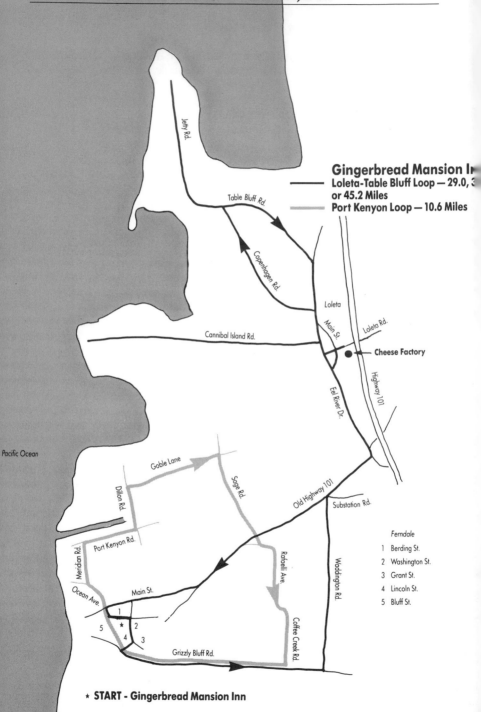

Gingerbread Mansion I
Loleta-Table Bluff Loop — 29.0, 3
or 45.2 Miles
Port Kenyon Loop — 10.6 Miles

Jetty Rd.

Table Bluff Rd.

Copenhagen Rd.

Loleta

Main St.

Loleta Rd.

Cannibal Island Rd.

Cheese Factory

Eel River Dr.

Highway 101

Pacific Ocean

Goble Lane

Sage Rd.

Old Highway 101

Substation Rd.

Dillon Rd.

Port Kenyon Rd.

Meridian Rd.

Raffaelli Ave.

Waddington Rd.

Ocean Ave.

Main St.

Ferndale

1 Berding St.
2 Washington St.
3 Grant St.
4 Lincoln St.
5 Bluff St.

Coffee Creek Rd.

Grizzly Bluff Rd.

★ START - Gingerbread Mansion Inn

beach on the Pacific Ocean side and on up to the end of the jetty; just remember that you must make the twisting, steep ascent to get back!

PORT KENYON LOOP (10.6 MILES)

Port Kenyon was once the seaport for the Ferndale dairies. Boats left daily for the overnight sail down the Eel River and down the coast to San Francisco. Floods have washed the entire port away, and the Eel River has since changed its course more than once, but the dairies go on and on. You can add this short loop to the Table Bluff Loop for 40+ or 50+ miles.

LOLETA-TABLE BLUFF LOOP

PT.-PT.	CUME	DIRECTION	STREET/LANDMARK
			From Gingerbread Mansion Inn
0.0	0.0	**R**	**Berding Street**
0.1	0.1	**R**	**Washington Street**; becomes **Grant Street**
0.4	0.5	**R**	**Lincon Street**
0.7	1.2	**L**	**Grizzly Bluff Road**
2.8	4.0	**L**	**Waddington Road**
2.8	6.8	**L**	**To Old Highway 101** at Substation Road (do NOT take Substation)
0.1	6.9	**R**	**Old Highway 101/Highway 211** (no sign)
0.9	7.8	**X**	**Eel River Bridge** *(Caution!)*
0.5	8.3	**L**	**At T** (no sign)
0.3	8.6	**L**	**Eel River Drive** at freeway interchange
1.5	10.1	**R**	**Main Street**
0.2	10.3		**Loleta** — grocery on left
0.3	10.6	**R**	**Loleta Road**
0.1	10.7	**R**	**Loleta Cheese Factory**
0.0	10.7	**L**	**Loleta Road**
0.2	10.9	**R**	**Eel River Drive**

LOLETA-TABLE BLUFF LOOP (CONT.)

PT.-PT.	CUME	DIRECTION	STREET/LANDMARK
0.4	11.3	L	**Copenhagen Road** (no sign, second left)
3.5	14.8	L	**Table Bluff Road**
1.4	16.2		**Table Bluff Park Overlook**
0.2	16.4		Top of hill — estuary view

Option:
Descend hill and ride out Jetty Road and return.
Approx 8.0 miles out and back.

0.0	16.4	R	**Table Bluff Road**
1.6	18.0	C	**Table Bluff Road** at Copenhagen (Sign facing Copenhagen reads: Highway 101 3.5 miles)
0.6	18.6	R	**Table Bluff Road** at Hookton Road
3.0	21.6	R	**Eel River Drive**

Option: To mouth of Eel River

1.2	22.8	R	**Cannibal Island Road** (8.2 miles out and back)
1.9	24.7	R	At freeway interchange
0.5	25.2	R	Over **Eel River Bridge** (*Caution!*) onto **Old Highway 101**
3.3	28.5	R	**Main Street**
0.3	28.8	L	**Ocean Ave.**
0.1	28.9	L	**Berding Street**
0.1	29.0		**Gingerbread Mansion** on right

PORT KENYON LOOP

PT.-PT.	CUME	DIRECTION	STREET/LANDMARK
			From Gingerbread Mansion Inn
0.0	0.0	L	**Berding Street**
0.1	0.1	R	**Ocean Avenue**
0.9	1.0	R	**Meridian Road**
0.9	1.9	R	**Port Kenyon Road**
0.5	2.4	L	**Dillon Road**
0.9	3.3	R	**Goble Lane**
2.5	5.8	R	**Sage Road**
0.8	6.6	L	**Rafaelli Avenue**
0.4	7.0	R	**Coffee Creek Road**
1.5	8.5	R	**Grizzly Bluff Road**
1.5	10.0	BR	**Bluff Street**; Short climb to good views of village and delta
0.5	10.5	C	**Ocean Avenue**
0.1	10.6	R	**Berding Street** **Gingerbread Mansion** on right

HIGHLAND DELL INN

Glenn Dixon and Anthony Patchett
21050 River Blvd., P.O. Box 370   Rates: $65-$115; Suites $140-$225
Monte Rio, CA 95462-0370   Bed & Breakfast Inn
800-767-1759; 707-865-1759   Full breakfast
Ambience: Old-fashioned Riverside Resort   Smoking permitted in
common areas

"**Welcome to Monte Rio,** Your Vacation Wonderland," reads the sign spanning California Highway 116. Well, "wonderland" may be stretching it a bit, but there's much about this little community snuggled on both sides of the Russian River to charm and delight.

There's the river itself, the backdrop for frenetic activity from May to October. Water lovers flock here for the canoeing and rafting, music lovers for the May and September festivals in nearby Guerneville, gourmands for the surprisingly good food at top-flight restaurants.

Cyclists riding through on the Santa Rosa Wine Country Century, with touring outfitters like Backroads, or on Almaden Cycle Touring Club's Russian River Rally are blown away by the scenic redwoods and coastside cliffs.

An ideal jumping-off point for independent riders heading to the coast or out on a "circuit" through the surrounding hills is the Highland Dell Inn, a perfect "base camp" on the south side of the river. Built in 1906 as a resort hotel, the Highland Dell is "the grand old lady on the river, and she deserves to be a quiet, relaxing B&B in her 90s," claims innkeeper Glenn Dixon.

Once the summer vacation destination of San Franciscans arriving by train, the inn has also been a bawdy house in the 1940s and '50s and a refuge for the love child and drug lifestyles of the '60s and '70s. As one guest put it, "History and karma echo through the corridors of this beautiful old inn."

(Alternative lifestyles still prevail in Monte Rio, and all persuasions of both life and style are welcome at Highland Dell Inn.)

Walking into the front lobby, I noticed that everything was just a little off-kilter. The doors slanted a bit, the floors sloped and some of the walls were a tad crooked. But the all-redwood construction is solid and everything is clean and freshly painted. The

lobby is dominated by a massive chandelier that consists of five individual crystal chandeliers suspended from another, balsa wood chandelier from Mexico.

The windows of the "Sun Room," where breakfast is served, presented great views of the Russian River meandering by. Framed black and white photos of the glory days of Monte Rio line the opposite wall.

Ornate and interesting art objects and antiques appear everywhere — fringed lampshades, procelain pedestals, carved wooden Buddhas, Greek gods and wood nymphs.

Downstairs, through a stained glass door, are four small single/ double rooms with private baths, telephones, queen-size beds and views of the woods or the river.

Upstairs are the suites, connected rooms you can rent individually or as a group or family. These include the Captain's Room with a king-size ship's cabin bed, an open steamer trunk in the corner, and a genuine Morris chair. The Dell Suite offers a sleigh bed, a river view and an attached living room with foldout sofabed, TV and VCR.

But the creme-de-la-creme is the 1300-square-foot Bohemian Suite, a penthouse taking up the entire third floor of the inn. Never mind the king-size antique brass bed; what really grabs you is the claret-red double-size bathtub with twin showers, assorted rubber play toys and round mirror on the ceiling directly above!

I spent the night in Room #3 on the ground floor. The queen bed was piled high with pillows. The walls were paneled in knotty pine, and the settle beneath the window was upholstered in chintz to match the drapes. But the centerpiece of the room was the huge lyre-shaped beveled mirror framed in massive wood on the wall above the bed. Richly filled chocolate truffles waited under the glasses by the in-room sink (an upgrade of the orginal).

The bathroom held a clawfoot tub with shower. A tray across the tub offered shampoo, bubble bath, a loofa sponge, and a rubber ducky. (All the tubs in the inn have rubber duckies, which are available for "adoption," according to the inn's guest literature. "Adoption papers" cost $5 each at the front desk.) A low wicker hamper held magazines handy to the tub for reading while soaking in a bubble bath.

Food on the Russian River is especially noteworthy. From Highland Dell it's a short walk down River Blvd. to the Village Inn for excellent pasta, chicken and seafood at reasonable prices (the desserts are special, too!)

On Saturday nights you can enjoy a gourmet feast from the Highland Dell's fixed-price menu. Or carboloading bicyclists may want to make the 6.3-mile trek to Occidental for old-fashioned fat-tube spaghetti at the Union Hotel or Negri's.

Breakfast at Highland Dell is a buffet affair on weekends. Weekdays, however, guests get to order their preferences in omelets or waffles. Choices for omelets run from green onions to chopped tomato to avocado and mushrooms, accompanied by your favorite cheese. Bon appetit! You're going to need the nourishment to get over Kings Ridge on the way to Fort Ross!

BIKING FROM HIGHLAND DELL INN

Terrain Climbing Kings Ridge on Fort Ross Road is a definite challenge: a 1300-foot gain in three miles! If climbing is your thing, you can find other precipitous walls to scale between Fort Ross and Bodega Bay. Some of them, like Fort Ross Road up from the coast, are featured in the "Terrible Two," quite likely California's most daunting double century. There's good touring to be had without all that verticality, however, as on the gentle climb to Occidental featured here.

Road Conditions Highway 116 is narrow and often shoulderless on the way to the coast, and all the backroads are typical country fare — often potholed, patched and always shoulderless.

Traffic Summer brings lots of tourists, which means lots of traffic. Guerneville is one big parking lot during the music festivals. Once you leave the town behind, however, traffic thins and is practically absent come September and October.

Nearest Bike Shop
Mike's Bikes
16434 Highway 116
Guerneville, CA
707-869-1106

Best Time To Ride September-October ("Secret Summer" on the Russian River)

Mountain Biking Opportunities Armstrong Redwoods State Park in Guerneville and Austin Creek State Recreation Area just above it have bike-legal trails. You can buy a map for $.50 at the Armstrong entry station. One warning from Almaden Cycle Touring Club riders who've been there: Stay off McCray Ridge Road — zealously guarded private property!

ARMSTRONG REDWOODS STATE PARK (15.1 MILES)

This circuitous but relatively flat route to Guerneville and back evolved from years of Russian River Rallies put on by Almaden Cycle Touring Club. It's great for either skinny or fat tires, and the fatties can continue up the Austin Creek Trail.

FORT ROSS CIRCUIT (43.6 MILES)

Although the Russians landed at Bodega Bay in 1809, Fort Ross, 22 miles to the north, became their southernmost outpost. From here they shipped furs and oil north to Sitka. For a few rubles, you can pick up a cassette and take the walking tour of the lovingly restored fort in about half an hour. The last time I was there a small store provided some calorie replacement, and the restrooms were a rider's delight.

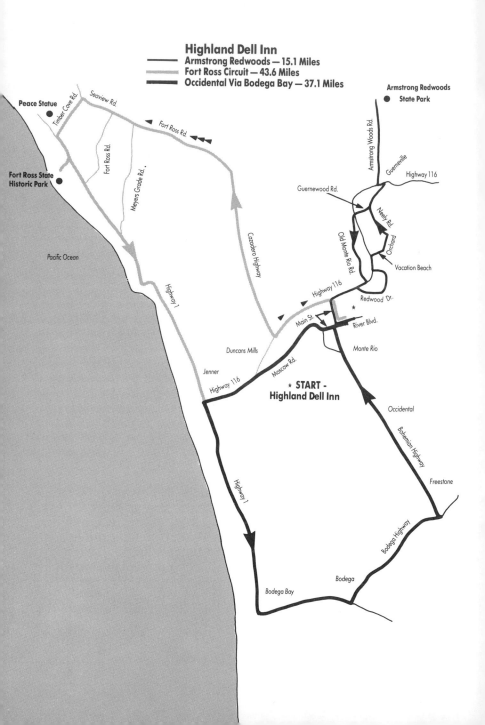

Highland Dell Inn
Armstrong Redwoods — 15.1 Miles
Fort Ross Circuit — 43.6 Miles
Occidental Via Bodega Bay — 37.1 Miles

Peace Statue

Timber Cove Rd.

Seaview Rd.

Fort Ross Rd.

Fort Ross State
Historic Park

Fort Ross Rd.

Meyers Grade Rd.

Cazadero Highway

Pacific Ocean

Highway 1

Armstrong Redwoods
State Park

Armstrong Woods Rd.

Guerneville

Highway 116

Guernewood Rd.

Neely Rd.

Old Monte Rio Rd.

Orchard

Vacation Beach

Highway 116

Redwood Dr.

Main St.

River Blvd.

Duncans Mills

Monte Rio

Jenner

Highway 116

Moscow Rd.

★ START -
Highland Dell Inn

Occidental

Bohemian Highway

Freestone

Highway 1

Bodega Highway

Bodega

Bodega Bay

This route avoids the 2.6-mile drop on Fort Ross Road from Meyers Grade to Highway 1, mostly because condensation from the redwood trees tends to make the steepest pitches "slick as whale snot." Instead, I prefer to ride the four miles of open country on Timber Cove Road, with its access to Bufano's renowned Peace Statue.

The return from Fort Ross down Highway 1 deserves special mention. It's 12.5 miles of absolutely gorgeous scenery. I am not exaggerating. Of all the vistas I've ridden a bike past, the sheer cliffs and crashing surf along this section of the California Coast Highway continue to blow me away.

OCCIDENTAL VIA BODEGA BAY (37.1 MILES)

Riding this popular loop counterclockwise lets you head straight down the coast with the wind at your back to Bodega Bay, where lunch can feature fresh seafood. Plan to eat here because Bodega and Freestone have few services, and it can be a long haul to the delis of Occidental.

ARMSTRONG REDWOODS

PT.-PT.	CUME	DIRECTION	STREET/LANDMARK
			From Highland Dell Inn
0.0	0.0	R	**River Blvd.**
0.1	0.1	R	**Main Street** at Bohemian Highway
0.1	0.2	X	**Russian River**. Access to walkway is via bike path alongside River Blvd. at corner.
0.1	0.3	R	**Highway 116**; grocery on left
0.5	0.8	R	**Redwood Drive**. Ride around the golf course.
0.8	1.6	R	**Highway 116**
0.9	2.5	R	**Vacation Beach**. No sign - 0.1 mile past Cnopius Road
0.1	2.6	X	Russian River
0.1	2.7	L	**Orchard**
0.5	3.2	L	**Neely Road**
1.2	4.4	L	**Highway 116**
0.1	4.5	X	Russian River
0.1	4.6	R	**Armstrong Woods Road**

ARMSTRONG REDWOODS (CONT.)

PT.-PT.	CUME	DIRECTION	STREET/LANDMARK
			Guerneville — stores, cafes, delis
2.3	6.9		**Armstrong Redwoods State Park Entrance.** Trail maps available at kiosk
0.5	7.4	U	**Armstrong Tree**
2.8	10.2	L	**Highway 116** in Guerneville
0.1	10.3	X	Russian River
0.2	10.5	R	**Neely Road**
0.3	10.8	R	**Guernewood Road**
0.2	11.0	R	**Summer crossing** (200 yards gravel)
0.1	11.1	X	Russian River
0.1	11.2	L	**Highway 116**
0.1	11.3	R	**Old Monte Rio Road**
2.5	13.8	R	**Highway 116/River Road**
1.0	14.8	L	**Main Street** in Monte Rio
0.1	14.9	X	Russian River
0.1	15.0	L	**River Blvd.** at Bohemian Highway
0.1	15.1	L	**Highland Dell Inn**

FORT ROSS CIRCUIT

PT.-PT.	CUME	DIRECTION	STREET/LANDMARK
			From Highland Dell Inn
0.0	0.0	R	**River Blvd.**
0.1	0.1	R	**Main Street** at Bohemian Highway
0.1	0.2	X	Russian River. Access to walkway is via bike path alongside River Blvd. at corner.
0.1	0.3	L	**Highway 116.** Turn right for grocery
2.9	3.2	R	**Cazadero Highway**
7.0	10.2	BL	**Fort Ross Road.** General Store on left. *Begin 1300' climb!*
3.0	13.2	BR	**Fort Ross Road** at Meyers Grade Road
0.5	13.7	R	**Seaview Road**
4.0	17.7	L	**Timber Cove Road**
3.0	20.7	L	**Highway 1. Bufano Peace Statue** 1.0 mile to north (right)

FORT ROSS CIRCUIT (CONT.)

PT.-PT.	CUME	DIRECTION	STREET/LANDMARK
2.0	22.7	R	**Fort Ross State Historic Park**
0.5	23.2	C	Bike path/walkway to **Visitor Center** — restrooms, snack bar
0.0	23.2	U	Return on bike path
0.5	23.7	R	**Highway 1**
12.0	35.7		**Jenner** — Stores, deli, cafe
0.5	36.2	L	**Highway 116**
3.7	39.9	R	**Moscow Road** at **Duncans Mills**; espresso bar, general store, railroad musuem
3.4	43.3	L	**Main Street.** Market on left
0.1	43.4	X	Bohemian Street at Bohemian Highway
0.1	43.5	C	**River Blvd.**
0.1	43.6	L	**Highland Dell Inn**

OCCIDENTAL VIA BODEGA BAY

PT.-PT.	CUME	DIRECTION	STREET/LANDMARK
			From Highland Dell Inn
0.0	0.0	R	**River Blvd.**
0.1	0.1	BR	**Main Street** at Bohemian Highway; market on right
0.1	0.2	R	**Moscow Road**
3.4	3.6	L	**Highway 116** **Duncans Mills** — Espresso bar, general store, railroad musuem
3.7	7.3	L	**Highway 1**
9.5	16.8		**Bodega Bay** — Delis, seafood restaurants
5.1	21.9	L	**Bodega Highway**
0.2	22.1		**Bodega** — Bar only - water, restrooms
3.4	25.5	L	**Bodega Highway**
1.5	27.0	L	**Bohemian Highway**
0.2	27.2		**Freestone** — General Store
3.5	30.7		**Occidental** — delis, Italian restaurants
6.3	37.0	R	**River Blvd.** at Main Street
0.1	37.1	L	**Highland Dell Inn**

PUDDING CREEK INN

Garry and Carole Anloff
700 North Main Street
Fort Bragg, CA 95437
800-227-9529; 707-964-9529
Ambience: Casual Victorian Whimsy

Rates: $65-$125
Bed & Breakfast Inn
Full breakfast
No smoking

Choosing a bed-and-breakfast inn on the Mendocino coast is a tough decision. From Fort Bragg down to Elk, B&Bs line the village streets and country roads. Some are right in the middle of the tourist hustle and bustle of the Mendocino art colony. Others sit at the end of long dirt roads in the backcountry. Some, like Heritage House, so charmingly depicted in the movie "Same Time Next Year," are scandalously expensive. Others are quite affordable.

I chose Pudding Creek Inn in northern Fort Bragg for three reasons: innkeepers Garry and Carole Anloff were kindly disposed to hosting bicyclists, their location gave me a scenic ride down to the action in Mendocino, and their rates were much more reasonable than those further south.

Not that Fort Bragg doesn't have its attractions. Noyo Harbor, just down the road a piece, offers salty atmosphere and terrific seafood cuisine. The Skunk Railroad (so named, I've heard, because the mix of Diesel and gas it once ran on meant you could smell the train before you saw it) is a delightful way to return from the 34-mile bike ride inland to Willitts. A fine museum occupies a lovingly refurbished former lumber company guest house. And the small downtown area holds enough galleries and craft shops to satisfy any "pro" shopper.

Of special note to bicyclists is the Fort Bragg Bakery on Franklin Street, one block east of Main, just south of Laurel. Here you can buy breads and pastries made on the premises, or sit down to a full lunch after your ride.

Arriving at Pudding Creek Inn, I was pleasantly surprised by the casual ambience. Surrounded by Queen Anne decor and Victorian memorabilia, Garry Anloff greeted me in denim cut-offs.

Actually, I was received by a small greeting committee: in addition to Garry, I met his charming 4-year-old daughter, and Max, the family's Labrador Retriever, who put his paws up on the half-door shelf to sniff out this new acquaintance. Another pet, Puddin'

the cat, came with the inn as part of the escrow agreement when the Anloffs purchased it in 1991.

Named for the creek that flows to the Pacific just north of town, the inn itself is a rambling affair of two separate buildings joined by a garden along the passageway between them. Rows of bright fuschias, begonias and geraniums line the gravel pathway. Here wine and munchies are served during "social hour" from 5:00 to 6:00 daily. Sipping Chardonnay I discovered a fascinating oral history record of Fort Bragg on the counter near the front of the garden.

In 700 Main on the south side of the garden are the Anloff's residence, the office, dining room and kitchen, where a display case holds a mannequin dressed in Victorian wedding finery.

Four guest rooms upstairs include the Potpourri, done in white wicker, the Spinning Room, with a spool bed, an authentic spinning wheel and an authentic rubber ducky resting on the rim of the clawfoot tub, the School Room in traditional schoolroom beiges and browns, and Grandma's Attic with brass queen bed and wedding ring quilt.

The building next door, 710 Main, holds six rooms. Mine was downstairs, in the Countess Room. A canopied queen bed draped with lace curtains was surrounded by rich redwood-paneled walls. Two easy chairs sat next to the bay window. An antique oval mirror stood in the corner. A fire was laid in the wood-burning fireplace, behind a huge Victorian fan.

The room was full of little out-of-the-way nooks and crannies, and many details that weren't immediately obvious would suddenly catch my attention later. One of these was the hummingbird mobile hanging over the bed: two birds hovering over a piece of driftwood. Another was the brocade lace wallpaper in the bathroom.

There were guests already checked into the Count's Room, but pictures of it told me it too was paneled in highly varnished redwood and contained many fine details. Upstairs I got a peek at the Buttercup Room, all in yellow, and Victorian Valentine, a honeymooners' romantic retreat in pink and lace.

In back of 710, a separate Recreation Room provided an entertainment center, soft and hot drinks, a huge library and no less than four versions of Trivial Pursuit. In the corner another display case was jammed with antique cameras and a collection of ladies' accessories — gloves, beaded handbags, a fan.

The dining room deserves special mention. Light streamed in through a bay window curtained in lace onto the pastel Queen Anne chairs and the spool tables covered with embroidered tablecloths. Each table held a copy of a "quiz" that asks, "Just how smart are you?" Sample question: If you had 17 sheep and all but 9 died, how many were left? (The answers are on the back.)

Breakfast was buffet style from a sideboard in the kitchen. I couldn't resist sampling nearly everything on the menu of the day: OJ; strawberry yogurt in sherbet glasses and topped with granola, fresh banana slices and strawberry slivers; apple strudel; sour cream blintzes topped with strawberries; Canadian bacon; English muffins; and a choice of tea, coffee, decaf or cocoa. That should be enough to carry a cyclist to Mendocino!

BIKING FROM PUDDING CREEK INN

Besides the rides listed here, you can also ride to Willitts, timing your trip to return on the Skunk Train, which will deposit you just a few blocks from Pudding Creek Inn. Or you can explore Noyo Harbor, on both sides of Noyo Bridge south of town, then continue south to tour the Mendocino Coast Botanical Gardens.

Terrain Surprisingly easy-rolling for the California coast, although you will climb going inland, or out to and from Point Cabrillo.

Road Conditions Highway 1 is part of the official Pacific Coast Bicycle Route, and for the most part it is well paved and shouldered. Some roads inland deteriorate rapidly as they rise into the redwoods, a factor of climate as much as neglect. The climate is basic fog, which will no doubt be a factor when you ride.

Traffic The perennial logging trucks are joined now by lumber trucks headed out from the mill in Fort Bragg. Then there's the tourist traffic around the state parks and in downtown Mendocino. When I was there, though, I found the road through the Mendocino Headlands free of any vehicles.

Nearest Bike Shop
Fort Bragg Cyclery
557 S. Franklin Street
Fort Bragg, CA 95437
707-964-3509

Best Time To Ride Late spring (best for the Botanical Gardens) through autumn

Mountain Biking Opportunities You can take the old logging road north of Fort Bragg (just past the Beachcomber Motel) and ride along the beach for miles. Or ask Garry how to get to the Skunk Railway tracks so you can ride along Pudding Creek on the train's route. Then there's the Canyon Trail at Russian Gulch State Park, two miles north of Mendocino, about seven miles south of Fort Bragg on Highway 1.

For the more technically oriented, Jackson State Forest offers an "unlimited" number of miles of trails in 46,000 acres off Highway 20 between Fort Bragg and Willitts. Maps are available from the State Forestry Office in Fort Bragg.

MOUNTAIN BIKES: FERN CANYON (10.4 MILES OUT AND BACK)

Ascend from the beach entrance of Van Damme State Park through a rain forest to the Pygmy Forest off Little River Road. Then come back down! The trail splits for hikers and cyclists between Fern Canyon and the Pygmy Forest, so the going is fairly worry-free (although I did see hikers on the shorter, bikes-allowed section).

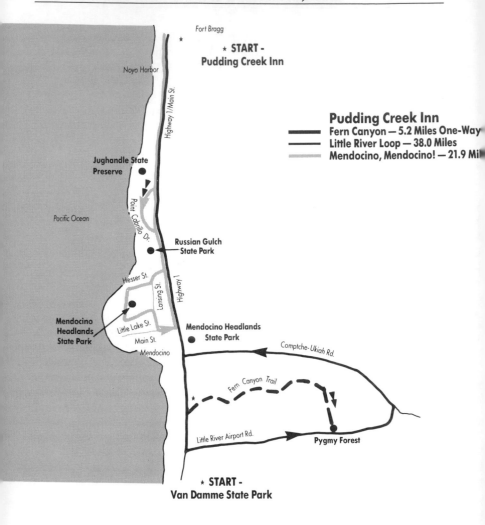

Fort Bragg

★ START -
Pudding Creek Inn

Noyo Harbor

Pudding Creek Inn
Fern Canyon — 5.2 Miles One-Way
Little River Loop — 38.0 Miles
Mendocino, Mendocino! — 21.9 Mi

Highway 1/Main St.

Jughandle State
Preserve

Point Cabrillo Dr.

Pacific Ocean

Russian Gulch
State Park

Highway 1

Hesser St.
Lansing St.

Mendocino
Headlands
State Park

Little Lake St.

Main St.

Mendocino

Mendocino Headlands
State Park

Comptche-Ukiah Rd.

Fern Canyon Trail

Little River Airport Rd.

Pygmy Forest

★ START -
Van Damme State Park

LITTLE RIVER LOOP (38.0 MILES)

This little inland loop south of Mendocino takes you past the pygmy forest in Van Damme State Park. It's worth a stop for a walk around the 0.3-mile boardwalk nature trail. You can also make the same side trips off Highway 1 as you would riding to Mendocino, adding just a few more miles to your ride.

MENDOCINO, MENDOCINO (21.9 MILES)

When the going gets tough on the Mendocino coast, the tough go shopping in Mendocino. Besides parting with your hard-earned cash for fine jewelry, crafts and works of art, you'll find plenty of culinary opportunities there as well, including some of the best ice cream I've ever put away on a bike tour!

On the way down or back, don't miss the opportunity to pedal down to Point Cabrillo or check out Russian Gulch State Park. Both offer terrific ocean views, and the tidepooling at Russian Gulch can also be rewarding.

FERN CANYON

PT.-PT.	CUME	DIRECTION	STREET/LANDMARK
			From Van Damme State Park Visitor Center, 0.1 miles inside park
0.0	0.0	**L**	**Campground road**; restrooms on left
0.8	0.8	**C**	**Fern Canyon Trail** (past gate)
1.8	2.6		**Fern Canyon Campground** — restrooms
1.2	3.8	**BR**	**Fern Canyon Trail** (bike-legal fork)
0.1	3.9		*Creek crossing! Use your granny gears for next 1.0 mile!*
1.1	5.0		**Pygmy Forest**
0.2	5.2		**Pygmy Forest Nature Trail**

LITTLE RIVER LOOP

PT.-PT.	CUME	DIRECTION	STREET/LANDMARK
			From Pudding Creek Inn
0.0	0.0	**L**	**Highway 1/Main Street**
5.4	5.4		**Jughandle State Preserve** on right

LITTLE RIVER LOOP (CONT.)

PT.-PT.	CUME	DIRECTION	STREET/LANDMARK
2.4	7.8		**Russian Gulch State Park** on right
1.3	9.1		**Mendocino** exit on right
3.4	12.5		**Van Damme State Park Beach** on right — Restrooms
0.5	13.0	L	**Little River Airport Road/Road 404**
2.8	15.8		**Pygmy Forest** on left
3.4	19.2	L	**Comptche-Ukiah Road**
5.8	25.0	R	**Highway 1**
0.3	25.3		**Mendocino Headlands State Park** on right
9.7	35.0		**Noyo Harbor** on left
3.0	38.0		**Pudding Creek Inn** on right

MENDOCINO, MENDOCINO!

PT.-PT.	CUME	DIRECTION	STREET/LANDMARK
			From Pudding Creek Inn
0.0	0.0	L	**Highway 1/Main Street**. Grocery store on left
5.4	5.4		**Jughandle State Preserve** on right
1.1	6.5	R	**Point Cabrillo Drive**
1.0	7.5		Caspar Beach Store
2.0	9.5	R	**Highway 1**
1.3	10.8	R	**Lansing Street**
0.5	11.3	R	**Hesser Street** around **Mendocino Headlands State Park**. Restrooms on right
1.0	12.3	C	**Little Lake Street**
0.4	12.7	R	**Lansing Street** to business district — delis, cafes, bistros, galleries, shops
0.1	12.8	L	**Main Street**
		IR	**Lansing Street**
0.3	13.1	L	**Highway 1**
5.7	18.8		**Noyo Harbor** on right
3.1	21.9	R	**Pudding Creek Inn** on right

TOMALES COUNTRY INN

Jo Anne Wallace and John McChesney/Laura Hoffman
25 Valley Street, P.O. Box 376
Tomales, CA 94971
707-878-2041
Ambience: Laid-back country

Rates: $70-$90
Bed & Breakfast
Expanded continental breakfast
No smoking

Little more than an intersection on Highway 1 just minutes from the Sonoma County line, Tomales is "a step out of the pushy present into a friendlier 1900," according to one Bay Area travel writer. As one local put it, "Tomales hasn't been spoiled by being yuppied up."

Protected by the planned land use restrictions of the California Coastal Zone and by its designation as a National Historic District, Tomales will change little. But that's not the only attraction for Northern California cyclists.

There are two reasons for this pedaling popularity: 1) the workouts and views to be had on the short, steep coastal hills, and 2) lunch at the Tomales Bakery, possibly the best fuel stop to be found north of San Francisco. Should you spend a night or two at the Tomales Country Inn, be sure to plan your rides so you're back at the Bakery in time to claim a piece of the foccaccio bread. Try the sun-dried tomato bread sticks, too!

The Tomales Country Inn sits on a little hilltop above the town park, on the other side of the highway from the bakery. Built around 1900 entirely of heart redwood in the Queen Anne tradition, the house still sports the original ship's lapstrake siding, cut shingles, and much of the gingerbread trim.

For years local artist Byron Randall owned the house and operated it as a combined "guest house" and art gallery. More a hostel than a country inn, the guest house operation took its toll on the building. In 1989 Randall sold the house to Jo Anne Wallace and John McChesney, two fugitives from the centers of power in Washington, DC, where they spent ten years with National Public Radio producing "Morning Edition" and "All Things Considered."

Their hard work turned the place into a first-class B&B. But it wasn't long before Wallace and McChesney found they missed the action of broadcasting. Today Jo Anne is general manager of KQED-FM in San Francisco, and John rejoined NPR as a West Coast news

correspondent. In their absence, you will be greeted by on-site innkeeper Laura Hoffman, also an artist whose studio is in the basement.

Meanwhile, Byron Randall still lives in a cottage on the property where he too paints every day. His paintings are everywhere in the Inn. My favorite is the one on the dining room wall — a peasant farmer pedaling a bike to market, his wares balanced all over the bike as well as on his head. When I expressed my admiration to Laura, she told me Byron often sells his paintings to guests, sometimes for very reasonable prices (and sometimes for extremely exorbitant ones!).

From the dining room, French doors lead to a big sunroom overlooking the park on one side and, on the other, the historic Tomales Presbyterian Church, built in 1886. Around the French doors is a wall of shelves stacked with books, everything from spy fiction to the latest in political thought. Inside, rattan furniture and a long banquette under the east windows invite relaxing. Stereo speakers surround the old brick fireplace, and abstract paintings adorn the walls.

There's more art to delight the eye in the garden: whimsical pre-Columbian style sculptures by Mary Fuller. Walk all the way around the lily pond and you can see the little figures change from different perspectives. Take a look in the kitchen window while you're at it and you'll see Byron's "World's Largest Collection of Potato Mashers" hanging in view.

The inn offers the hospitality of five guest rooms. The two on the first floor have private baths, while the upstairs rooms and "Attic" share a bath. All the rooms have hardwood floors spread with colorful rugs, down comforters on the beds, and more original paintings and other artwork.

I stayed in Room #6 on the first floor, sleeping warmly in its carved oak Victorian queen-size bed under a white lace-covered comforter. I loved the two antique cane chairs and the oak hotel dresser with raised mirror. Everything was simple and elegant — no extraneous gingerbread here!

The bathroom took up what looked to be a former walk-in closet. Wine and white tiles covered the floor, and the wine towels were a perfect color match. Above the sink, a huge oak-framed beveled mirror commanded attention.

But the best feature of Room #6 was the eastern exposure. I awoke before dawn and relished watching the sun rise over the far ridge.

Room #7 across the hall, with the same sunrise view, features a dramatic Eastlake walnut Victorian queen bed with ornate headboard and foot, and a matching marbletop dresser. The two cozy second-floor rooms are built into the gables of the roof. The eastern room is furnished with a double oak bed, hotel dresser and rocker. The west room has a double bed, marbletop walnut dresser, bedside chest and wicker chair.

For both space and privacy, stay in the Attic on top of the house. An arched Palladian window looks out over the gardens to the church, which is softly lit at night. There's a large oak library table, an oversized wicker chair and rocker, and a maple washstand.

Breakfast at Tomales Country Inn is often listed as "continental" but don't let that fool you into thinking you'll be hungry! Laura plied me with all the wholesome granola I could eat, along with bananas. Plus there was excellent juice, coffee or tea, fresh cantalope and whole-grain bread so warm it was crumbling and spilling its nuts, seeds and raisins. "Sometimes I make eggs too," she told me.

Please, no, I said to myself. I want to save room for what comes out of the Bakery's ovens today!

BIKING FROM TOMALES COUNTRY INN

Terrain The hills in West Marin County were once sand dunes, but you'd never know it now! Most of the roads that scale them are steep, but the uphill sections are generally short, and the downhills are a blast! Toughest climb is the "Marshall Wall" between Chileno Valley and Highway 1. The route described here descends the steepest section of the Wall.

Road Conditions Highway 1 continues its way down the coast with rare glimpses of shoulder, except occasionally when you pass through a town. Yet almost all the secondary roads are well graded and surfaces are relatively free of pock marks.

Traffic As in other tourist meccas, summer brings the most traffic, especially on Highway 1. The trick is to stay on the traffic-free paralleling or perpendicular local roads as much as possible.

Nearest Bike Shop Sadly, the world-famous Point Reyes Bikes in Point Reyes Station is no longer. The nearest "shop" is Trail Head Bike Rentals in Bear Valley (featured in Bear Valley Inn on page 167), nearly 20 miles south on Highway 1. No major repairs or parts are available.

Best Time To Ride May through October
     Summer months tend to be foggy and windy, while spring and fall (Indian summer) are usually milder.

Mountain Biking Opportunities It's an easy drive to Point Reyes National Seashore on the other side of Tomales Bay, or to the north end of the Bolinas Ridge Trail in the Golden Gate National Recreation Area. Pick up free bike trail maps at the Bear Valley Visitor Center, half a mile from Trail Head Bike Rentals.

CHILENO VALLEY (36.1 MILES)

     Riding through Chileno Valley, the phrase "bucolic wonderland" came to mind. It just couldn't be more charmingly rural. Warning: there are no services available on this ride, except in Tomales.

VALLEY FORD (29.3 MILES)

     Head for the ocean at Dillon Beach, then north to the hamlet of Valley Ford and back through the rolling hills. Suggestion: If it's foggy on the coast and you want to get an early start, do this ride in reverse. That way you'll pedal away from the fog to the sheltered valleys, returning when "the coast is clear."

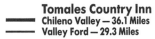

Tomales Country Inn
Chileno Valley — 36.1 Miles
Valley Ford — 29.3 Miles

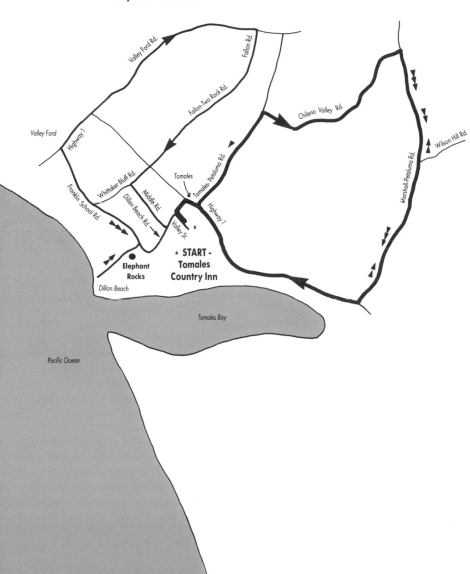

Valley Ford Rd.

Fallon Rd.

Fallon-Two Rock Rd.

Chileno Valley Rd.

Valley Ford

Highway 1

Wilson Hill Rd.

Marshall-Petaluma Rd.

Whitaker Bluff Rd.

Tomales

Tomales-Petaluma Rd.

Franklin School Rd.

Dillon Beach Rd.

Middle Rd.

Valley St.

Highway 1

Elephant Rocks

★ START -
Tomales
Country Inn

Dillon Beach

Tomales Bay

Pacific Ocean

CHILENO VALLEY

PT.-PT.	CUME	DIRECTION	STREET/LANDMARK
			From Tomales Country Inn
0.0	0.0	**L**	**Valley Street**
		IR	**Dillon Beach Road**. General store on left, deli on right, bakery across Highway 1 on left
0.1	0.1	**R**	**Highway 1**
0.3	0.4	**L**	**Tomales-Petaluma Road**
5.3	5.7	**R**	**Chileno Valley Road**. Laguna Lake on left.
9.6	15.3	**R**	**Marshall-Petaluma Road** at T *Two "walls": first right away, second in 9 miles for 1.5 miles, then steep descent for 1.5 miles.*
13.6	28.9	**R**	**Highway 1**
7.0	35.9		**Tomales** — Bakery on right
0.1	36.0	**L**	**Dillon Beach Road**. General store on right, deli on left
0.1	36.1	**L**	**Valley Street** to Tomales Country Inn at end

VALLEY FORD

PT.-PT.	CUME	DIRECTION	STREET/LANDMARK
			From Tomales Country Inn
0.0	0.0	**L**	**Valley Street**
		IL	**Dillon Beach Road**
2.4	2.4	**L**	**Dillon Beach Road** at Franklin School Road
1.4	3.8	**U**	**Dillon Beach.** Lawson's Store on left. *Steep climb!*
0.3	4.1		**Elephant Rocks** on right
1.1	5.2	**L**	**Franklin School Road**
5.0	10.2	**R**	**Highway 1**. Valley Ford Cafe, market and deli on left
1.8	12.0	**S**	**Valley Ford Road** at Highway 1 junction
7.1	19.1	**R**	**Fallon Road**; becomes **Fallon-Two Rock Rd.**
5.9	25.0	**X**	Highway 1
		C	**Whittaker Bluff Road**
1.4	26.4	**BL**	**Middle Road**
1.9	28.3	**L**	**Dillon Beach Road**
1.0	29.3	**R**	**Valley Street** to Tomales Country Inn at end

SAN FRANCISCO BAY AREA INNS AND RIDES

San Francisco conjures up images of the Golden Gate Bridge, Fisherman's Wharf, Chinatown, Union Square, Coit Tower and Telegraph Hill. Unfortunately, all these places are gridlocked with urban traffic and rife with streets and roads that make cycling more a chore than a joy. Hence this book does not visit the City, as nearly everyone in the Bay Area calls it.

Travel just a few miles along the coast north or south of the City, however, and you will find country roads, scenic seashores, and B&B inns to delight any vacationing cyclist.

To the north there's Point Reyes National Seashore, directly off Highway 1 in west Marin County. Sir Francis Drake made landfall here in 1579, on his quest for the Northwest Passage to Asia. The mountain biking and scenic road touring opportunities are so prolific here, I've included inns in two locations just adjacent to Point Reyes, in order to cover all the great rides.

To the south lies the San Francisco Peninsula's Coastside, with its ocean beaches and fine roads winding through the picturesque Santa Cruz Mountains. Climb through the redwoods to Skyline Drive and you will be rewarded with simultaneous views of San Francisco Bay to the east and the Pacific Ocean to the west.

Although you can ride nearly all year long here, the weather can be variable in any season. Fog can hug the coast for days on end in July, prompting Mark Twain to comment, "The coldest winter I ever spent was a summer in San Francisco." Yet when the fog clears, it often signals the onset of strong onshore winds. Winter can bring torrential rains, but recent droughts saw weeks of uninterrupted sunshine all along the coast.

When the sun gets its licks in, the lure of the beach can be hard to resist. Tomales Bay and Half Moon Bay can enjoy high temperatures spring through autumn, and the shoreline is just right for sunning, surfing, beachcombing, birdwatching or peoplewatching.

Spring and summer bring century season, with well-supported rides criss-crossing the mountains to the coast. Three popular favorites are the Sequoia Century, from the urban Peninsula to Coastside in early June; and in August, the Marin Century, featuring afternoon freewheeling ahead of the winds along Tomales Bay, and the Banana Classic, with its redwood-shaded climb up Tunitas Creek Road.

Country inns are enjoying a burgeoning popularity in the Bay Area, offering the privacy of remote locations combined with great touring opportunities and the casual California lifestyle. In Olema, just over the hill from Fairfax, the cradle of mountain biking on the slopes of Mt. Tam, **Bear Valley Inn** coexists with a mountain bike rental shop right next door. Innkeepers Ron and JoAnne Nowell have revived a turn-of-the-century farmhouse, filling it with antiques and operating the bike concession as an adjunct.

Dancing Coyote Beach allows guests to luxuriate in the ultimate privacy — no phones, no TV, no common rooms, just your own cottage, with a well-stocked kitchen and personal access to a private beach right on Tomales Bay. And all a short walk from the fine Czech restaurants for which Inverness is renowned.

Moving south, Bud and Lee Raynor at **Rancho San Gregorio** give their guests a refreshing appreciation of the ecology and value of the land in this still-bucolic rural outpost just 45 minutes from the City. Bird watchers are in their element here, and cyclists discover rural roads that appear forgotten by time.

Right smack in "downtown" Half Moon Bay, Simon and Ann Lowings' **Zaballa House** is an affordable way to explore redwood forests, ocean beaches, pumpkin patches, and gourmet restaurants from one restful spot. Just wandering through the neighboring nursery can induce symptoms of laid-back California relaxation.

FOR MORE INFORMATION ON BICYCLING IN THE SAN FRANCISCO BAY AREA:

Favorite Pedal Tours of Northern California by Naomi Bloom. Fine Edge Productions, Route 2, Box 303, Bishop, CA 93514.

Mountain Biking in the Bay Area, Volume One: South from San Francisco Bay and *Volume Two: North from San Francisco Bay* by Michael Hodgson and Mark Lord. Western Tanager Press, 111 Pacific Avenue, Santa Cruz, CA 95060.

Bay Area Bike Rides by Ray Hosler. Chronicle Books, 275 Fifth Street, San Francisco, CA 94103.

Cycling the San Francisco Bay Area by Carol O'Hare. Bicycle Books, Inc., P.O. Box 2038, Mill Valley, CA 94942.

Roads to Ride, A Bicyclist's Topographic Guide to Alameda, Contra Costa and Marin Counties by Grant Petersen and Mary Anderson. Heyday Books, Box 9145, Berkeley, CA 94709.

Roads to Ride South, A Bicyclist's Topographic Guide to San Mateo, Santa Clara and Santa Cruz Counties by Grant Petersen and John Kluge. Heyday Books, Box 9145, Berkeley, CA 94709.

BEAR VALLEY INN

Ron and JoAnne Nowell
88 Bear Valley Road, P.O. Box 33
Olema, CA 94950
415-663-1777
Ambience: Country Farmhouse

Rates: $70-$125
Bed & Breakfast
Full breakfast
Smoking outside only

Bicycles may be banned from dirt trails in most national parks, but not in Point Reyes National Seashore, where you can explore miles and miles of trails on fat tires. The center for all this two-wheel activity is Bear Valley, a little slip of a canyon just west of the village of Olema, at the junction of Sir Francis Drake Blvd. and Coast Highway 1.

Suppose you arrive in the area without a mountain bike to ride. No problem. You can rent one from Trail Head Rentals, which just happens to be next door to Olema's version of down-home bed-and-breakfasting, Bear Valley Inn. Both bike rental shop and inn are expertly guided by Ron and JoAnne Nowell, who have done a terrific job converting their 1899 farmhouse into a first-rate accommodation.

Ron told me it took some major work, including a new foundation. "Doors were boarded up, the floors had many, many coats of paint and the walls were covered with layers of wallpaper," he added. Today, all that's left of that stuff is the wallpaper surrounding the bay windows in the dining room. Throughout the house, the hardwood floors are enhanced with area and throw rugs, and all the warm colors are based on a scheme of wine red and green.

There are three guest rooms, all on the second floor. One offers a king-size bed under a double oak headboard and covered with a rose and beige comforter. An antique lace bedspread hangs on the wall above. Other antiques include a wine-colored wingback chair, a secretary desk and an old telephone table with a glass tiffany lamp. The floor is formally dressed in a purple and green oriental rug.

Another room features a double bed with a tall carved oak headboard and a wine-colored bedspread, an oak hotel dresser/washstand with brass drawer pulls and heart-shaped beveled mirror, and an oak rocker in the corner. A whimsical cabbage rose rug in

blue, gold, rose and pink complements the colors in the quilt on the wall.

My room was the one with the queen bed, a marvelous brass piece with a green and rose quilt comforter and wine-colored lace-trimmed pillow shams. A rose and green down comforter sat folded at the bottom of the bed. The windows were covered with lace shades framed by heavy lace-trimmed brocade curtains in a cabbage rose pattern. Both windows overlooked the garden.

The carpet, a white and red cabbage rose pattern, left just an inch or so of the highly varnished wood flooring visible at the perimeter. An antique chest of drawers stained wine red and topped with a tilting mirror faced the bed. On the top, a pink cut-glass carafe held drinking water. And a round antique oak side table held a brass lamp topped with a fringed Tiffany-style shade.

All the rooms share the single bath, which is also brimming with antiques. The clawfoot tub is wine red on the outside, and its feet are green. There's a handsome brass towel rack, an old medicine chest in the corner above the sink, an oak utility table, and, instead of an antique toilet tank on the wall, an oak planter, its "chain" a trailing pothos vine.

Downstairs, a combined living/dining room takes up the front of the house. The two are separated by a gigantic antique oak cabinet that faces the dining room. On the back, next to the front door, is a topographic map of Point Reyes National Seashore, so you can see what kind of terrain your next ride holds in store for you. On top of the cabinet sits a small collection of Spanish conquistador helmets. A brass coat rack nearby holds binoculars that guests can borrow for bird or whale watching.

In the dining room, the oval oak table, extended to its full length, is surrounded by a mixed collection of oak farmhouse kitchen chairs. A small covered dish of chocolate chip cookies is always on the table. A dropleaf table in the corner holds a tray of coffee and tea for guests to help themselves. Afternoons, lemonade or iced tea is also up for grabs.

In the living room a huge brick fireplace with oval hearth is surrounded by plush easy chairs — one deep rose, the other dark blue — opposite a matching dark blue settee. All are adorned with lace antimacassars. A round oak coffee table is stacked with copies of such magazines as *National Geographic, Outside, Bicycling, Backpacker,* and books with titles like, *More to the Point, Lesser Known Aspects of the Point Reyes National Seashore, Marin Coast, The Enchanted Coast,* and *Last Stage For Bolinas.*

Outside, a country garden leads to a small apple orchard. A weathered round picnic table is surrounded by benches and lawn chairs, and trellises filled with ivy frame the pathways. A giant cedar graces the parking area; its branches hang so low that I couldn't drive my bike-topped car beneath it.

Just steps around the corner on Highway 1 lies Olema, the last outpost of civilization before Highway 1 skirts Stinson Beach and heads to the Golden Gate.

I was delighted to discover the Olema Inn still serving outstanding gourmet dinners for reasonable prices. Their wine list is also excellent; be sure to ask what other labels besides those listed are available by the glass. There's also a cafe and a deli across the street, for your on-bike goodies.

Not that you'll need much in the way of extra fuel after breakfast at Bear Valley Inn. When I appeared in the living room in the morning, JoAnne greeted me with a champagne flute full of fresh orange juice, then brought out a pot of Earl Grey tea. When I'd settled down at the table, she served me an Apple Walnut Buttermilk Cake (see recipe section) made with apples from the inn's own trees, along with plenty of nuts and seeds sprinkled on top. The cake was accompanied by a bowl of yogurt with chunks of fresh banana and strawberry swimming in it. Yum!

BIKING FROM BEAR VALLEY INN

Terrain Riding inland from Olema is not as arduous as it sounds; Point Reyes-Petaluma Road and the Cross-Marin Bike Trail are easy grades with just a few little "bumps." Off road, there are quite a few ups and downs on the Olema Valley Trail, and transferring to the Bolinas Ridge Trail is an arduous ascent.

Road Conditions Sir Francis Drake Blvd. between Fairfax and Olema is a nightmare of rough surface, potholes and narrow lanes. The County of Marin is attempting to do something about this; when I last rode through Lagunitas there was construction, presumably to widen and smooth the roadway. At any rate, the Cross-Marin Bike Trail, from Samuel P. Taylor Park down to Platform Bridge Road, is an excellent alternate, well maintained, shady and scenic.

Traffic Only Highway 1 and Sir Francis Drake Blvd. offer any competition for the roadway. Again, the Cross-Marin Bike Trail is a sensible alternate for Sir Francis Drake, and Highway 1 traffic doesn't build up until some time after noon.

Nearest Bike Shop No major repairs or parts are available at Trail Head Rentals, which is closed on Wednesdays. The closest pro bike shop is Sunshine Bikes in Fairfax.

Best Time To Ride May through October
   Fog is always a factor this close to the coast, but clear days occur all year long.

Mountain Biking Opportunities There are miles and miles of trails open to bikes in the Point Reyes National Seashore. Pick up free bike trail maps at the Bear Valley Visitor Center, half a mile from Bear Valley Inn, or from Ron at Trail Head Rentals.

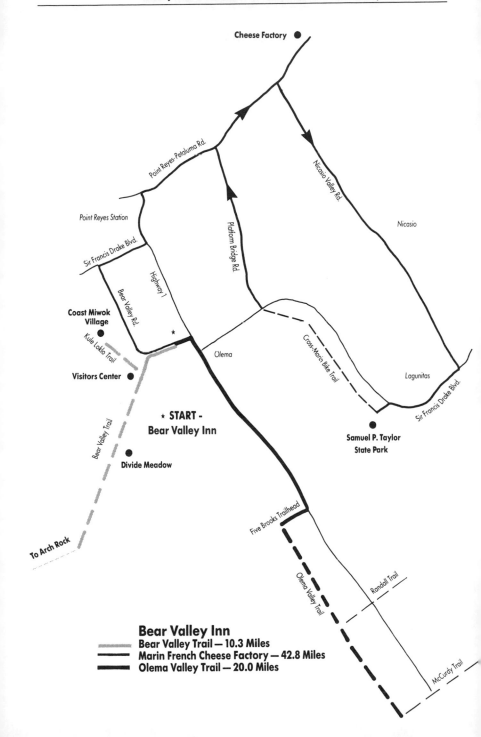

Cheese Factory ●

Point Reyes-Petaluma Rd.

Nicasio Valley Rd.

Point Reyes Station

Nicasio

Sir Francis Drake Blvd.

Highway 1

Platform Bridge Rd.

Bear Valley Rd.

Coast Miwok Village ●

Kule Lokla Trail

Olema

Visitors Center ●

Cross-Marin Bike Trail

Lagunitas

Bear Valley Trail

Sir Francis Drake Blvd.

★ **START - Bear Valley Inn**

Divide Meadow ●

● **Samuel P. Taylor State Park**

To Arch Rock

Five Brooks Trailhead

Olema Valley Trail

Randall Trail

McCurdy Trail

Bear Valley Inn
Bear Valley Trail — 10.3 Miles
Marin French Cheese Factory — 42.8 Miles
Olema Valley Trail — 20.0 Miles

MOUNTAIN BIKES: BEAR VALLEY TRAIL (10.3 MILES)

Even the most timid beginner can enjoy this off-road excursion, which rolls through shady Bear Valley. Take a lock with you so you can leave your bike and hike the last mile to Arch Rock on the coast. Then, when you return to the Visitor Center, ride out to Kule Loklo, the Coast Miwok Village project on the edge of Bear Valley Road.

MARIN FRENCH CHEESE FACTORY (42.8 MILES)

Established in 1865, the Thompson family's "Rouge et Noir" Cheese Company produces "authentic" French cheeses from traditional recipes with traditional cultures. Every day they open their tasting room, deli and private picnic grounds to the public. Bicyclists are especially welcome. Sample all you want, then buy a snack-size wheel of Camembert, Brie, Schloss or Breakfast Cheese, some bread or crackers and a cold drink for lunch. On the way back from the Cheese Factory, you'll roll through Nicasio Valley, a ranching community that's changed little since the turn of the century.

MOUNTAIN BIKES: OLEMA VALLEY TRAIL (20.0 MILES)

This is a solid intermediate ride, a good workout for experienced off-road riders. The trail takes off from Five Brooks Stables, an easy (but often trafficky) 3.6 miles south of Olema and Bear Valley Inn on Highway 1. From Olema Valley Trail you can ride up the Randall Trail or McCurdy Trail at the end to Bolinas Ridge, an option only advanced mountain bikers used to long arduous miles should attempt.

BEAR VALLEY TRAIL

PT.-PT.	CUME	DIRECTION	STREET/LANDMARK
			From Bear Valley Inn
0.0	0.0	**R**	**Bear Valley Road**
0.5	0.5	**L**	**Visitors Center** — restrooms, maps, information
0.4	0.9	**C**	**Bear Valley Trail**
1.6	2.5		**Divide Meadow**; restrooms on right
1.6	4.1	**U**	**End of bike trail**

Option: Lock your bike to bike rack and hike to **Arch Rock** (1 mile).

BEAR VALLEY TRAIL (CONT.)

PT.-PT.	CUME	DIRECTION	STREET/LANDMARK
3.6	7.7		**Visitors Center** — restrooms. Continue through parking lot.
0.1	7.8	L	**Kule Loklo Trail**
0.9	8.7	U	**Coast Miwok Village**
0.9	9.6	L	**To Bear Valley Road**
0.2	9.8	R	**Bear Valley Road**
0.5	10.3	L	**Bear Valley Inn**

MARIN FRENCH CHEESE FACTORY

PT.-PT.	CUME	DIRECTION	STREET/LANDMARK
			From Bear Valley Inn
0.0	0.0	R	**Bear Valley Road**
2.2	2.2	R	**Sir Francis Drake Blvd.**
0.8	3.0	L	**Highway 1**
		X	Bridge
0.1	3.1		**Point Reyes Station**
0.1	3.2	L	**Highway 1** — Delis, cafes, bakery, market, taqueria, craft shops, florists, produce, ambience
0.2	3.4	R	**Highway 1**
0.5	3.9	R	**Point Reyes-Petaluma Road**
3.1	7.0	L	**Point Reyes-Petaluma Road** at Platform Bridge Road
6.4	13.4	L	**Cheese Factory** — Samples, deli, restroom, picnic area
0.0	13.4	R	**Point Reyes-Petaluma Road**
3.3	16.7	L	**Nicasio Valley Road**
3.2	19.9		**Nicasio** — no services
4.4	24.3	R	**Sir Francis Drake Blvd.**
2.1	26.4		**Lagunitas** — grocery/deli on right
2.7	29.1	L	**Samuel P. Taylor State Park Entrance**
0.4	29.5	R	**To Group Campground**; water on left
0.3	29.8	C	**Cross-Marin Bike Trail**; restrooms on right in campground

MARIN FRENCH CHEESE FACTORY (CONT.)

PT.-PT.	CUME	DIRECTION	STREET/LANDMARK
3.5	33.3	L	**At end of trail**
		IL	On access road (no sign)
		IL	**Sir Frances Drake Blvd.**
0.1	33.4	L	**Platform Bridge Road**
2.4	35.8	L	**Point Reyes-Petaluma Road**
3.1	38.9	L	**Highway 1**
0.5	39.4	L	**Highway 1**
0.1	39.5	L	**Highway 1; Point Reyes Station**
0.2	39.7	R	**Highway 1**
0.1	39.8	X	Bridge
		IR	**Sir Francis Drake Blvd.**
0.8	40.6	BL	**Bear Valley Road**
2.2	42.8	L	**Bear Valley Inn**

OLEMA VALLEY TRAIL

PT.-PT.	CUME	DIRECTION	STREET/LANDMARK
			From Bear Valley Inn
0.0	0.0	L	**Bear Valley Road**
0.1	0.1	R	**Highway 1; Olema** — Cafe on right, market on left
3.6	3.7	R	**Five Brooks Trailhead sign**
1.0	4.7	L	**To Trailhead** at parking lot
0.2	4.9	R	**At Y** onto singletrack (Sign on left is hard to see.)
2.5	7.4		**Randall Trail Trailhead**; turn left for Bolinas Ridge
2.7	10.1	U	**End of bike trail**
5.2	15.3	L	**At Y** onto dirt road (sign on right)
0.1	15.4	R	**To parking lot**
0.2	15.6	R	**To Highway 1**
1.0	16.6	L	**Highway 1**
3.6	19.9		**Olema** — cafe, market
0.1	20.0	L	**Bear Valley Road**
		IR	**Bear Valley Inn**

DANCING COYOTE BEACH

Bobbi Stumpf/Sherry King
12794 Sir Francis Drake Blvd., P.O. Box 98   Rates: $95-$125
Inverness, CA 94937   Resort Cottages
415-669-7200   Breakfast fixings provided
Ambience: Seaside Cottage Retreat   Smoking on beach only

How would you like to snuggle up in your own private little cottage by a secluded beach? Go tidepooling. Ride your mountain bike along beach cliffs with bays, estuaries, points and peninsulas spread at your feet. Cook your own meals (or not, as you prefer), and then light a fire to ward off the evening's foggy chill.

All this can be yours at Dancing Coyote Beach, on the edge of tiny Inverness, smack on the shore of Tomales Bay. Instead of providing all the attention other B&Bs lavish on you, Dancing Coyote gives you, first and foremost, privacy. No one dares to intrude on your solitude, even to leave a bonbon on your pillow.

Yet all the amenities you'd expect from a B&B are there: A fire laid in the fireplace, ready to be lit. Everything you need to prepare a complete breakfast, at any time of the morning (or afternoon or evening) you desire. And more, including your own personal beach just outside the door.

Actually, there are four cottages. Acacia, Beach and Birch Tree are two-story affairs, with living room and kitchen downstairs, bed and bath upstairs. Skye is a studio with a loft bed, an outdoor shower overlooking the bay, and an extra-large deck.

My cottage for the night was Birch Tree, and it was as close to perfect as any beach lover could ask for. Skylights above the tiny living room extended as windows on the wall above the fireplace. These could be covered with shades you pull up, rather than down, by means of ropes tied off sailboat fashion on grommets on the wall. Bare beams and whitewashed paneling added to the seaside decor.

Snuggled up to the hearth were a loveseat sofa and a wicker easy chair with ottoman. The mantel held a small collection of seashells, above which a colorful lithograph depicted a Victorian seashore resort.

The equally tiny kitchen had a tile floor under a well-worn round butcher-block table. On the table a tide calendar lets guests plan

their own beach and tidepooling excursions. A half-sized refrigerator, range, oven and sink took up the opposite wall. Cooking utensils and fixings for breakfast occupied the fridge and the closet next to it. Need more food for breakfast? Just ask Sherry in the Manager's Cottage, or leave her a note.

It was just a step from the kitchen to the little deck with its two well-weathered deck chairs and small collection of bleached bones on the ledge (one looked like it might be a section of a shark's jaw). A step off the deck and you're on the beach where more bones might be waiting for discovery.

The second story was an open loft overlooking the fireplace and windows. The queen bed was spread with a down comforter. The antique dresser had a basket-woven framed mirror on it. And more skylights added light to the scene. On the other side of the loft a settee sat under a skylight in a romantic little nook. A built-in bookshelf offered puzzles, games, books and magazines. Lots of soft pillows and lights controlled by a dimmer switch added to the romance.

More skylights appeared in the bath, above the shower. And although the bathroom was also small, there were enough towels and shelves to make using it convenient and comfortable.

In front of the cottages and just next to the beach, a green lawn invited relaxing. A common deck held more chairs. On either side two portable, hooded white wicker loveseats looked out over the bay, and a hammock hung between two giant cedars.

All this is right in the middle of charming little Inverness, where you can shop in the market for on-bike snacks or the fixings for a complete meal. Or have dinner at one of the two Eastern European gourmet restaurants — Vladimir's across from the market on Sir Francis Drake Blvd., or Manka's, down the road a piece and up a short hill.

For breakfast, I found more than enough to fuel me for a day's mountain biking on Point Reyes trails: croissants with butter and blueberry jam, low-fat granola laced with yogurt (a choice of two flavors), a pint carton of orange juice and tea.

For other tastes, there were fresh eggs with which to make an omelet or French toast, a chocolate-chocolate chip muffin, a jar of coffee beans and the implements to grind and drip them, and half a loaf of sliced sourdough bread.

BIKING FROM DANCING COYOTE BEACH

Terrain There are quite a few steep surprises on the roads through Point Reyes National Seashore, not the least of which is the final climb to Point Reyes Lighthouse and the series of ridges to be scaled on the way to McClure's Beach.

Road Conditions No shoulders, very few potholes and mostly smooth surface pretty much sum up the situation. Near the points and beaches, the road may be wet from fog or spray.

Traffic The height of the tourist season is, as usual, high summer, when traffic must make Sir Francis Drake Blvd. seem like a freeway. I've never witnessed this situation, however, probably because I've only biked in Point Reyes in May, June or October.

Nearest Bike Shop Sadly, the world-famous Point Reyes Bikes in Point Reyes Station is no longer. The nearest "shop" is Trail Head Bike Rentals in Bear Valley (featured in Bear Valley Inn on page 167). No major repairs or parts are available.

Best Time To Ride May through October
The fog and wind are generally worst during summer, but the weather patterns on the North Coast are never consistent enough to rely on.

Mountain Biking Opportunities There are miles and miles of trails open to bikes in the Point Reyes National Seashore. For more information, see pages 160 and 170. Pick up free bike trail maps at the Bear Valley Visitor Center.

DRAKE'S BEACH/POINT REYES LIGHTHOUSE (23.4, 34.8, 44.4 OR 54.8 MILES)

Options abound on the out-and-back route through Point Reyes National Seashore. Simply head to Drake's Beach for lunch and a history lesson on Drake's circumnavigation and return for less than 25 miles but still plenty of climbing. Add the trip out to the lighthouse for 32 miles and a lot more climbing. And tack on the trip out Pierce Point Road to McClure's Beach for an additional 18+ miles of even more climbing. (I suppose those who really love pain could also nip down to Heart's Desire Beach in Tomales Bay State Park on the way out Pierce Point Road for a truly horrendous return back up, but count me out!) All the roads are dotted with historic ranches in continuous operation since the mid 1800s.

MOUNTAIN BIKES: DRAKE'S ESTERO (22.2 MILES)

"Estero" is the Spanish word for "estuary", a place where fresh and salt water meet, and therefore always rich bird habitat. On this ride you'll not only glimpse fantastic vistas from the clifftops, you'll also swoop down to the estero itself to spy on egrets and herons. Along the way you'll pass through many stiles and gates. Be sure to close the gates behind you. You'll soon see why as you share the trails and scenery with impressively large herds of cows.

POINT REYES STATION (12.4 MILES)

Short and flat but worth the trip to explore one of the funkiest settlements on the California coast. A stop in the used book store, the bakery and the feed store (yes, the feed store!) are absolutely required.

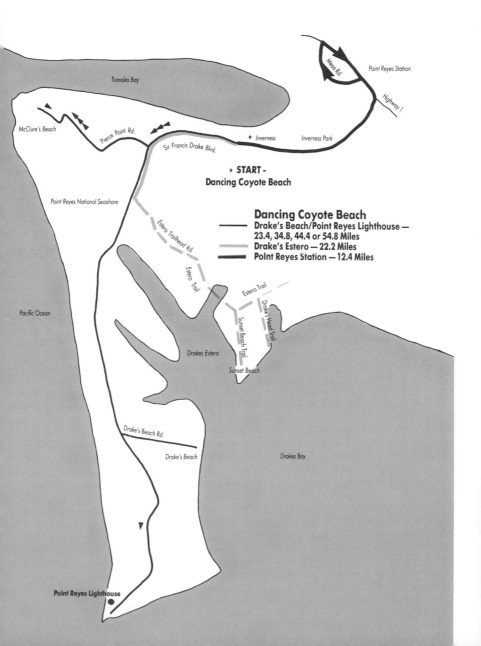

Point Reyes Station

Mesa Rd.

Highway 1

Tomales Bay

McClure's Beach

Pierce Point Rd.

Sir Francis Drake Blvd.

★ Inverness

Inverness Park

★ **START -**
Dancing Coyote Beach

Point Reyes National Seashore

Estero Trailhead Rd.

Dancing Coyote Beach
Drake's Beach/Point Reyes Lighthouse —
23.4, 34.8, 44.4 or 54.8 Miles
Drake's Estero — 22.2 Miles
Point Reyes Station — 12.4 Miles

Estero Trail

Estero Trail

Drake's Head Trail

Pacific Ocean

Sunset Beach Trail

Drakes Estero

Sunset Beach

Drake's Beach Rd.

Drake's Beach

Drakes Bay

Point Reyes Lighthouse

DRAKE'S BEACH/POINT REYES LIGHTHOUSE

PT.-PT.	CUME	DIRECTION	STREET/LANDMARK
			From Dancing Coyote Beach
0.0	0.0	**R**	**Sir Francis Drake Blvd.**
McClure's Beach Option:			
2.4	2.4	**R**	**Pierce Point Road**
1.7	4.1		**Tomales Bay State Park/Heart's Desire Beach Turnoff** — *steep downhill and uphill return!*
7.6	11.7	**U**	**McClure's Beach**
9.3	21.0	**R**	**Sir Francis Drake Blvd.** to continue route to Drake's Beach and/or Lighthouse, or **turn left** and pedal 2.4 miles back to Dancing Coyote Beach
10.1	10.1	**L**	**Drake's Beach Road**
1.6	11.7		**Drake's Beach** — Visitor's Center, restrooms, cafe
0.0	11.7	**U**	**Drake's Beach Road**
1.6	13.3		**Sir Francis Drake Blvd.** Turn **right** and pedal 10.1 miles back to Dancing Coyote Beach, or follow Lighthouse option:
Lighthouse Option:			
1.6	13.3	**L**	**Sir Francis Drake Blvd.**
5.3	18.6	**C**	Through gate at parking lot; restrooms
0.4	19.0		**Point Reyes Lighthouse;** Visitors Center
0.0	19.0	**U**	Back through gate
0.4	19.4	**L**	**Sir Francis Drake Blvd.**
5.3	24.7	**C**	**Sir Francis Drake Blvd.** at Drake's Beach Road
10.1	34.8	**L**	**Dancing Coyote Beach**

DRAKE'S ESTERO

PT.-PT.	CUME	DIRECTION	STREET/LANDMARK
			From Dancing Coyote Beach
0.0	0.0	**R**	**Sir Francis Drake Blvd.**
4.6	4.6	**L**	**Estero Trailhead Road**
0.6	5.2	**R**	**Parking Lot**—pit toilets. Begin trail here.
2.4	7.6	**C**	**Sunset Beach Trail** where Estero Trail turns left
1.5	9.1	**U**	**Sunset Beach**
1.5	10.6	**R**	**Estero Trail**
0.6	11.2	**R**	**Drake's Head Trail**; no sign; many choices
1.4	12.6	**U**	**At End** — Vista Point onto Drake's Head
1.4	14.0	**L**	**Estero Trail**
0.6	14.6	**R**	**Estero Trail** at Sunset Beach Trail
2.4	17.0	**L**	**Estero Trailhead Road** at parking lot
0.6	17.6	**R**	**Sir Francis Drake Blvd.**
4.6	22.2	**L**	**Dancing Coyote Beach**

POINT REYES STATION

PT.-PT.	CUME	DIRECTION	STREET/LANDMARK
			From Dancing Coyote Beach
0.0	0.0	**L**	**Sir Francis Drake Blvd.**
0.1	0.1		**Inverness** — Market on left; deli, restaurants on right
2.7	2.8		**Inverness Park** — Bakery, grocery on right
1.3	4.1	**L**	**Highway 1**
		X	Bridge
0.5	4.6	**L**	**Highway 1. Point Reyes Station** — Shops, delis, bakery, more — explore!
0.2	4.8	**R**	**Highway 1**
0.3	5.1	**L**	**Highway 1** at Point Reyes-Petaluma Road
1.1	6.2	**L**	**Mesa Road**
1.5	7.7	**R**	**Highway 1**
		IL	**Highway 1**
0.5	8.2	**X**	Bridge
		IR	**Sir Francis Drake Blvd.**
1.3	9.5		**Inverness Park**
2.8	12.3		**Inverness**
0.1	12.4	**R**	**Dancing Coyote Beach**

RANCHO SAN GREGORIO

Bud and Lee Raynor
Route 1, Box 54, 5086 La Honda Road   Rates: $80-$135
San Gregorio, CA 94074   Bed and Breakfast Inn
415-747-0810   Full Breakfast
Ambience: Family Farm   Smoking outdoors only

If you're looking for a town called San Gregorio, don't blink! Even if you manage to stay wide-eyed all the way down Highway 84, you'll never find it. Although it does boast a post office, a general store and a state beach, San Gregorio is more a state of mind than one particular place. And that state of mind is tied to the land.

At Rancho San Gregorio, Bud and Lee Raynor work the land, as they have since buying "Raynor Ranch" in the early 1970s and building their Spanish mission-style home. Here they raised five children who have since gone on to raise families of their own. Then, as now, the Raynors' lives centered around the growing seasons and the well-being of their livestock.

The surrounding grounds and San Gregorio Creek give one the feeling of remote country living here, yet Rancho San Gregorio is right on State Highway 84 just four miles west of La Honda, smack dab in the middle of one of Bay Area bicyclists' best-loved routes, with access to Skyline, the coast, and some of the most scenic and challenging roads in our state.

Riding up Highway 84 from the ocean, the first thing you see at Rancho San Gregorio is the big white barn, which once served as home for all the Raynors while Bud, a now-retired contractor, built the house. Now the barn is a "recreation hall" reminiscent of summer camps, and one of its most frequent uses is as a dance floor and reception area for weddings. It's also a great place to securely store your bike.

Today Bud and Lee's sleeping quarters are once again in the barn and guests have free reign of the house, including the big country kitchen and the sitting room crammed with books, games and a video library. The decor is American Southwest, emphasized by the heavy redwood beams, bright terra cotta tile floors, carved oak antiques and colorful cactus courtyard and herb garden.

Each room is named for a local creek, and I got "el numero uno," the San Gregorio Room, formerly the family's master bedroom. Actually it's sitting room and bedroom combined, with a view over the back lawn, gazebo and picnic area to the creek below. Sliding glass doors in both bathroom and bedroom lead to the deck. A mini-fridge is stocked with bottled water, beer, soda (diet and regular) and mineral water. Snack crackers, tea, Sanka, a hot pot and thick crockery mugs sit close by.

A huge antique armoire holds two thick terry robes and a warm mohair shawl for snuggling up on foggy coastside nights. A wood-burning stove also stands ready to stave off typical Northern California chills.

While waiting for dinner guests to arrive, Bud and Lee took us on a walking tour of their "spread." As we walked and chatted, the tang of sea air drifted in from the beach five miles down the road.

We hiked through the pasture to the creek where years ago their kids had dammed up a swimming hole. "The creek runs all year," Bud told me, "even in drought." Then it was back through the apple orchard and along the berry patches about to burst forth with ollaliebarries, logan berries and raspberries. In season, "I just let guests pick them and take them home," Bud said.

I was fortunate to have received a dinner invitation from the Raynors in order to meet members of their family and some friends from out of town and up the coast. If you're looking for dinner in San Gregorio, however, be prepared to do some traveling. I whole-heartedly recommend two restaurants in Pescadero: Duarte's, which specializes in artichoke dishes and homemade pies, and Dinardi's, also known as "the Greek restaurant" among hungry and appreciative cyclists.

Breakfast, on the other hand, was a simple matter of tumbling down to the Rancho San Gregorio kitchen. We helped ourselves to coffee or tea from the sideboard and sat at the big oak table chatting while Bud and Lee demonstrated their teamwork at stove and sink.

At Lee's invitation, we moved to the long dining table to start with juice and muffins (apparently the result of Bud's culinary talent, since his chef's apron read: "A good innkeeper is worth his weight in muffins."). Next came crepes drenched in a glaze of fresh local strawberries. Prefer a lower fat/higher carbohydrate meal? Help yourself to boxed cereal or granola. Or ask for several slices of Bud's homemade bread. And be sure to include "dessert," a smoothie blended from bananas, more fresh strawberries, o.j. and yogurt.

One last note about San Gregorio: don't drink the water! The drinking water at Rancho San Gregorio is quite palatable, but the straight well water throughout the community is rather brackish. It's safe to drink but tastes horrendous. If you're looking to fill water bottles at the San Gregorio Store, buy it in bottles rather than take it from the tap.

BIKING FROM RANCHO SAN GREGORIO

Terrain Basically, it's all up to the east and the Santa Cruz Mountains skyline, and all down to the west and the coast, although the north-south oriented coastline has its ups and downs on Highway 1 and Stage Road.

Road Conditions Most of Highways 84, 35 and 1 have good surface and a broad enough shoulder to maneuver safely; however, the shoulder often disappears at creeks and severe switchbacks. Stage and Alpine Roads are pockmarked with holes and patches; an alert eye and a pinch of caution are advised on the descents.

Traffic Unless you've arrived on a particularly busy weekend, you'll find most of the roads here blessedly free of traffic, especially off the state highways.

Nearest Bike Shop
A Bicyclery in Half Moon Bay
432 Main Street
Half Moon Bay, CA 94019
415-726-6000

Best Time To Ride May through October

Mountain Biking Opportunities If you're on the Windy Hill Loop and would like to check out some more singletrack, ride across Highway 35/Skyline Drive at the top of Crazy Pete Road to Russian Ridge Open Space Preserve. Ride south on these trails and you can connect with Skyline Ridge Open Space Preserve across Alpine Road, then again with trails in Montebello Open Space Preserve across Skyline and Page Mill Road. Lost? Check in with the rangers at their tiny office in Skyline Preserve. Better yet, contact the Midpeninsula Open Space District at 201 San Antonio Circle, Mountain View, CA 94040, 415-949-550, for maps.

PIGEON POINT LIGHTHOUSE LOOP (45.2 MILES)

This ride has something for everyone: redwood trees, farm-land, seacoast, mountains, steep climbs, fast descents, county parks, history, and perhaps best of all, good food in Pescadero. For a shorter version, minus the lighthouse and the rollers on Cloverdale Road, ask Lee Raynor for a copy of her "My Favorite Loop" map.

SKYLINE VISTA LOOP (27.1 MILES)

I scouted this ride the day after an extremely rare June rain-storm, and the views of San Francisco Bay from Skyline were so stupendous, they just about knocked me off my bike! A lot mel-lower but always soul-refreshing is Old La Honda Road, a true coun-try lane connecting two state highways. Take food and plenty of water on this outing; once you leave La Honda there is no place to buy (without deviating from the route) until you return. You might also want to take a lock (and walking shoes) in order to visit the

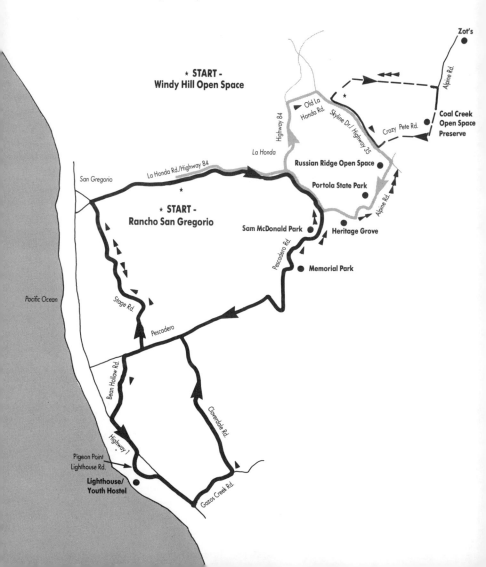

Rancho San Gregorio
Pigeon Point Lighthouse Loop — 45.2 Miles
Skyline Vista Loop — 27.1 Miles
Windy Hill Loop — 11.3 Miles

Zot's

★ START -
Windy Hill Open Space

Old La
Honda Rd.

Highway 84

Skyline Dr./ Highway 35

Alpine Rd.

Crazy Pete Rd.

Coal Creek
Open Space
Preserve

La Honda

La Honda Rd./Highway 84

San Gregorio

Russian Ridge Open Space

Portola State Park

Alpine Rd.

★ START -
Rancho San Gregorio

Sam McDonald Park

Heritage Grove

Pescadero Rd.

Memorial Park

Stage Rd.

Pescadero

Pacific Ocean

Bean Hollow Rd.

Cloverdale Rd.

Highway 1

Pigeon Point
Lighthouse Rd.

**Lighthouse/
Youth Hostel**

Gazos Creek Rd.

Heritage Redwood Grove near the bottom of Alpine Road, a rewarding stop.

MOUNTAIN BIKES: WINDY HILL LOOP (11.3 MILES)

This is still one of my favorite off-road rides in the Bay Area, even after many repetitions over many years. From Rancho San Gregorio I recommend driving up to Skyline; you can park at Windy Hill Open Space picnic area. Normally we start in Portola Valley at a local watering hole called The Alpine Inn (formerly Risotti's and known affectionately as Zot's). Adding the paved miles from the lower trailhead to Zot's, where cold beer awaits, makes the distance a full 15 miles.

PIGEON POINT LIGHTHOUSE LOOP

PT.-PT.	CUME	DIRECTION	STREET/LANDMARK
			From Rancho San Gregorio
0.0	0.0	R	**La Honda Road/Highway 84**
2.2	2.2	R	**Pescadero Road**
1.1	3.3	R	**Pescadero Road** at Y. *Climb Haskins Hill*
0.5	3.8		**Sam McDonald Park** on right
3.8	7.6		**Memorial Park** on left
1.4	9.0		Loma Mar Store on left
6.3	15.3		**Pescadero** on right at Stage Road (best place to buy lunch to eat at the Lighthouse beach; see services below)
0.5	15.8	L	**Bean Hollow Road**
2.4	18.2	L	**Highway 1**
3.5	21.7	R	**Pigeon Point Lighthouse Road**
0.5	22.2		**Pigeon Point Lighthouse/Youth Hostel**
		C	**Pigeon Point Lighthouse Road**
0.5	22.7	R	**Highway 1**
2.0	24.7	L	**Gazos Creek Road**
2.1	26.8	C	**Cloverdale Road**
6.0	32.8	L	**Pescadero Road**
0.7	33.5	R	**Stage Road**

PIGEON POINT LIGHTHOUSE LOOP (CONT.)

PT.-PT.	CUME	DIRECTION	STREET/LANDMARK
			Pescadero — Duarte's Tavern on right (sit- down meals/artichoke soup and pie); Arcangeli (a.k.a. Norm's Grocery) on left (great breads and pastries).
		C	**Stage Road**
7.3	40.8	R	**La Honda Road/Highway 84** San Gregorio Store on Stage Road across Highway 84
4.4	45.2	R	**Rancho San Gregorio**

SKYLINE VISTA LOOP

PT.-PT.	CUME	DIRECTION	STREET/LANDMARK
			From Rancho San Gregorio
0.0	0.0	R	**La Honda Road/Highway 84**
3.7	3.7		**La Honda** — Pioneer Market on left (last services before return)
3.3	7.0	R	**Old La Honda Road**
2.6	9.6	R	**Skyline Drive/Highway 35. Windy Hill Open Space** picnic area on left (no water or restrooms)
4.4	14.0		Last vista point on left
1.3	15.3	R	**Alpine Road** **Russian Ridge Open Space** on immediate right — restrooms but no water
3.4	18.7		Entrance to **Portola State Park**
2.8	21.5		**Heritage Grove** on left
7.4	22.7	R	**Pescadero Road** at Y
1.1	23.8	L	**La Honda Road** Turn right for La Honda and Pioneer Market.
3.3	27.1	R	**Rancho San Gregorio**

WINDY HILL LOOP

PT.-PT.	CUME	DIRECTION	STREET/LANDMARK
			From Windy Hill Open Space Picnic Area
0.0	0.0	**R**	**Skyline Drive/Highway 35**
0.6	0.6	**R**	**Trailhead** on north side of hill; long, scenic downhill!
1.9	2.5	**R**	**At Y**; tight switchbacks lead to creek crossing.
0.2	2.7	**X**	**Corte Madera Creek**
0.2	2.9	**R**	**Alpine Road** (paved) For a side trip to Zot's, turn left on Alpine for 1.9 miles.
2.2	5.1	**C**	**Alpine Road** (dirt) beyond pipe gate
1.3	6.4	**R**	Into **Coal Creek Open Space Preserve**; singletrack trailhead just beyond third or fourth fenced-off "reconstruction area" — easy to miss
0.3	6.7	**BR**	**At Y** Bear left for direct connection to Crazy Pete Road that skips additional singletrack.
0.4	7.1	**C**	**Crazy Pete Road** beyond trailhead stile. Becomes paved and climbs steeply to Skyline
0.4	7.5	**R**	**Skyline Drive/Highway 35**
3.8	11.3	**R**	**Windy Hill Open Space Picnic Area**

ZABALLA HOUSE

Simon and Anne Lowings
324 Main Street
Half Moo Bay, CA 94019
415-726 9123
Ambience: Seaside cottage

Rates: $65-$150
Bed & Breakfast Inn
Full breakfast
No smoking

Half Moon Bay is for relaxing. No matter how stressed out I feel, when I hit this thriving coastal community, I just naturally kick back and forget all my cares. From the fine restaurants in town to the expansive State Beaches along the Pacific Ocean to the surrounding pumpkin fields and berry patches, the pace is leisurely and the attitude is laid back.

The pervasive easy-does-it aura flows right through the front door of Zaballa House, "the oldest building still standing in Half Moon Bay." This sunny seaside retreat was built circa 1859 for his family of seven by Estanislao Zaballa, Half Moon Bay's first city planner, who owned part of the original Miramontes Land Grant, a general store, several stables and a drinking spot on Main Street.

Today Zaballa House sits at the north end of Main Street, surrounded by the seedlings, saplings and other plants of the Flora Farm Nursery. A white picket fence separates the small parking lot from the grounds. And just across the street is one of the best pasta restaurants you could ever ask for when carboloading for the next day's ride.

The present owners, Ann and Simon Lowings, have long since shed any pretense of maintaining the "stiff upper lip" of their native Great Britain in exchange for the Half Moon Bay lifestyle, setting the tone for the easy-going ambience at Zaballa House.

I arrived after an energetic ride to Skyline and was eager to lose the dust and sweat of the road. Kerry, the Simons' capable assistant, immediately showed me to my room, where a double whirlpool bath awaited. What a blessing!

Once refreshed, I took the time to look around. Room #4 was small, like all the first-floor rooms (the ones upstairs are a good bit larger). Delicate pastel colors and flowers dominated the decor. A white rattan bed, a loveseat and a window bench were the only furnishings.

ZABALLA HOUSE

"Oldest House in Town"
Bed and Breakfast

With its broad pale pink terazzo tiles surrounding the tub, the bathroom outdid the bedroom. At each of the two high windows — inside the room — hung a planter box filled with blooming pansies, petunias and more.

All the windows faced west, and the bright afternoon sun was all the light I needed for making notes, reading and making myself presentable for the complimentary sherry, port, white wine, cheese and crackers Kerry was putting out in the hallway between the dining room and front parlor.

Dinner followed at Pasta Moon across the street, just one of Half Moon Bay's culinary delights. You can also choose from Mexican, Thai, Japanese and a wonderful bakery just a block from the bike shop that makes delicious foccacio bread. And most are within walking distance from Zaballa House.

Breakfast was decidedly wholesome, featuring a variety of local berries and fresh melons, a choice of sweet breads, muffins or granola with milk, all served buffet style. OJ and hot coffee sat ready on the big dining table and on two smaller tables, one in the dining room and one at the front of the house off the parlor. Kerry put the finishing touch on the meal with her own recipe for Eggs Florentine made to individual orders.

Half Moon Bay offers other pursuits besides eating and riding. Of course, there are the beaches, four of them, with parking lots, restrooms and a picnic area. The closest is a mile due west of Main Street. Parking costs, but bikes and pedestrians can enter the beach area free, and there's a mile-long coastside trail (eventually to be extended to all the way north to Moss Beach) that cyclists share with walkers, skaters and the like, as well as horses on a parallel dirt trail.

Along the way to the beach, you'll pass the Andreotti Family Farm on Kelly Street. There are animals kids love to pet, and on weekends their homegrown produce is for sale in the barn.

Obester Winery, on Highway 92 about two miles up the hill from town, invites you to bring your own clean empty bottles and fill them with wine on "Bottle Your Own" days.

Finally, there's the annual Pumpkin Festival just before Halloween. The traffic can be horrendous, but the pumpkins — and festivities — are enough to attract several organized club rides from the San Francisco Peninsula.

BIKING FROM ZABALLA HOUSE

Terrain The town of Half Moon Bay is flat as a pancake, but once you take any road leading out of town, including Highway 1, it's all up and down. Some of the ups, as on Tunitas Creek and Lobitos Creek roads, are quite strenuous.

Road Conditions The state highways are generally in good repair, especially Highways 1 and 35, which have generous shoulders in most areas. Highway 92 can get a bit narrow on the trip down from Skyline, but it's easy to pace yourself with the traffic. Off the beaten path on the backroads, especially Tunitas Creek Road, expect rough pavement and one-lane roadway at times. Another major consideration on all coastside roads is fog, which can obliterate all visibility and render you invisible to motorists. It can also make for heavy condensation, creating slippery road surfaces. Most fog will clear by mid-morning, so if the conditions look iffy, the best advice is to wait.

Traffic Highways 1 and 92 are Half Moon Bay's only connections to San Francisco, and commercial traffic is accordingly thick. In addition, there's a great deal of tourist traffic, including trailers, along Highway 1. Again, things are different on the backroads, where passing cars are unusual to rare.

Nearest Bike Shop
A Bicyclery in Half Moon Bay
432 Main Street
Half Moon Bay, CA 94019
415-726-6000

Best Time To Ride Spring, summer or fall, March through November

Mountain Biking Opportunities If you're heading out by bike to ride in Purisima Creek Redwoods Open Space Preserve, you may want to make a side excursion into the new Burleigh-Murray State Park, which has a few miles of newly opened trails. Or you can simply take your mountain bike to the beach and explore the cliff heights south of the main parking lot, or take the Coastside Trail north and explore beyond the paved pathway (taking care to respect restricted access to private property).

COASTSIDE CREEKS AND CANYONS (27.4 MILES)

Charge up your climbing muscles for this challenging exploration of the backroads south of Half Moon Bay. For those who'd rather forgo the exposed descent into and resultant climb out of Lobitos Creek Canyon, there's an almost-as-scenic bailout on Lobitos Creek Cutoff (you'll cut four miles of up and down from your route, but keep in mind you'll also miss the redwoods on Tunitas Creek). Pack plenty of food and water on this ride; there are no food establishments outside of Half Moon Bay. And if you're tempted to do it in reverse, keep in mind that the climbing on Lobitos Creek Road is exponentially steeper in the eastbound direction.

MOUNTAIN BIKES: PURISIMA CREEK OPEN SPACE PRESERVE (27.1 OR 10.4 MILES)

Climb an old logging road through old-growth redwoods, then return down technical singletrack. You can ride to the trailhead at the junction of Higgins-Purissima and Purissima roads by following the directions for the first 5.5 miles of Coastside Creeks and Canyons, then return the way you came or via Purissima Road. If you drive, keep in mind that the parking area at the trailhead is small.

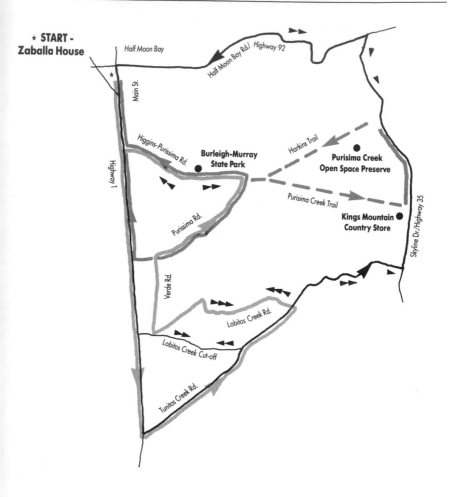

Zaballa House

Coastside Creeks and Canyons — **27.4 Miles**
Purisima Creek Open Space Preserve — **27.1 or 10.4 Miles**
Tunitas Creek Loop — **30.0 Miles**

TUNITAS CREEK LOOP (30.0 MILES)

Of the many roads running from Coastside to Skyline Drive on the crest of the Santa Cruz Mountains, Tunitas Creek has to be the most beautiful. Although there are 2.8 miles of greater than 10% grade about halfway up, they are pleasantly shaded by towering redwoods growing along tiny, log-jammed Tunitas Creek. About 3.5 miles up, look for a plank bridge on the right and yellow chalk marks warning you to "gear down next 2.8 miles," a favor bestowed by the route markers for a local century, the Banana Classic.

Once on Skyline, don't miss the opportunity to sample the homemade bread and double-fudge brownies at the Kings Mountain Country Store, which politely requests you remove cleated shoes before treading on their beautifully finished hardwood floors. You will doubtless meet other Bay Area cyclists at this favorite stop, where you can even buy a patch kit or spare tube if you have need.

Given clear weather, within a mile beyond the Country Store you'll begin to glimpse views of San Francisco Bay on the east and the Pacific on the west. This is the only stretch of Skyline from which both are visible.

COASTSIDE CREEKS AND CANYONS

PT.-PT.	CUME	DIRECTION	STREET/LANDMARK
			From Zaballa House
0.0	0.0	**R**	**Main Street**. Services on right
1.0	1.0	**L**	**Highway 1**
7.9	8.9	**L**	**Tunitas Creek Road**
Bailout:			
1.7	9.6	**L**	**Lobitos Creek Cut-off**
2.0	11.6	**C**	**Verde Road**
3.7	12.6	**L**	**Lobitos Creek Road**
4.0	16.6	**S**	**Verde Road**
1.8	18.4	**R**	**Purissima Road**
3.5	21.9	**BL**	**Higgins-Purissima Road** at Open Space Entrance (no sign)
4.5	26.4	**R**	**Main Street**. Deli, bike shop, bakery on left
1.0	27.4	**L**	**Zaballa House**

PURISIMA CREEK REDWOODS

PT.-PT.	CUME	DIRECTION	STREET/LANDMARK
			From Zaballa House
0.0	0.0	R	**Main Street**. Deli, bike shop, bakery on right
1.0	1.0	L	**Higgins-Purissima Road**
1.6	2.6		**Burleigh-Murray State Park** entrance on left
2.9	5.5	L	**Purisima Creek Open Space Preserve**. Begin **Purisima Creek Trail**
4.5	10.0	L	**Skyline Drive/Highway 35**
2.0	12.0	L	**Purisima Creek Open Space Preserve**. Follow signs to **Harkins Trail**. Note: Great food and clean restrooms are just beyond the open space parking lot at Kings Mountain Country Store.
3.8	15.8	R	**Purisima Creek Trail**. To parking area
0.1	15.9	L	**Purissima Road**
3.7	19.6	R	**Highway 1**
6.5	26.1	R	**Main Street Exit**. Deli, bike shop, bakery on left
1.0	27.1	L	**Zaballa House**

TUNITAS CREEK LOOP

PT.-PT.	CUME	DIRECTION	STREET/LANDMARK
			From Zaballa House
0.0	0.0	R	**Main Street**. Deli, bike shop, bakery on right
1.0	1.0	L	**Highway 1**
7.9	8.9	L	**Tunitas Creek Road**. *Steep climb begins in 3.0 miles*
9.1	18.0	L	**Skyline Drive/Highway 35**
2.5	20.5		**Kings Mountain Country Store** on left
4.3	24.8	L	**Half Moon Bay Road/Highway 92**. *Caution — high winds!*
5.0	29.8	L	**Main Street**
0.2	30.0	R	**Zaballa House**

"SUPERIOR" CALIFORNIA INNS AND RIDES

Where, you may well ask, is "Superior" California? The name is not an official one (hence the quotation marks), and I confess that I am not the one who coined it. That honor belongs to Chuck Elliot, aka Bodfish, the poet laureate of the California touring cyclist, both on and off the road.

Superior California lies north of the nine-county Bay Area and east of the Pacific Coast. It is characterized by rural communities interspersed with endless national forests, designated wildernesses and open rangeland. It contains magnificent Mount Shasta, volcanic Mount Lassen, the relatively lower altitude mountains of the Northern Sierra Nevada, and the scenic Feather River Canyon.

If you're an avid mountain biker, you'll find endless logging roads, jeep tracks and singletrack trails to explore. The rivers run swift here into mid-August, making whitewater rafting and kayaking a thrilling adventure. Anglers, power boaters and windsurfers relish the waters of mighty Lake Shasta.

More characteristic of the Pacific Northwest than sunny California, this is prime bicycle touring country. Instead of being too hot, summer presents the finest weather for cycling. The roads are clean and, for the most part, well maintained. Traffic rarely achieves the congestion of urban areas, even in popular tourist spots such as Lake Almanor (one exception may be the Avenue of the Giants). And the scenery is unmatched in both variety and beauty.

Cycling at high altitudes such as encountered in the backcountry described by Bodfish can easily exhaust "flatland" cyclists who are not accustomed to it. Take precautions: Drink extra liquids to avoid dehydration in the dryer air. Apply plenty of sunscreen to ward off the stronger ultraviolet rays. Dress in or carry extra layers of clothing for sudden changes in weather. And take it easy for at least the first day or two to acclimate your cardiovascular system to the lower atmospheric pressure.

The inns of Superior California are as varied as the terrain and the scenery. You can experience the old-fashioned gentility of a large resort hotel, the coziness of a Victorian B&B, the rustic charm of a backcountry mountain biking resort, or the down-home atmosphere of a former working horse ranch.

On the edge of the magnificent redwoods lining the Avenue of the Giants, **Benbow Inn** brings back memories of the Twenties,

Thirties and Forties with its charming Tudor architecture and gracious amenities, from full-service dining room to bellhops summoned with a ding from the main desk.

At the northern tip of Lake Almanor, **The Bidwell House** in Chester is a B&B housed in a historic summer home updated to provide every modern convenience. Ride out from here to the backcountry and return to be pampered in luxurious style.

The Feather Bed in Quincy is a fine example of early California Victorian architecture in the midst of the Feather River Country. Hosts Bob and Jan Janowski are continuing a B&B tradition by providing the small comforts that make a country inn memorable.

Experience the flavor of the old West at **Mount Shasta Ranch Bed & Breakfast**, a former horse breeding farm within sight of the magnificent mountain and just off the best cycling routes. Bill and Mary Larson have created the perfect combination of comfort and decor to provide guests with affordable elegance.

Exclusively for mountain bikers, from curious novices to adventure-seeking trail hounds, **Otter Bar Lodge** on the banks of the (California) Salmon River puts guests up in a rustic resort and guides them on logging roads and single tracks in the Klamath National Forest.

FOR MORE INFORMATION ON BICYCLING IN SUPERIOR CALIFORNIA:

California Dream Cycling with Bodfish, Cycling in the Shadow of Shasta, and *Cycling The California Outback with Bodfish* by Chuck Elliot. Bodfish Books, P.O. Box 69, Chester, CA 96020.

Mount Shasta Area Mountain Bike Map by Sig Orwig, 163 Shasta Avenue, Mount Shasta, CA 96067.

BENBOW INN

Patsy and Chuck Watts
445 Lake Benbow Drive
Garberville, CA 95542
707-923-2125
Ambience: Tudor Mansion

Rates: $98-$175; Cottage $260
Destination resort
European Plan
No smoking

Old-fashioned gentility is the hallmark of the Benbow Inn, a fine example of Tudor architecture tucked among the redwoods just south of the town of Garberville and the world-famous Avenue of the Giants.

Arrival at the Benbow brings out the bellhop for your luggage, followed by complimentary brisk tea and crumbly scones served in the lobby beginning at 3:00 p.m. Actually, you can check in any hour of the day or night. There is always a desk clerk on duty.

The lobby is a great place to hang out anytime; guests never seem to tire of exploring all the nooks and crannies. "So much visual stimuli all at once," was how one fellow guest put it. There are rich medieval tapestries, an antique hobby horse, and an intricate lovebird cage (containing paper lovebirds, alas!). And all around you the beauty of highly polished cherrywood wainscoting.

On the stairway landing sits a rather large dog bed occupied by Bijou, the Watts' Afghan, who has an intriguing habit of winning guests over with her soulful eyes. "Please do not feed me, even if I beg," says the caption to her portrait in the inn's brochure.

Outside, a stone walkway skirts the expansive terrace, manicured lawn, and honeymoon cottage as it wends its way to a swimming beach on the Eel River, where the water was too low and the temperature too cool to tempt anyone late in the season. Many guests did take advantage of the deck chairs spread around the lush lawn to curl up in the sunshine with an absorbing book.

The Benbow provides a broad range of rooms to suit most budgets. The largest rooms, facing the terrace and garden, are spacious, with woodburning fireplaces, private entrances, patios or balconies, and TVs and VCRs. However, every room in the inn has a private bath, telephone, air conditioning and central heating.

My rather small room was tastefully decorated and comfortable. No space was left unutilized. Dormer windows overlooked

the cottage, terrace and river. A hand-painted design dressed up the back of the door. The floral wallpaper and blue tiling in the tiny bathroom gave it an organized look. A basket full of complimentary goodies, including a plastic tote bag and shoeshine cloth, sat on a shelf. A decanter of sherry and two glasses sat on the sideboard, beneath a small library of paperbacks (mostly romances).

The queen bed, with brass and walnut headboard, was covered with a dark green and wine quilted comforter and beige shams in an opposing-colored print. After dinner, I found the bed turned down and chocolates on the pillows. In the bath, used towels had been replaced with clean ones.

Food at the Benbow was quite good. The dinner menu features pastas, grill and seafood. I splurged on stuffed roast venison served with red potatoes and a creamless sauce. It was excellent! The wine list specializes in Northern California vintages by the bottle or glass. And there's a complimentary after-dinner glass of port waiting for each guest in the lobby at 9:00.

Lunch is served daily from June to mid-September, and a champagne brunch is available on Sunday mornings. Breakfast is also served early on Sunday, and all morning every other day. The menu ranges from breakfast parfait (fruit, yogurt and granola swirled together) to a heart-healthy vegetable fritata made with low-fat cheese and no-yolk eggs.

Reservations are requested for dinner, but other meals are on a first-come, first-served basis.

BIKING FROM BENBOW INN

Terrain While the U.S. 101 freeway undulates over some pretty hefty hills, the Avenue of the Giants parallels it via a much gentler path. Still, you'll find you're steadily rising as you pedal north. To the south, there are some steeper pitches on the way to Leggett.

Road Conditions Good to excellent, although there is nary a shoulder to be found off the freeway.

Traffic Highway 101 and its alternates are designated part of the official Pacific Coast Bicycle Route, which doesn't prevent the motorized competition from gawking and filling the road with all sorts of tourist traffic, from Winnebagos to motorcycles. And don't forget the logging trucks!

Nearest Bike Shop
Bill Staples
East Branch Road
Garberville, CA 95542
707-923-2659

Best Time To Ride Summer through early autumn

Mountain Biking Opportunities Just behind the inn, an old dirt road now closed to motor traffic circles and climbs above the river and around the dam that forms Benbow Lake, eventually descending to a cobble beach along the river on the other side of the lake. It's about an eight-mile round-trip ride with good views of Benbow Valley, Benbow Lake and the redwoods. You can do it on one of the inn's red Bridgestone cross-bikes if you didn't bring your own mountain bike along.

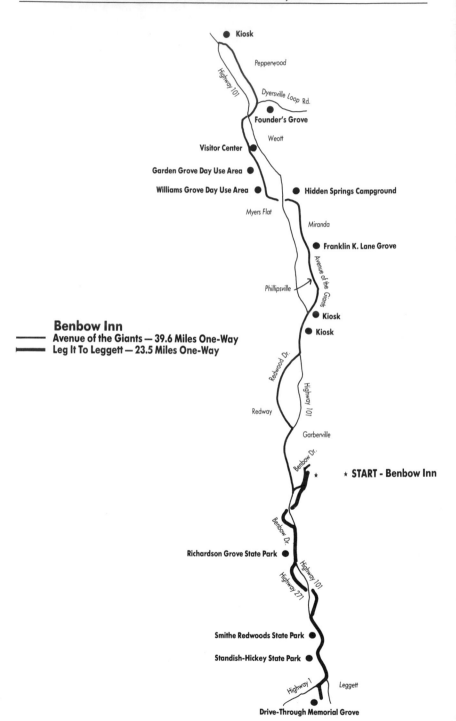

Kiosk

Pepperwood

Highway 101

Dyersville Loop Rd.

Founder's Grove

Weott

Visitor Center

Garden Grove Day Use Area

Williams Grove Day Use Area

Hidden Springs Campground

Myers Flat

Miranda

Franklin K. Lane Grove

Avenue of the Giants

Phillipsville

Kiosk

Kiosk

Benbow Inn
Avenue of the Giants — 39.6 Miles One-Way
Leg It To Leggett — 23.5 Miles One-Way

Redwood Dr.

Highway 101

Redway

Garberville

Benbow Dr.

★ ★ **START - Benbow Inn**

Benbow Dr.

Richardson Grove State Park

Highway 101

Highway 271

Smithe Redwoods State Park

Standish-Hickey State Park

Highway 1

Leggett

Drive-Through Memorial Grove

AVENUE OF THE GIANTS (39.6 MILES ONE WAY)

With the help of a shuttle, you can ride this renowned road through Humboldt Redwoods State Park in either direction, or if you have all day and don't mind long distances, ride it both ways for the full effect of those magnificent Sequoia trees. You can pick up an "Auto Tour" pamphlet at a small kiosk on either the north or the south end. Plan to take a lock and allow enough time to dismount and walk in some of the groves. I'd especially recommend visiting the informative Founder's Grove, about 10 miles from the north end. You'll also find plenty of refueling opportunities up and down the Avenue, from markets to cafes and delis.

LEG IT TO LEGGETT (23.5 MILES ONE WAY)

There are three state redwood parks along Highway 101 south of Benbow on the way to Leggett, where Highway 1 begins its winding way to the coast. Except for the alternate Route 271 around Piercy, it's almost all downhill, meaning an uphill trek on the way back, should you choose to do the 47-mile round trip.

AVENUE OF THE GIANTS

PT.-PT.	CUM E	DIRECTION	STREET/LANDMARK
			From Benbow Inn
0.0	0.0	L	**Benbow Drive**
0.2	0.2	R	**Highway 101 North**
3.9	4.1	R	**Garberville Exit/Redwood Drive.** All services in Garberbille
2.8	6.9	X	Highway 101
2.2	9.1		**Redway** — Cafe, market, restaurant
		R	**Follow signs to 101 North**
		IL	**Onto Freeway**
1.0	10.1		Map kiosk on right
2.3	12.4	R	**Avenue of the Giants exit**
0.4	12.8		Pamphlet kiosk on right
2.1	14.9		**Phillipsville** — Market on left
0.4	15.3		**Franklin K. Lane Grove** (restrooms may be closed)
3.4	18.7		**Miranda** — Cafe on right, market on left

AVENUE OF THE GIANTS (CONT.)

PT.-PT.	CUME	DIRECTION	STREET/LANDMARK
5.2	23.9		**Hidden Springs Campground** — uphill to restrooms
1.1	25.0		**Myers Flat** — Cafe and tourist traps on left
1.0	26.0		**Williams Grove Day Use Area** on left — picnic tables, restrooms, water
2.0	28.0		**Garden Grove Day Use Area** on left — picnic tables, restrooms
1.0	29.0		**Visitor Center** on right — picnic tables, restrooms
1.6	30.6		**Weott** — Turn right for general store.
2.0	32.6		Turn right at Dyersville Loop Rd. for **Founder's Grove**
4.5	37.1		**Pepperwood** — No services — good place to turn around
2.5	39.6		**North end pamphlet kiosk.** Last chance to turn around before freeway

LEG IT TO LEGGETT

PT.-PT.	CUME	DIRECTION	STREET/LANDMARK
			From Benbow Inn
0.0	0.0	**L**	**Benbow Drive**
		X	Highway 101
0.3	0.3	**R**	**Benbow Drive** at golf course
3.9	4.2	**L**	**Highway 101 South** (*Caution!*)
1.9	6.1		**Richardson Grove State Park** on right — Picnic areas, restrooms
1.6	7.7	**R**	**Highway 271/Piercy exit**
3.4	11.1	**X**	Under Highway 101
0.1	11.2	**IR**	**Highway 271**
2.5	13.7	**L**	**Highway 101 South**
5.0	18.7		**Smithe Redwoods State Park** — Viewing area on right
2.6	21.3		**Standish-Hickey State Park** on right
1.6	22.9	**R**	**Leggett/Highway 1 exit**
0.1	23.0	**IL**	**Drive-Through Tree Road**. Market, diner on right
0.5	23.5	**R**	**Drive-Through Memorial Grove**. Can ride through for half price, or just turn around and head back to Benbow!

THE BIDWELL HOUSE

Mike and Susi Gillum
1 Main Street
Chester, CA 96020
916-258-3338
Ambience: Collector's Retreat

Rates: $60-$135
Bed & Breakfast Inn
Full Breakfast
Smoking outside only

Two major attractions lure cyclists to Chester. The first is Lake Almanor, a recreational treat for the angler, boater, boardsailer and nature enthusiast as well. The second is...Bodfish country!

Let me explain. Bodfish is the nom de plume of Chuck Elliot, an early mountain biking pioneer by virtue of the fact that he insisted on riding his road bike on the dirt in some of California's most remote territory. Besides writing books about the backroads and trails he has discovered, Chuck and his wife Lisa Jo Sedlacek run off-the-beaten dirt cycling events from their home base, which just happens to be...Chester.

So if dirt is your thing, you'll fall in love with Bodfish country. And if first-class accommodations are what you seek, you don't have to search far for The Bidwell House, located on the north end of Chester at Number One Main Street.

Back in the days before Lake Almanor was created by damming the Feather River, General John Bidwell, the founding father of the city of Chico, built his wife Annie a summer home at Big Meadow (which now lies beneath the lake).

"We just discovered Annie's diary in the archives at Chico State," Susi Gillum told me, "and we're busy revising a lot of our history!"

After Annie passed on, the house was acquired by prominent cattle ranchers, who moved it out of the path of flood to its present location on Main Street. Since that time it's been a dress shop, a real estate office, a beauty parlor, and now a newly renovated bed-and-breakfast inn.

The Gillums and their partners have invested heavily in reconstruction and in a collection of fine antiques and reproductions. There are 14 units, including three "honeymoon" rooms in a separate cottage. Most have their own private entrances. The new L-shaped addition surrounds the patio and gardens, with four rooms overlooking garden and croquet court from bay windows.

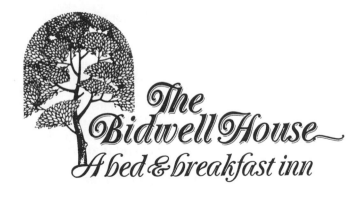

The
Bidwell House
A bed & breakfast inn

When you walk into the front lobby, the first thing that catches your eye is the old sleigh filled with pine cones, pumpkins, flowers, or whatever the season calls for. It sets the tone for the fine details brought to bear in every room, each decorated around a singular theme.

My room was Hunter's Glen, a peaceful combination of muted greens, reds and browns dominated by the brass queen bed and a huge armoire. A world globe stood on a walnut stand next to the small secretary-style desk. An old-fashioned lectern held the guest book, which contained some rather "revealing" entries! And in the corner an authentic turn-of-the-century (or older) Morris chair tempted me to find out how the gentry relaxed before the advent of the Barcalounger.

The doors to both room and bathroom were massive blocks of stained oak, as was the wainscoting around the windows. And the bathroom was an artful blend of old and new, with a modern pedestal sink, sunken Jacuzzi tub and an antique lowboy table holding an old brass-framed shaving mirror.

Another fine detail not used during my stay, but ready for any guest who wishes to have breakfast in bed: a dumbwaiter hatchway, locked from outside, through which room service can be delivered without disturbing the occupants.

There are three public rooms — the lobby, the dining room, and the sun porch, furnished with card tables and well stocked with games, puzzles and a television set. Susi serves cheese and crackers here in the late afternoon. Guests are also welcome in the kitchen, where they can help themselves to coffee or tea after

7:00 a.m. The refrigerator is also available for your own beer, wine or soft drinks (the inn has no liquor license).

The Bidwell House may be the last house on the way out of town on Highway 36, but it's within easy walking distance from excellent dining at the Chester Saloon, cited in *Northern California Best Places* for its fine Italian food.

Then there's breakfast at The Bidwell itself. First there's fresh fruit cocktail and all the o.j. and coffee or tea you can drink. The whole grain French toast is dotted with seeds and wheat berries and accompanied by sausage and bacon. Go ahead and ask for seconds, thirds if you plan to follow the demanding route of the Humbug-Humboldt Loop on Bodfish's Sierra Nevada Mountain Metric.

BIKING FROM THE BIDWELL HOUSE

Terrain Here at the headwaters of the Feather River, you're riding in the "saddle" between the Sierra Nevada and the Cascades. On pavement this translates to fairly rolling terrain, making the going difficult only when headed into the wind. On the other hand, there are plenty of steep climbs off pavement.

Road Conditions The state and county highways circling Lake Almanor are in excellent shape, with generous shoulders along Highway 89 and enough room for all kinds of users. Indian Valley's roads are suprisingly good for their rural character. And the dirt roads into the Humbug and Humboldt drainages are wide and graded for daily use. One down note: Circling Lake Almanor was the first time I'd spotted broken glass north of Lake Tahoe.

Traffic Chester is a mill town, so lumber and logging trucks are a fact of life. Otherwise, you'll enounter heavy tourist traffic at the height of the season at Lake Almanor, yet rarely see another vehicle in Indian Valley.

Nearest Bike Shop
Coming soon:
Bodfish Bicycles
opening in early 1994
(look behind the supermarket)

Also:
Barretts Bike Barn
330 Feather River Drive
Chester, CA 96020
916-258-3428

Best Time To Ride September (after the tourists go home)

Mountain Biking Opportunities Another mind boggler. Consult Bodfish's *Cycling the California Outback* (second edition just out in 1993), as well as *California Dream Cycling*. Pick up Forest Service maps of Lassen National Forest at the Ranger Station on Highway 36 just west of town.

MOUNTAIN BIKES: BODFISH'S SIERRA NEVADA MOUNTAIN METRIC (60.5 MILES)

"No pavement!" That's the rallying cry at the start of this annual Bodfish event held every Memorial Day Sunday, starting from the Roadside Rest Area nine miles south of Chester on the west side of Highway 89. If you can't get reservations at The Bidwell House for Memorial Day Weekend so you can enjoy the fantastic support the Almanor Wheelpeople give on this ride, my advice is to wait a month or so before tackling it yourself. That gives the snow a chance to melt, and to cease falling from the sky, which it can still do up here at the end of May. Regardless of when you do it, you'll relish the fine scenic opportunities from Humbug Summit, and the 20-some odd miles of downhill back to the start from Humboldt Summit.

INDIAN VALLEY (22.6 MILES)

Vastly more scenic than Sierra Valley to the south, Indian Valley is a flat-to-rolling ride. If you like, you can ride the relatively easy 26 miles from The Bidwell House down the west side of the lake to Greenville (keep in mind this will add 52 miles if you ride down and back up). Or simply drive to Greenville and start out there, like my cue sheet does.

LAKE ALMANOR CIRCUMCYCLE (33.6 MILES)

Here's a round-the-lake ride you don't have to scale passes or cover long miles to do. The lake may be a tourist mecca, but the roads around it will take you to secluded wooded areas where you

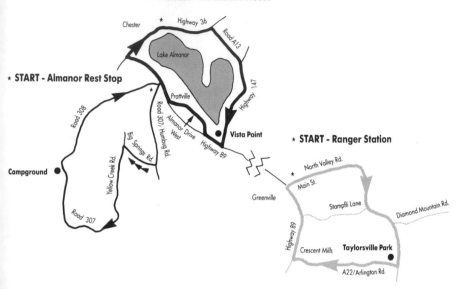

The Bidwell House
Bodfish's Sierra Nevada Mountain Metric — 60.5 Miles
Indian Valley — 22.6 Miles
Lake Almanor Circumcycle — 33.6 Miles

may just spot deer or other wildlife. From the south side you'll also get a few good peeks at Mount Lassen to the north.

BODFISH'S SIERRA NEVADA MOUNTAIN METRIC (HUMBUG-HUMBOLDT LOOP)

PT.-PT.	CUME	DIRECTION	STREET/LANDMARK
			From Almanor Rest Stop nine miles south of Chester on the west side of Highway 89
0.0	0.0	**R**	**Dirt road behind picnic area**
1.5	1.5	**L**	**Road 307/Humbug Road**
10.0	11.5	**R**	**Big Springs Road** — through scenic Humbug Valley
5.0	16.5	**SL**	**Yellow Creek Road**
10.0	26.5	**R**	**Road 307** to Humbug Summit
4.0	30.5	**BR**	**Road 307.** *Do NOT take the road to Stirling City!*
6.0	36.5	**R**	**Blue Meadows Junction.** *Do NOT follow signs to Butte Meadows!*
4.0	40.5	**L**	**Road 308** at campground — head downhill
20.0	60.5	**R**	**Almanor Rest road**

INDIAN VALLEY

PT.-PT.	CUME	DIRECTION	STREET/LANDMARK
			From Forest Service Ranger Station, Main Street, Greenville, 26 miles south of Chester on Highway 89
0.0	0.0	**L**	**Main Street.** Becomes **North Valley Road**
8.1	8.1	**C**	**North Valley Road** at Stampfli Lane
1.7	9.8	**R**	**North Valley Road** at Diamond Mountain Road — cross bridge
1.0	10.8	**S**	**North Valley Road** at sign: Taylorsville 1 mile
1.0	11.8	**R**	**A22/Arlington Road** at Taylorsville Park — pit toilets on left

INDIAN VALLEY (CONT.)

PT.-PT.	CUME	DIRECTION	STREET/LANDMARK
0.5	12.3		**Taylorsville** — Indian Valley Museum and general store on left
4.8	17.1	R	**Highway 89**
0.8	17.9		**Crescent Mills** — General store, saloon on right
4.5	22.4		**Greenville**
0.2	22.6	R	**Main Street** — Cafe, general store on right; ranger station on left

LAKE ALMANOR CIRCUMCYCLE

PT.-PT.	CUME	DIRECTION	STREET/LANDMARK
			From The Bidwell House
0.0	0.0	L	**Highway 36/Main Street**
4.7	4.7		Rest Area (restrooms) at 4.7 miles
0.2	4.9	R	**Road A13**
3.8	8.7	R	**Highway 147**. Cafe on left on A13 just before intersection
4.2	12.9		BP Gas Station with grocery store on left
2.0	14.9		Picnic area (pit toilet) on right
0.8	15.7		Vista point with view of Lassen on right
0.4	16.1	R	**Highway 89**
0.3	16.4		Picnic area on right (pit toilets)
5.3	21.7	R	**Almanor Drive West**
0.7	22.4	L	At T (no sign). **Prattville**
0.6	23.0		**Plumas Pines Resort** — Snack bar, grocery on left, restaurant on right
1.2	24.2	R	**Highway 89**
5.5	29.7	R	**Highway 36**
2.8	32.5		**Chester** — all services
1.1	33.6	L	**Bidwell House**

THE FEATHER BED

Bob and Jan Janowski
542 Jackson Street, P.O. Box 3200
Quincy, CA 95971
916-283-0102
Ambience: Early American

Rates: $70-$100
Bed & Breakfast Inn
Full Breakfast
No smoking

Tales of both wonder and woe have been told by cyclists who have pedaled the hills and valleys of Feather River Country. Yet in spite of unpredictable weather (which Californians from more southern climes are just not used to), steep climbs, shoulderless highways and fast-moving logging trucks, all agree it is a fantastically beautiful place to ride a bicycle.

Towns are far apart and cities are unheard of. The air carries a refreshing tang of smog-free cleanliness, while the wild and scenic Feather River and its tributaries provide a rich and varied terrain to explore both on and off the pavement.

As the Plumas County seat, Quincy is pretty much the administrative center for Feather River Country. It's even got a shopping strip, about a mile and a half outside town in East Quincy. Otherwise, things are pretty much the way they were 20 years ago. In fact, one of the most controversial issues of the day is whether or not to install the town's first traffic light out by the high school.

In the midst of this easygoing environment sits The Feather Bed, a stately Queen Anne Victorian one block beyond the Courthouse on Jackson Street. Built by Edward Huskinson in 1893, the house has been a bed and breakfast inn since 1979.

When I arrived, there was bustling activity next door, where new owners Bob and Jan Janowski were putting up two new cottages for their inn, one with complete disabled access, the other specifically for families.

Buffy the Siamese cat was first to the door when I rang the bell. She was followed closely by Jan, who immediately showed me around the three common rooms in the main house. The front parlor has a phone (although you can request one for your room), a tape player and a small collection of reading material. In the sitting room you can sit and read the latest edition of the San Francisco Chronicle at the antique oak clawfoot table. Or you can help yourself to wine by the glass or a cup of sun tea from the

adjacent kitchen to go with the complimentary chocolate chip cookies. Just beyond is the dining room, with three tables for serving breakfast.

All seven guest rooms at The Feather Bed have private access, either up outdoor stairways, through the back of the house, or in the cottage. So it was outside and up the back stairs to the Gladys-Reid room, where Huskinson's daughter grew up. She loved it because it basked in the late afternoon sun.

Like all the other rooms, the Gladys-Reid was extremely spacious, with a private bath, floral wallpaper and wall-to-wall carpeting. A queen bed with a white cast iron headboard was spread with forest green and tan quilts. The antique furniture included a handsome sideboard with fold-out desk and a bottom cupboard stacked with magazines and travel books. An antique radio sat on top, in front of dark green glass tiles. A sitting area on the other side of the room was furnished with two wing-back easy chairs and a small vanity dresser with a mirror.

The bathroom had built-in oak cupboards and a two-sided brass-framed shaving mirror suspended on an accordian bracket above the sink. A basket of rolled towels sat on the floor, ready for use in conjunction with the clawfoot tub/shower.

Of the other rooms, Barrett's Room, named for the Huskinsons' son, is the most elaborate, with a Franklin stove and clawfoot tub/ shower. Edward's Suite has a separate sitting room and a fireplace. There's also the air-conditioned Jennie's Sewing Room, and the Morning Room with a private balcony. Most desirable, however, is the secluded Sweetheart Cottage with private deck, clawfoot tub and wrought iron queen bed.

Venturing out from The Feather Bed leads guests first to the front porch with its full complement of rattan furniture — perfect for relaxing with a glass of iced sun tea and peoplewatching at the Courthouse across the street. From there it's a short walk to the Plumas County History Museum on the corner of Jackson and Bradley streets. Pick up a Heritage Walk Brochure and tour all the old Victorian and early 20th century buildings of the town. For an extra-fun tour, do it on The Feather Bed's one-speed Schwinn Twin tandem.

The Feather Bed will make sure you leave in the morning with a full load of bike-fueling carbohydrates. Served by Bob, our breakfast began with blackberry smoothies, all nonfat and made from wild blackberries grown in back of the inn. Along with my fellow guests — a couple from Santa Cruz who were emigrants from British Columbia — I then dug into blackberry cobbler, followed by tomato-basil fritata with sausage, and raspberry-walnut muffins.

BIKING FROM THE FEATHER BED

Terrain The altitude may be below 5,000 feet, but never forget that you're still in the Sierra Nevada. If you do forget, the climb to Bucks Lake — not to mention the hairy descent — will remind you!

Road Conditions As usual, state highways are in fairly good condition, as is Big Creek Road up to Bucks Lake. You'll encounter some bumpy spots near the pass on Bucks Lake Road, along with narrow lanes and a sharp dropoff to the right.

Traffic Unless there's a major golf tournament happening at Graeagle (where there are three courses), the traffic will be moderate to light. Logging trucks are a daily fact of life, although they do lighten up on the weekends.

Nearest Bike Shop
Sierra Mountain Sports (2 blocks from The Feather Bed)
501 W. Main Street
Quincy, CA 95971
916-283-2323

Best Time To Ride Late summer (mid-August through early September)

Mountain Biking Opportunities The best off-road riding seems to be out of Greenville, 23 miles north of Quincy on Highway 89. Pick up a copy of the Plumas National Forest Map from the Ranger Station on Lawrence Street in Quincy. I was privileged to receive a copy of ride suggestions written up by the Greenville District's Fuels Management Officer, one Joe Castillo, and a fellow named Ken Roby. Hopefully there are more copies around. (Thanks, Marcia!)

BUCKS LAKE LOOP (33.1 MILES)

In *California Dream Cycling*, Bodfish recommends taking this scenic loop the counterclockwise way, to avoid the hair-raising descent on Bucks Lake Road (featuring a precipitous dropoff without benefit of guardrails). My preference is to take it clockwise to avoid climbing that 15+% grade.

SCENIC FEATHER RIVER HIGHWAY (63.8 MILES)

Cycle America tourists and Olympic racers alike can occasionally be spotted freewheeling down Highway 89 through the Feather River Canyon. If you want to follow in their draft, your best bet is the 28 or so miles between Quincy and Graeagle, where the terrain is relatively rolling and the scenery typical of the region. You'll find plenty of intriguing food stops in Blairsden, as well as a market in Graeagle and a good deli in Mohawk. If you'd like to get some serious climbing in, strike out from Mohawk for Plumas Eureka State Park.

INDIAN VALLEY (22.6 MILES)

See write-up under Biking from The Bidwell House, page 209.

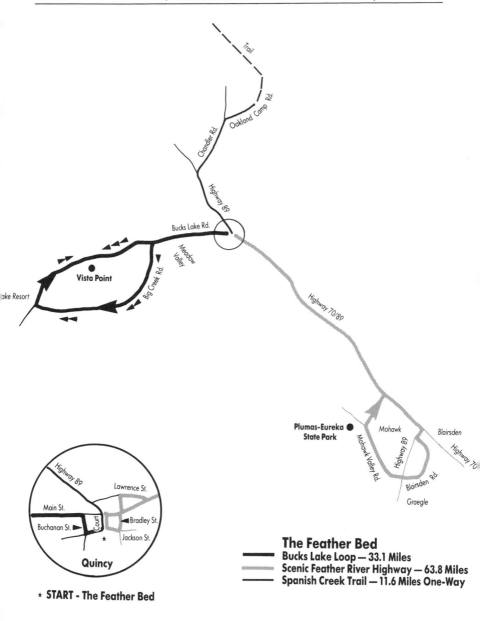

Trail

Oakland Camp Rd.

Chandler Rd.

Highway 89

Bucks Lake Rd.

Meadow Valley

Big Creek Rd.

Vista Point

ake Resort

Highway 70/89

Plumas-Eureka ●
State Park

Mohawk

Blairsden

Mohawk Valley Rd.

Highway 89

Blairsden Rd.

Highway 70

Graegle

Highway 89

Lawrence St.

Main St.

Court

Bradley St.

Buchanan St.

Jackson St.

★

Quincy

★ START - The Feather Bed

The Feather Bed
Bucks Lake Loop — 33.1 Miles
Scenic Feather River Highway — 63.8 Miles
Spanish Creek Trail — 11.6 Miles One-Way

MOUNTAIN BIKES: SPANISH CREEK TRAIL (APPROX. 23.2 OR 6.8 MILES)

This delightful and often technical singletrack parallels the railroad grade along Spanish Creek between Oakland Camp and the fishing access at the end of Old Keddie Road, which you will have a hard time finding by car. So my advice is to drive or ride up to Oakland Camp via Chandler Road and head out from there. In September of 1993 the Forest Service had removed the bridge just beyond Oakland Camp, but at that time of year fording the creek was not difficult. Besides, there's a good chance a new bridge will have appeared since then.

BUCKS LAKE LOOP

PT.-PT.	CUME	DIRECTION	STREET/LANDMARK
			From The Feather Bed
0.0	0.0	L	**Jackson Street**
0.1	0.1	R	**Buchanan Street**
0.1	0.2	L	**Main Street**; becomes **Bucks Lake Road**
7.0	7.2		**Meadow Valley** — market on right
2.2	9.4	L	**Big Creek Road**
9.5	18.9	R	**Bucks Lake Road**
0.5	19.4		**Bucks Lake Resort** — store, restaurant
0.7	20.1		**Lakeside Resort** — market
3.5	23.6		**Pass/Vista Point** — pit toilet. *Begin 3.0-mile downhill/15+% grades!*
9.3	32.9	R	**Buchanan Street**
0.1	33.0	L	**Jackson Street**
0.1	33.1	R	**The Feather Bed**

SCENIC FEATHER RIVER HIGHWAY

PT.-PT.	CUME	DIRECTION	STREET/LANDMARK
			From The Feather Bed
0.0	0.0	R	**Jackson Street**
0.1	0.1	L	**Court Street**
0.1	0.2	R	**Main Street**
2.5	2.7	C	**Highway 70/89**
28.5	31.2	R	**Highway 89** at Highway 70 junction
0.2	31.4	L	**Blairsden Road** in **Graegle**
			Restaurants, market in **Blairsden**
1.1	32.5	X	Highway 89 in Graeagle — market 0.2 miles to the left
0.1	32.6	C	**Mohawk Valley Road**
1.0	33.6	R	**Mohawk Valley Road** in **Mohawk**. Deli on right. **Plumas-Eureka State Park** up steep hill on left
0.6	34.2	L	**Highway 89**
26.8	61.0	C	**Lawrence Street** in Quincy
2.5	63.5	L	**Bradley Street**
			Murals on right on either side of Main
0.2	63.7	R	**Jackson Street**
0.1	63.8	L	**The Feather Bed**

MOUNTAIN BIKES: SPANISH CREEK TRAIL

PT.-PT.	CUME	DIRECTION	STREET/LANDMARK
			From The Feather Bed
0.0	0.0	S	**Court Street**
0.1	0.1	BL	**Highway 89**
4.0	4.1	R	**Chandler Road**
2.8	6.9	BL	**Oakland Camp Road** at Y at one-lane bridge (no sign)
1.0	7.9	X	**Spanish Creek** into camp
0.3	8.2	L	**At trailhead**
3.0	11.2		Single track becomes jeep road
0.4	11.6		Pavement — U-turn and reverse route to Oakland Camp and Quincy

MOUNT SHASTA RANCH

Bill and Mary Larsen
1008 W. A. Barr Road
Mount Shasta, CA 96067
916-926-3870
Ambience: Family Ranch

Rates: $45-$85
Bed & Breakfast Inn
Full Breakfast
Smoking on front porch and patio only

Drive north or south on Interstate 5 through the Sacramento River Valley and you cannot escape the impact of Mount Shasta, looming nearly 14,000 feet above you. Riding a bicycle in the area merely serves to increase the impact of that amazing snow-capped peak. You meander along a quiet country road, casually turn a corner and wham! There it is in all its splendor. Ride a mile or two further, turn another corner, and the mountain seems to have changed ever so slightly, just enough to give you a new perspective.

One perspective of Mount Shasta you're sure to appreciate is the view from the front porch, or perhaps from your own room, at Mount Shasta Ranch. Built in 1923 as the headquarters of a vast thoroughbred horse ranch, this "down-home" B&B offers all the amenities of the most elegant inns for a surprisingly reasonable price (there's no extra charge for the panoramic view).

Today all that remains of the ranch is the main house — a fine example of 1920s Dutch colonial architecture, the carriage house and a separate cottage. A stay in any of the three will transport you back to the ranching days of 75 years ago without denying you a single comfort or convenience.

The common rooms in the main house have open log beams throughout. The huge dining room overlooking the lawn is adjacent to a recreation room with pool table, ping pong table and piano. Centered around a massive stone fireplace, the living room is stacked with magazines and games. Drinks and snacks are available in the kitchen, and a hot tub spa awaits your pleasure on the south patio.

Upstairs the guest rooms all have 12-foot ceilings, private baths, quilt-covered queen beds, and views of the mountain.

My room in the carriage house was one of five above what's now the garage. A sink and mirror took up one corner of the room, while I had the choice of two shared bathrooms just down the hall.

At the north end of the carriage house was a common kitchen with double sink, large refrigerator, stove/range and a large table. The whole setup is perfect for clubs or touring groups, who can just take over and treat the Carriage House as a base camp.

Families might prefer the cottage, with its two bedrooms (one has a queen bed, the other a set of twin beds), sofabed in the tiny living room, and fully equipped kitchen.

For nearly 15 years Bill and Mary Larsen raised a small mob of foster kids at Mount Shasta Ranch. Finally, "we found ourselves alone," Bill told me. The next step became obvious as offer after offer for the spread came from enterpreneurs eager to open a B&B. "We didn't want to sell," Bill said, "so we opened the B&B ourselves."

As a former art teacher, Mary relishes the job of decorating. Much of her artwork hangs in the public rooms of the main house, and her refined taste is reflected in the choices of antiques, wallpapers and other art objects throughout the inn. When I admired a handsome folding hand loom displayed on the main house's stairway landing, Bill said, "Oh, Mary picked that up at a garage sale."

I wondered if garage sales were also her source for the inviting rocker and armchair, the huge antique dresser and matching mirror, the carved cherry bed frame, or the collection of straw hats hung on the wall in my room.

The town of Mount Shasta City, just half a mile up the road, has attracted an assortment of New Agers and other alternative lifestyle folks. They live congenially alongside the ranchers and loggers who have been there for generations, and the combination makes for a happy choice of places to dine and relax.

You can buy sushi and Thai noodles at just about any deli. Or you can sit down to a sumptuous dinner at Bellissimo's, which Mary calls "the best restaurant between San Francisco and Ashland." Unfortunately, Bellissimo's was closed when I was there, so I opted for Lily's, whose chef once worked at Bellissimo's. I was not disappointed, and neither will you be, especially if you order anything from the Mexican or pasta parts of the menu.

The breakfasts at Mount Shasta Ranch rival anything you can buy in town, though. As Terry, the cook, puts it, "My philosophy is, if you leave my breakfast table hungry, it's your own fault." We started with fruit cup laced with coconut shavings, orange juice from a huge pitcher and tea or coffee. Then out came extremely generous western omelets wrapped in flour tortillas and topped with mild salsa, accompanied by peppery ranch-style hash brown potatoes.

But no meal can hold a candle to the scenery. Every time I looked up, there was Mount Shasta warming my aesthetic awareness. Best of all was the magnificent after-dinner sunset spraying pink and lavender on the thunderclouds that had spit a few drops of rain with the last light and now hovered like a shawl over the peak.

BIKING FROM MOUNT SHASTA RANCH

Terrain Everything from dead flat to maddeningly steep. If you take the Everett Highway to Panther Meadows, you'll climb for your life! On the other hand, the dirt roads into the McCloud River Falls area are essentially level.

Road Conditions Old Stage Road, paralleling Highway 5, is in excellent condition, but the streets in Mount Shasta, McCloud and Weed could use some work.

Traffic Downtown Mount Shasta and Weed Blvd. are thick with hustle and bustle. Once outside of town, though, there's so little traffic, it can get downright lonely.

Nearest Bike Shop
Doctor Bicycle's Cyclery
412 N. Mount Shasta Blvd.
Mount Shasta, CA 96067
916-926-4951

Best Time To Ride July through mid-September

Mountain Biking Opportunities I defer to the expert on cycling in the shadow of Shasta: Bodfish recommends heading for Gumboot Lake, at the headwaters of the South Fork of the Sacramento River. It's about a 20-mile drive from Mount Shasta City, up a paved road that ends at a campground. For more information, consult Bodfish's *Cycling the California Outback* and the excellent *Mount Shasta Area Mountain Bike Map* available at Doctor Bicycle's Cyclery.

If you prefer to ride out from Mount Shasta Ranch, take W.A. Barr Road to Castle Peak Road and strike out for the peak. For a more laid-back ride, simply take the circuit around Lake Siskiyou, just a mile or so south of Mount Shasta Ranch.

MOUNTAIN OR ROAD BIKES: MCCLOUD RIVER FALLS (48.0 MILES)

If you're not feeling energetic enough to scale 4,770-foot Snowman Hill Summit on your clunker, you can follow these directions by car to McCloud and ride from there or from Cattle Camp at the south end of the scenic dirt road. On the other hand, if you're riding a road touring bike, I'd recommend entering from the north end and heading down the paved road to the Lower Falls, then attempting the Upper Falls on the dirt, which is well-graded gravel and flat. On a mountain bike, however, I'd definitely start at the south end for the best Shasta views.

WANDERING TO WEED (31.0 MILES)

This little explorer goes to the old timber town of Weed. Along the way you can hike the trails of the Rupp Nature Study Area or tour the oldest fish hatchery in California. Don't miss the Sisson Museum next to the hatchery, where you can pick up photocopies of "tourmaps" for the area for a dime apiece. There's also the cute little Lumbertown Museum in Weed, a good rest stop at the turnaround.

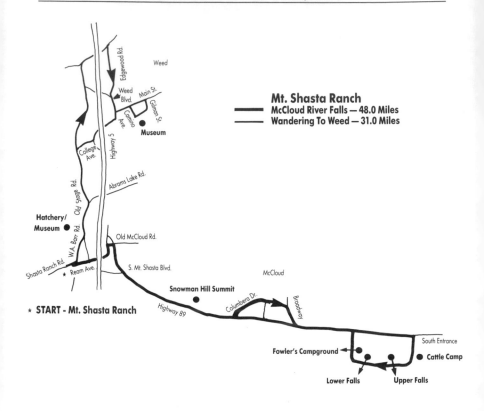

Weed

Edgewood Rd.

Weed Blvd.

Main St.

Gilman St.

Camino Ave.

College Ave.

Highway 5

Old Stage Rd.

Abrams Lake Rd.

Museum

Mt. Shasta Ranch
McCloud River Falls — 48.0 Miles
Wandering To Weed — 31.0 Miles

Hatchery/ Museum ●

W.A. Barr Rd.

Shasta Ranch Rd.

★ Ream Ave.

Old McCloud Rd.

S. Mt. Shasta Blvd.

McCloud

Snowman Hill Summit ●

Highway 89

Columbera Dr.

Broadway

South Entrance

★ **START - Mt. Shasta Ranch**

Fowler's Campground ●

● **Cattle Camp**

Lower Falls

Upper Falls

MCCLOUD RIVER FALLS

PT.-PT.	CUME	DIRECTION	STREET/LANDMARK
			From Mount Shasta Ranch driveway
0.0	0.0	R	**Shasta Ranch Road**
		C	**Ream Avenue**
		X	Under Highway 5, over railroad tracks
0.9	0.9	R	**Old McCloud Road**
0.1	1.0	R	**S. Mt. Shasta Blvd.** to end
1.6	2.6	L	**Highway 89**
5.0	7.6		Snowman Hill Summit
3.5	11.1	L	**Columbera Drive**
1.5	12.6		**McCloud** — Stonybrook Restaurant, historic church on left — plus another Shasta view
0.1	12.7	L	**Quincy Avenue**
0.2	12.9	R	**At T** (no sign). Mac's Delicatessen on left
0.1	13.0	R	**Broadway**
0.1	13.1	L	**Highway 89**
5.2	18.3		**Lower Falls**/west entrance on right
4.6	22.9	R	**South Entrance.** Scenic drive is marked with binoculars. Cattle Camp on left — pit toilets
2.0	24.9		**Lakin Dam turnoff** on left — good riverside singletrack to explore. DO NOT CROSS Bigelow Bridge — private property.
1.5	26.4	L	**To Upper Falls.** Follow binocular signs to singletrack, super river overviews.
2.0	28.4	L	**Fowler's Campground.** Road becomes paved
0.1	28.5	R	Singletrack to Lower Falls, picnic area, swimming access
0.1	28.6	L	Paved road to Highway 89
1.5	30.1	L	**Highway 89**
5.3	35.4		**McCloud turnoff** on right
10.0	45.4	R	**Mt. Shasta Blvd.**
1.6	47.0	L	**Old McCloud Road**
0.1	47.1	L	**Ream Avenue**

MCCLOUD RIVER FALLS (CONT.)

PT.-PT.	CUME	DIRECTION	STREET/LANDMARK
0.9	48.0	C	**Shasta Ranch Road**
		IL	**Mt. Shasta Ranch** driveway

WANDERING TO WEED

PT.-PT.	CUME	DIRECTION	STREET/LANDMARK
			From Mount Shasta Ranch driveway
0.0	0.0	**R**	**Shasta Ranch Road**
		IL	**W.A. Barr Road**
0.5	0.5	**L**	**Old Stage Road. State Fish Hatchery & Sisson Museum** on left, **Rupp Nature Study Area** on right
3.3	3.8	**L**	**Old Stage Road** at Abrams Lake Road
9.6	13.4	**L**	**At T** (no sign — follow sign to Edgewood)
0.1	13.5	**R**	**Under Highway 5**
0.1	13.6	**R**	**Edgewood Road**
3.0	16.6	**L**	**Weed Blvd.** at freeway ramp
0.5	17.1	**L**	**Main Street** —deli, saloon, restaurants
0.5	17.6	**R**	**Main Street** at Mercantile Building
0.1	17.7	**R**	**Gilman Street. Weed Historical Lumber Town Museum** on left at intersection
0.2	17.9	**R**	**Camino Avenue**
0.1	18.0	**L**	**Main Street**
0.2	18.2	**L**	**Weed Blvd.**
0.4	18.6	**R**	**College Avenue**
2.4	21.0	**L**	**Old Stage Road**
6.2	27.2	**R**	**Old Stage Road** at Abrams Lake Road
3.3	30.5	**BR**	**W.A. Barr Road**
0.5	31.0	**R**	**Shasta Ranch Road**
		IL	**Mount Shasta Ranch** driveway

OTTER BAR LODGE

Peter and Kristy Sturges
10426 Salmon River Rd.
Forks of Salmon, CA 96031
916-462-4772
Kayaking & mountain bike resort

Rates: $1050 for 7 days
3 full meals a day
Smoking permitted outside

How would you like to spend a whole week in a rustic B&B-type atmosphere, whiling away entire days cycling dirt roads in some of the most remote, most beautiful forests and canyons in Northern California?

Taking dips in swimming holes seemingly designed for the purpose? Spending a day river rafting between rides? Eating three sumptuous gourmet meals a day (some of them on the trail)? Enjoying a massage, a cedar-lined, wood-fired sauna or solar-heated hot tub at the end of each exuberant day?

Yes to all the above? Then head north beyond (way beyond) the northernmost B&B in this book to Otter Bar Lodge, nestled on the California Salmon River, just beneath the Oregon border between the Marble Mountain and the Trinity Alps.

During the high-water months between April and July, Otter Bar is one of the premier river kayaking resorts in the country. But come August the water tends to get a bit low for whitewater adventure, and Otter Bar turns into a mountain biking mecca.

Owned and operated by Peter and Kristy Sturges, Otter Bar spreads out over 30 acres (including three-quarters of a mile of the river itself), surrounded by countless miles of fire roads and singletrack trails in the 1.7 million-acre Klamath National Forest.

The lodge is built to "bring the outside in," with 12-foot windows in the living room and French doors leading from each room to a deck. Blond oak floors laid with colorful throw rugs dominate the 3,000-square-foot interior.

Three of the four bedrooms are double occupancy, decorated with B&B-type details. The dorm room sleeps four, two on loft beds with furniture built in underneath. Everyone sleeps under a down comforter during the crisp mountain nights. The three bathrooms are shared by all.

OTTER BAR LODGE

During your week-long stay, a guide will take you on rides to remote mountaintops like Blue Mountain Ridge, where you'll spend the night in a cabin with a 360° view of the surrounding backcountry. You can ride every mile of these excursions (and add more if you like), or you can "sag out" at any time you like, hopping into one of the trucks or vans that carries gear and meals to your destinations.

One of the rides terminates at Soames Bar, where an inflated raft waits to take you down the river for an afternoon of Class III (i.e., moderate) whitewater. Hardshell kayaking lessons are always available at the lodge — no extra charge.

You can bring your own bike (and reap a $50 discount) or use one of the bikes from Specialized or similar top-of-the-line company that the Sturges replace yearly. There's always at least one mountain bike pro on hand to offer instruction for novices or coaching to those who'd like to improve their skills. (Past "pros" have included mountain bike originators and gurus Scot Nicol, Joe Breeze and Jeff Lindsay).

Otter Bar Lodge is a minimum 2.5-hour drive from Eureka or the Mt. Shasta area, 7.5 hours from San Francisco, and 8 hours from Portland, Oregon. Fly into Eureka and they'll pick you up at the airport for a small additional fee. There are only 12 beds, so reserve well in advance.

WINE COUNTRY INNS AND RIDES

In 1838 General Mariano Vallejo arrived from Southern California as military governor of a tumultuous Mexican colony headquartered in a backwater town called Sonoma. With him came grape vines from the mission padres of the south, the humble beginnings of Northern California's most romantic, most legendary industry.

By 1858 both the Napa and Sonoma valleys were producing wine commercially. Today some three million people a year descend on Napa Valley alone, eager to sample the good life epitomized by the sprawling vineyards and imposing winery buildings that spread up and down the 35-mile-long strip between the Mayacamas and the St. Helenas.

In all fairness, some of the best California wines are not produced, or even grown, in Napa County. Indeed, nearly all of California, from Simi Valley in the south to the Sierra foothills to the Mattole Valley in the north, may in truth be called "Wine Country." But Napa and Sonoma possess the cachet, the romance of renowned winery names and the infamous intrigues that have combined to turn California wines into a smashing marketing success.

The valleys, hillsides, roadways and byways of both counties are virtually covered with vineyards. In the spring the mustard seeds bloom, turning the entire region into a gigantic sheet of brilliant yellow. In fall the vine leaves turn to muted reds, bronzes, oranges and tawny browns, California's smugly secret reply to the autumn colors of the East Coast.

Need it be mentioned that bicycling here is an especially delicious treat? Well-maintained roads roll through hills and valleys to reveal patterns of vineyards against a backdrop of rugged mountains. Wineries beckon with tasting rooms and guided tours. Fine restaurants and little out-of-the-way markets offer culinary delights to be matched only in similar territory in Italy and France.

A word or two regarding wine tasting and cycling: These suggestions, offered by the folks at Sunrise Winery in Cupertino (a long way south of Napa and Sonoma) will help you minimize the dangers of guiding two wheels down the road with the fruit of the vine in your bloodstream:

1) When you first arrive at a winery, put off tasting until your pulse has settled down to its resting rate. 2) Try to eat lunch, or at least a nutritious snack, before you belly up to the tasting bar. 3) When you do taste, take just a few sips of each sample, clearing your palate with plenty of water and breadsticks in between to help counter the effects of the alcohol.

If you love to ride centuries, the Napa Valley Century, held in late August, will treat you to all the sights of the Valley, with outstanding food at highly supported rest stops. In early May the Santa Rosa Wine Country Century offers much the same for the Alexandar and Dry Creek valleys of Sonoma County.

Along with all this marvelous food and drink comes B&B hospitality with its own unique flavor. Ranging from down-home Americana to early 20th century Arts and Crafts to elegantly whimsical Victorian, these inns extend the Wine Country experience for any lucky guest.

Hope-Merrill House in Sonoma County's rural Geyserville, sits at the gateway to the Alexander and Dry Creek valleys, far from the mad whirl of Napa yet blessed with some of the finest wines to come out of the region. Innkeeper Kim Taylor specializes in providing guests with picnic lunches and wines made from grapes grown in her own backyard. Across the street, sister inn Hope-Bosworth House offers similar delights on weekends and all summer long.

Just south of bustling St. Helena in the middle of Napa Valley, **The Ink House** stands in the midst of acres of vineyards. A visit here simply must include time spent in the cupola, with its 360-degree view of the surroundings. Hosts Ernie Veniegas and Jim Annis have created an unpretentious Victorian ambience that refuses to take itself too seriously.

Larry and Norma Barnett operate **Thistle Dew Inn**, just off Sonoma's historic town plaza, for the gardener and gourmand in each of us. Larry's inventive evening hors d'oeuvres and breakfasts are the highlight of this Craftsman-era B&B.

And in quiet, unpretentious Yountville, off the beaten track of wineries and fine shops, **The Webber Place** is artist Diane Bartholomew's haven of Americana collected in an authentic 1850s farmhouse.

FOR MORE INFORMATION ABOUT BICYCLING IN WINE COUNTRY:

Cyclist's Route Atlas, A Guide to Yolo, Solano & Napa Counties by Randall Gray Braun. Heyday Books, Box 9145, Berkeley, CA 94709.

Grape Expeditions, Bicycle Tours of the California Wine Country by Lena Emmery and Sally Taylor, 756 Kansas Street, San Francisco, CA 94017.

North San Francisco Bay/Sacramento Bicycle Touring Map. Krebs Cycle Products, P.O. Box 7337, Santa Cruz, CA 95061.

Bicycle Rides in and around Napa Valley prepared by Napa Bicycle Club. Order from Eagle Cycling Club, 3335 Solano Avenue, Napa, CA 94558.

Cycling the San Francisco Bay Area by Carol O'Hare. Bicycle Books, Inc., P.O. Box 2038, Mill Valley, CA 94942.

HOPE-MERRILL HOUSE

Kim Taylor
21253 Geyserville Avenue, P.O. Box 42
Geyserville, CA 95441
800-825-4233; 707-857-3356
Ambience: Country Victorian

Rates: $95-$125
Bed & Breakfast Inn
Full breakfast
No Smoking

Want to do some **Wine Country cycle touring** without congested traffic, ostentatious wineries, and overpriced tourist traps? Head for Alexander Valley, Dry Creek Valley and the countryside around Geyserville. Here you'll discover out-of-the-way wineries whose vintages are every bit as remarkable as those in neighboring Napa Valley. You'll also find endless vineyards to pedal through. And in Geyserville — as rural as any French farming village — you'll have a choice of two delightful B&Bs.

Both the Hope-Merrill House and the Hope-Bosworth House across the street are owned by Rosalie and Robert Hope and operated by their very able daughter, Kim Taylor. During summer months, both houses are open to guests all week long. Off-season (after the harvest and crush), Hope-Bosworth is only open on weekends.

A Queen Anne Victorian, Hope-Bosworth was built in 1904 entirely of heart redwood from plans early settler George M. Bosworth mail-ordered from a "pattern book." The original oak grain woodwork still dominates throughout the house. Polished fir floors, antique light fixtures and warm-toned wallpapers enhance the furnishings in each room.

Hope-Merrill is an Eastlake Stick Style Victorian built around 1885 by land developer J.P. Merrill. The most striking feature of the interior is the original Lincrusta Walton wainscoting that dominates the downstairs entrance, staircase and upstairs hallway. All the rage at the end of the last century, this linoleum made from chemically treated wood fibers gives the walls a highly embossed "leather look" that complements the original quarter-sawn oak grain doors and woodwork.

Adding to the overall effect is an eclectic range of silk-screen wallpapers designed by Bruce Bradbury for each of the guestrooms, the parlor and the dining room. It's the dining room that provides the most fascinating chapter in the Hopes' scrapbook describing

Bed & Breakfast

the house's restoration and subsequent first place in a national competition. After raising the ceiling (as in all the rooms) to its original 12-foot height, they topped the red paisley wallpaper with a gilt frieze and papered the ceiling with "stars," hanging a brass chandelier in the center.

The ceiling is almost enough to detract from the handsome blond oak table and eight oak and cane chairs, not to mention the marbled steel fireplace and tile hearth, and the bay window on the opposite wall. This is where Kim serves up a family-style breakfast at 9:00 every morning. Ours featured homemade apple sauce, almond poppyseed cake, fluffy silver dollar pancakes with homemade grape jam (from the grape arbor out back) and plum preserves (from the tree in the yard).

The parlor also has bay windows framing five matching pieces of Victorian furniture upholstered in red velvet. The wallpaper is a "busy" blue and white floral design that manages not to detract from the rich redwood plank floors covered with a multicolored paisley oriental carpet.

All the guest rooms in Hope-Merrill House have queen beds and private baths. There's one guest room downstairs, the Peacock Room, next to the stuffed peacock under the stairs. It boasts a lavish rose wallpaper, a tile and redwood fireplace, and redwood

French doors leading to a private bath with marble sink and sunken whirpool tub.

My room, named Bachelor Button for the bright blue flowers in the wallpaper, had a plain queen bed with an antique lace coverlet spread over a down comforter. The redwood-sashed windows were shaded with quilted fabric pull shades. A handsome dresser of old oak with two keepsake drawers built in at the top held a tilting harp-shaped mirror. The far wall held three Renoir reproductions next to three of Maxfied Parrish. The "chimney" wall held a collection of sillhouettes of Victorian characters painted on glass over other background paintings or photos.

The private bath was across the hall, where the dark green wallpaper beautifully offset the redwood wainscoting and woodwork. Above the redwood shutters on the window was a stained glass fleur-de-lis. But the best pieces were the clawfoot tub with brass shower fixtures that delivered a satisfyingly strong spray, and the black and glass industrial-strength Dixie cup dispenser mounted on the wall above the sink.

Among the other rooms was Briar Rose, with climbing rose wallpaper and a "hex sign" design at the ceiling, wicker loveseat, chair, chaise and tables, and a small crystal chandelier made into a table lamp. On the oak dresser sat a vase of dried roses next to a silver hand mirror, small oval mirror, and pin cushion made of buttons.

Carpenter Gothic's wallpaper was a seashell design, and a matching spread and comforter graced the carved oak throne bed. In the adjacent bath a whirlpool tub sat beneath a skylight, and there was also a glass-enclosed stall shower.

Geyserville is small enough to roll up the sidewalks every night at dusk, if there were sidewalks to roll! There's little else besides the two Hope houses to provide entertainment. If you're seeking an elegant meal, the best bet is the Madrona Manor on Dry Creek Road, a bit of a drive but well worth it. But if you'd rather stick close to where you sleep, there's another Victorian about a ten-minute walk up Geyserville Avenue from the inns. This is Hoffman House, and for gourmands it is a wonderful discovery.

All this quiet country atmosphere may be soon disappear. Just north of the Hope-Merrill House a new housing tract is rapidly rising. Development, alas, has come to Geyserville.

BIKING FROM HOPE-MERRILL HOUSE

Terrain Stick to the valleys and the occasional climb you encounter will be a refreshing exercise. Take on the challenge of The Geysers, however, and you will suffer...I promise!

Road Conditions West Dry Creek Road is only one and a half lanes or narrower for more than five miles, whereas Dry Creek Road on the east side of the valley is a broad highway with ample shoulders.

Geysers Road gets narrower and rougher the further from civilization you wander, but once it turns back toward Alexander Valley, the pavement is new and the descent a great deal smoother than you might have anticipated.

Then there's Old Redwood Road between Windsor and Healdsburg, which suffers from years of neglect, with the result that the shoulder often disappears or is far too rough to ride comfortably or often even safely. And, of course, Highway 128 is virtually shoulderless, in tried-and-true CalTrans fashion.

Traffic Healdsburg is the bottleneck of the Sonoma wine country; the traffic backs up all the way through town, then miraculously disappears out in the valleys.

Nearest Bike Shop
Spoke Folks Cyclery
Center Street at Matheson
Healdsburg, CA
707-433-7171

Best Time To Ride September crush time through mid-November for autumn colors

Mountain Biking Opportunities Mountain bike history buffs will delight in riding the trails of Annadel State Park, once the home of the Rockhopper, a pioneering pre-NORBA race and source of the name of a popular frame model. Access is through Spring Lake Park, off Montgomery Road east of Santa Rosa, approximately 25 miles south of Geyserville.

ALEXANDER VALLEY TO CHALK HILL (39.3 MILES)

Don't let the word "hill" frighten you off; the only nontrivial climb on Chalk Hill Road is half a mile of 6% or so grade; the rest is rolling and downhill to the outskirts of Windsor. On the way out you may want to stop at a winery or two for a taste (I heartily recommend the whites at Alexander Valley Vineyards). On the way back, you can stop at Healdsburg Plaza for a gourmet lunch.

EASTSIDE, WESTSIDE, ALL AROUND DRY CREEK VALLEY (42.7 MILES)

This is it, folks...the ultimate wine country ride. As you follow the roads on the edge of the valley, you'll gaze out over acres of vineyards. You'll also pass some excellent wineries. My favorite is Hop Kiln, occupying what was once a processing plant for beer hops (the kiln chimneys still stand above the main building), and today producing as fine red wines as you'll taste anywhere in Napa or France. Their picnic grounds make a great lunch stop (you can order a picnic lunch from Kim at Hope-Merrill House); or you can wait for the gourmet goodies around Healdsburg Plaza.

THE GEYSERS (49.7 MILES, OR 45.9 MILES IN SUMMER)

Geyserville derives its name from The Geysers, natural geothermal vents high in the Mayacamas Mountains. High is the operative word here; this ride is only for those with strong thighs and/or low granny gears. As you ascend toward the pass, you'll spot the maze-like pattern of pipes which trap thermal energy for the PG&E plant that is hidden from view.

Do not attempt this ride in high summer, or anytime the temperature threatens to climb above the 70s; the road is exposed to the fierce sun and there is no food or water to be had until you get back down to the Jimtown Store.

In summer months the bridge connecting Washington School Road with River Road will be open, allowing you to trade the traffic on Highway 101 into Cloverdale for the backroads, eliminating 3.8 miles in the process.

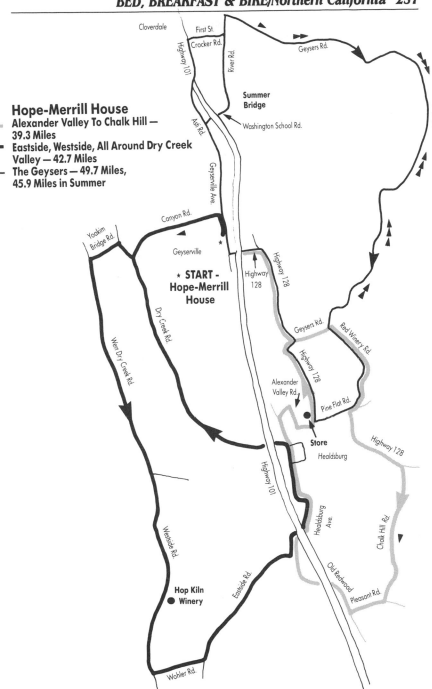

Hope-Merrill House
**Alexander Valley To Chalk Hill —
39.3 Miles**
**Eastside, Westside, All Around Dry Creek
Valley — 42.7 Miles**
**The Geysers — 49.7 Miles,
45.9 Miles in Summer**

ALEXANDER VALLEY TO CHALK HILL

PT.-PT.	CUME	DIRECTION	STREET/LANDMARK
			From Hope-Merrill House
0.0	0.0	R	**Geyserville Avenue**
0.2	0.2	L	**Highway 128**; Geyserville market on right
0.9	1.1	R	**Highway 128** at Geyserville Grange (River Road and Moody Lane)
3.7	4.8	L	**Geysers Road**
0.6	5.4	R	**Red Winery Road** at Y
2.3	7.7	R	**Pine Flat Road**
0.3	8.0	L	**Highway 128** at stop sign (Jimtown Store straight ahead in 0.3 miles)
3.2	11.2	S	**To Chalk Hill Road.** No sign except to Santa Rosa (century markers may be painted in roadway)
0.2	11.4	BR	**Chalk Hill Road**
8.1	19.5	R	**Pleasant Road**
1.0	20.5	R	**Old Redwood Road**
0.1	20.6		Market on left
0.4	21.0		Windsor Plaza on left
2.0	23.0	X	Highway 101
0.1	23.1	BR	**Old Redwood Highway** at Eastside Road
0.3	23.4		Market on right
1.3	24.7	X	Highway 101
0.7	25.4	BL	Cross Russian River
0.6	26.0	C	**Healdsburg Avenue** at Mill Street
0.2	26.2	R	**Matheson Street/Town Square** Bike shop on right at Center Street
		IL	**Center Street** — Salame Tree Deli on right
0.1	26.3	L	**Plaza Street** — Samba Java on right
0.1	26.4	R	**Healdsburg Avenue** — sweet shop on right
2.8	29.2	R	**Alexander Valley Road**
3.3	32.5	L	**Highway 128.** Alexander Valley Market on left
1.8	34.3	R	**Highway 128** at Estancia Vineyards

ALEXANDER VALLEY TO CHALK HILL (CONT.)

PT.-PT.	CUME	DIRECTION	STREET/LANDMARK
0.2	34.5	L	**Highway 128** at Geysers Road
3.7	38.2	L	**Highway 128** at Geyserville Grange
0.9	39.1	R	**Geyserville Avenue** — market on left
0.2	39.3		**Hope-Merrill House** on left

EASTSIDE, WESTSIDE, ALL AROUND DRY CREEK VALLEY

PT.-PT.	CUME	DIRECTION	STREET/LANDMARK
			From Hope-Merrill House
0.0	0.0	L	**Geyserville Avenue**
0.7	0.7	L	**Canyon Road**
2.2	2.9	R	**Dry Creek Road**
0.3	3.2	L	**Yoakim Bridge Road**
0.6	3.8	L	**West Dry Creek Road**
8.8	12.6	R	**Westside Road**
5.2	17.8		**Hop Kiln Winery** on left — tasting, picnic area
3.4	21.2	L	**Wohler Road**
0.1	21.3	X	Russian River
0.8	22.1	L	**Eastside Road**
6.4	28.5	L	**Old Redwood Highway**
0.3	28.8		Market on right
1.3	30.1	X	Highway 101
0.7	30.8	BL	Cross Russian River
0.6	31.4	C	**Healdsburg Avenue** at Mill Street
0.2	31.6	R	**Matheson Street/Town Square** Bike shop on right at Center Street
		IL	**Center Street** — Salame Tree Deli on right
0.1	31.7	L	**Plaza Street** — Samba Java on right
0.1	31.8	R	**Healdsburg Avenue** — sweet shop on right
1.0	32.8	L	**Dry Creek Road**
3.2	36.0		Dry Creek General Store on right
3.8	39.8	R	**Canyon Road**

EASTSIDE, WESTSIDE, ALL AROUND DRY CREEK VALLEY (CONT.)

PT.-PT.	CUME	DIRECTION	STREET/LANDMARK
2.2	42.0	R	**Geyserville Avenue**
0.7	42.7		**Hope-Merrill House** on right

THE GEYSERS

PT.-PT.	CUME	DIRECTION	STREET/LANDMARK
			From Hope-Merrill House
0.0	0.0	L	**Geyserville Avenue**
0.7	0.7	C	**Geyserville Avenue** at stop sign
2.7	3.4	C	**Asti Road**

In summer, when River Road Bridge is open:

1.6	5.0	R	**Washington School Road**
0.6	5.6	X	Russian River (summer bridge)
0.1	5.7	C	**River Road**
4.4	10.1	R	**Geysers Road**

All other times of year:

3.2	6.6	C	**Highway 101**
5.3	11.9	R	**First Street** in Cloverdale
0.5	12.4	X	Russian River
		C	**Crocker Road**
0.5	12.9	L	**River Road**
1.0	13.9	R	**Geysers Road**
14.3	28.2	L	**Geysers Road** at Geysers Resort Road. *Gear down! (You did save a gear to shift down to, didn't you?)*
13.7	41.9	L	**Red Winery Road**
0.3	42.2	S	**Highway 128**
0.3	42.5		Jimtown Store on right — cold drinks!
0.5	42.7	R	**Highway 128**
2.0	44.7	R	**Highway 128**
0.2	44.9	L	**Highway 128**
3.7	48.6	L	**Highway 128**
0.9	49.5	R	**Highway 128/Geyserville Avenue**
0.2	49.7		**Hope-Merrill House** on left

THE INK HOUSE

Ernie Veniegas and Jim Annis
1575 St Helena Highway
St. Helena, CA 94574
800-553-4343; 707-963-3890
Ambience: Elegant (and fun) Victorian

Rates: $95-$155
Bed & Breakfast
Expanded continental breakfast
Smoking on veranda only

In 1884, long before wine became king in the Napa Valley, cattle baron Theron J. Ink was one of the wealthiest men in the area. He owned the livery stable in St. Helena. His land holdings extended beyond Howell Mountain to Pope Valley; he built precipitous Ink Grade so he could ride directly through them. He served as county supervisor for more than one term. And his palatial 64,000-square-foot mansion in the middle of his Valley "spread" was the site of many an elaborate party.

Today Ink's mansion is still far enough from the center of bustling St. Helena that it sits in the middle of seemingly endless vineyards. It has been a bed-and-breakfast inn for the past 20 years, operated by partners Ernie and Jim since 1990.

When they took possession, the house was practically bare. "I think there was one bed upstairs, and two or three rugs on the floors," Ernie recalls. What they've done with the place since then is just amazing. There's no doubt that, when you step into The Ink House, you enter the Victorian era. But instead of doing it in deadly earnest, you should be prepared for some good old-fashioned, whimsical fun.

When I arrived, Jim was on hand to show me around. We started with the wraparound veranda furnished in front of the house with white wicker chairs and woven throw rugs. These give way to deck chairs on the south side. The two "family dogs," yellow Lab Mike and sheepdog Maxine, hold sway in back, while the north side overlooks Whitehall Vineyards across Whitehall Lane.

Solid oak floors, oriental rugs and 12-foot ceilings give the two parlors downstairs a feeling of both coziness and roominess. The smaller front parlor contains a grand piano and a grandfather clock. In the rear parlor is a vintage-1890s pump organ, a beautiful "Sultan" chair upholstered in rich dark blue brocade, a high-back chair, and no less than four loveseats, all arranged around a brick fireplace with an oval beveled mirror above the mantel. Between the

two connected parlors is a large serving table set with complimentary sherry and brandy.

The entire effect is enhanced by a plethora of small pieces, like the lacquered oriental occasional table beside an Empire-era carved oak chair, a rectangular gilt-framed beveled mirror above the red brocade loveseat, a cherrywood lowboy table in the corner, and several curved ottomans handy to the chairs or loveseats.

Beneath the red-velvet-carpeted oak staircase is a modern touch-tone telephone on a deacon bench ("from my church," confessed Jim) beneath an antique crank wall phone. Next to it sits a steamer trunk covered with a leopardskin and a collection of Winnie the Pooh dolls.

The most intriguing room in the house has got to be the observatory in the square-shaped cupola three flights up and then further up a small spiral staircase. With windows covering all four walls, it affords a full 360-degree view of Napa Valley, including Mt. Veeder to the west, Mt. St. Helena to the east, and vineyards as far as the eye can see. According to Ernie, there have been several marriage proposals up here.

If you can manage to tear your eyes away from the view, you'll discover a chess table and small collections of foreign currency, antique brass dollhouse furniture and antique toys, including a horse-drawn red fire engine.

After all this, even the elegantly furnished guest rooms — all with private baths and queen beds — seem a bit aniticlimatic. But here you'll also find countless little details to delight the eye.

I stayed in the Rose Room, which held a carved cherrywood bed made with a white comforter and lace pillow shams. A Teddy bear in a sailor outfit sat next to a bunny rabbit on the pillows. The carved wood canopy above the headboard matched the wainscoting at the ceiling as well as the headboard. A damask curtain draped from it behind the bed for a truly romantic effect.

Cabbage rose wallpaper, hand-painted roses on a hurricane lamp, rose-print upholstery on the settee beneath the east window, and a still life of a rose on the wall carried out the theme of the room. Two brocaded Queen Anne chairs sat at the north window, and a heavy sideboard served as a dresser, which held a decanter of sherry and two sets of Russian Matryoshka dolls.

Don't let The Ink House's claim of a "continental breakfast" put you off. You'll get more than enough to prepare you for an "upvalley" bike ride. Served in the elegant dining room, our breakfast consisted of fresh fruit, juice, filled croissants or brioches, Danish pastry and coffee and tea. "You can't leave till it's all gone," Jim told us. So naturally we just had to clean the plates.

BIKING FROM THE INK HOUSE

Note: Should you find yourself at The Ink House without your bicycle, the inn has a few 18-speeds to lend. That many gears should get you up the hills on these rides.

Terrain Napa Valley is flat as a board, but unfortunately, that's where the most popular wineries — and therefore the crowds — are. So it behooves cycle tourists to seek out hillier roads. Among these is Petrified Forest Road beyond Franz Valley School Road, and Howell Mountain Road, a relatively gentle climb to Angwin, but steeper beyond.

Road Conditions Shoulders on Highway 128/29 are sporadic at best and are particularly absent between The Ink House and St. Helena. Backroads like White Cottage Road, Ink Grade, and Franz Valley Road are narrow and often bumpy. Franz Valley School Road is especially narrow on the Sonoma County side.

Of special note are the railroad tracks, slanted at a rather haphazard angle across Whitehall Road, in front of The Ink House. Please use extra caution when crossing them onto Highway 29.

Traffic From noon through the evening the traffic in St. Helena and Calistoga is jampacked. Morning hours are surprisingly light, so it makes sense to get out into the hills early.

Nearest Bike Shop
St. Helena Cyclery
1150 Main Street
St. Helena, CA 94574
707-963-7736

Best Time To Ride Mid-October to mid-November when the vines have turned to brilliant fall colors

Second Best Time To Ride Mid-March to early May when the mustard is in bloom in the vineyards and the Valley is blanketed in brilliant yellow

Mountain Biking Opportunities The truly ambitious may want to climb Sugarloaf Mountain between Mt. St. Helena and Pope Valley. The dirt road takes off from the end of Aetna Springs Road, a left turn about five miles north of Ink Grade on Pope Valley Road. On the trail, turn left at Oat Hill Road to descend Livermore Road to Highway 29, or take Oat Hill Road to Butt Canyon Road and on to Middletown, where I'm told there is a good deli.

FRANZ VALLEY (42.7 OR 52.7 MILES)

Many a high-tone winery in Napa Valley maintains a prolific vineyard somewhere in Franz Valley. Up here it's a lot more like what Napa Valley used to be before the wine industry became a mega-marketing enterprise. Along the way you'll pass Bale Grist Mill State Historic Park between St. Helena and Calistoga. This living history project features a restored grain mill with a 36-foot waterwheel and three-story milling structure. Apparently, they'll even grind your grain for you!

The climber's option up Petrified Forest Road leads you to the Petrified Forest, a private-enterprise attraction that showcases the forest that was buried in ash and pumice when Mt. St. Helena erupted many centuries ago. On the way back, just before Calistoga, you can visit Old Faithful Geyser, which shoots a plume of steam and water at some 40-minute intervals. This one is private-enterprise too.

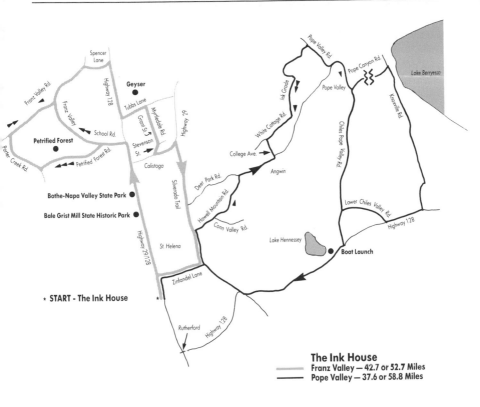

The Ink House
Franz Valley — 42.7 or 52.7 Miles
Pope Valley — 37.6 or 58.8 Miles

POPE VALLEY (37.6 OR 58.8 MILES)

This relatively easy route over Howell Mountain to Pope Valley takes you down Ink Grade, the road Mr. Ink built to ride horseback from The Ink House in St. Helena to his lands in Pope Valley. Once on the other side of the mountain, you'll roll for miles through some of California's most scenic countryside, coming out at little Lake Hennessey.

FRANZ VALLEY

PT.-PT.	CUME	DIRECTION	STREET/LANDMARK
			From The Ink House
0.0	0.0	L	**Highway 29/St. Helena Highway**
			Caution! Slanting railroad tracks!
			Becomes **Main Street** in St. Helena
1.1	1.1		Market on left
0.5	1.6		**St. Helena** — all services; St. Helena Cyclery on right
4.2	5.8		**Bale Grist Mill State Historic Park** on left
1.5	7.3		**Bothe-Napa Valley State Park** on left
3.6	10.9		**Calistoga** 0.2 miles to right of light
1.0	11.9	L	**Petrified Forest Road** — cafe on left
0.6	12.5	R	**Franz Valley School Road**

Climbers Option (adds 10 miles):

0.6	12.5	C	**Petrified Forest Road**
2.8	15.3		**Petrified Forest** on right
1.1	16.4	R	**Porter Creek Road**
3.1	19.5	R	**Franz Valley Road**
3.0	22.5	C	**Franz Valley Road** at Franz Valley School Road

4.4	16.9	R	**Franz Valley Road**
3.6	20.5	R	**Spencer Lane**
1.4	21.9	R	**Highway 128**
4.2	26.1	L	**Tubbs Lane**. Grocery on right corner
0.5	26.6		**Old Faithful Geyser** on left
0.1	26.7	R	**Myrtledale Road**. Becomes **Grant Street** at Greenwood Road

FRANZ VALLEY (CONT.)

PT.-PT.	CUME	DIRECTION	STREET/LANDMARK
1.5	28.2	**BR**	**Stevenson Street**
0.1	28.3	**L**	**Lincoln Avenue/Highway 29.** Turn right and ride 0.2 miles for downtown **Calistoga**
0.5	28.8	**R**	**Silverado Trail**
12.0	40.8	**R**	**Zinfandel Lane**
1.4	42.2	**L**	**Highway 29/St. Helena Highway**
0.5	42.7	**R**	**The Ink House** at Whitehall Lane

POPE VALLEY

PT.-PT.	CUME	DIRECTION	STREET/LANDMARK
			From The Ink House
0.0	0.0	**L**	**Highway 29/St. Helena Highway.** *Caution! Slanting railroad tracks!*
0.5	0.5	**R**	**Zinfandel Lane**
1.4	1.9	**L**	**Silverado Trail**
2.1	4.0	**R**	**Howell Mountain Road**
1.2	5.2	**L**	**Howell Mountain Road** at Conn Valley Road
3.1	8.3	**R**	**Howell Mountain Road** at Deer Park Road
1.3	9.6		**Angwin**; Pacific Union College on right; College Market on left (closed on Saturdays)
0.5	10.1	**L**	**College Avenue**
0.8	10.9	**R**	**White Cottage Road**
1.2	12.1	**L**	**Ink Grade** (no sign — look for yellow "trucks not recommended" sign on Ink Grade)
4.2	16.3	**R**	**Pope Valley Road**
1.8	18.1	**C**	**Chiles Pope Valley Road** at Howell Mountain Road in Pope Valley. Pope Valley Market on left — closed Saturdays

POPE VALLEY (CONT.)

PT.-PT.	CUME	DIRECTION	STREET/LANDMARK
Lake Berryessa Option: (adds 21.2 miles)			
1.9	20.0	L	**Pope Canyon Road**
8.5	28.5	R	**Knoxville Road**
13.0	41.5	R	**Highway 128**
3.0	44.5	R	**Lower Chiles Valley Road**
3.5	48.0	L	**Chiles Pope Valley Road**
Main Route:			
8.7	26.8	BR	**Chiles Pope Valley Road** at Lower Chiles Valley Road
3.7	30.5	R	**Highway 128**
0.7	31.2		Lake Hennessey Boat Launch on right — pit toilets
3.2	34.4	R	**Silverado Trail/Highway 128.** *Do NOT follow Highway 128 sign to Rutherford!*
1.3	35.7	L	**Zinfandel Lane**
1.4	37.1	L	**Highway 29/St. Helena Highway**
0.5	37.6	R	**The Ink House** at Whitehall Lane

THISTLE DEW INN

Larry and Norma Barnett
171 West Spain Street
Sonoma, CA 95476
707-938-2909
Ambience: Turn-of-the-Century Arts & Crafts

Rates: $100-$135
Bed & Breakfast
Full breakfast
Smoking outdoors only

If there is a cradle of modern California history, it is in the town of Sonoma. Here it was that the Spanish missionaries established their northernmost outpost in 1823. In 1838 General Mariano Vallejo arrived to serve as military governor and proceeded to promote alliances with the United States. It didn't take long for the growing gringo population, upset with restrictions on land acquisition, to revolt.

In ten short minutes, on June 14, 1846, the rebels captured two sleeping guards, Vallejo surrendered, the Bear Flag was raised, and a free and independent Republic of California was declared.

All of this took place on Sonoma Plaza, just blocks from where Thistle Dew Inn takes you back to more recent history in "the authentic style of 1910 California." Here are two historic Sonoma houses combined into one B&B experience. The cottage was built at the site in 1869 and moved back from the street to make room for the 1905 house, originally a few blocks away, to occupy the front of the lot.

All the furniture in both houses is authentic quarter-sawn Arts and Crafts, sometimes called "Mission Oak," designed by early 20th Century artisans like Limbert and the Stickleys (father and son). Aghast at how frivolous and ostentatious Victorian decor had become, these avant garde designers stuck to the principle of "Form Follows Function." To them, the most beautiful item was the most useful.

Simple lines, earth tones, brass and copper and a somewhat Southwest flavor dominate the style, about which you can learn more by browsing through the beautifully produced auction catalogs innkeepers Norma and Larry Barnett have collected. You'll find these in the living room at the center of the front house. Here stark white paneled walls rise to high wainscoting, above which hang a classic Georgia O'Keefe-type longhorn steer skull, an Indian winnowing basket and a handwoven fan.

The decor is decidedly low-key and designed for comfort: plush couches and chairs, a Franklin stove in the fireplace, and three elegant Mission Oak side tables lined up to form a center coffee table. There's an impressive collection of jigsaw puzzles on a small table in one corner.

Entry to the dining room is through a marvelous Mission Oak door featuring carved spindles at least three feet long. Two sets of chairs surround the huge oval table, on which six long white tapers sit in large crystal candle holders.

All the guest rooms at Thistle Dew feature queen beds, private baths, ceiling fans, and central heat/air. Two rooms are in the front house. Rose Garden has tons of natural light, and a classic Amish Fan quilt on the bed. Cornflower features a garden view from a large window and a Broken Star quilt.

Under renovation during my stay, the back cottage will grow to five or six rooms in 1994, with many changes. My room, Jasmine, with its large glass French door, private entrance and two-step access to Larry's cactus garden, will probably be the least affected. The bed is a Craftsman classic with headboard of quarter-sawn slats, and the thin mauve and white quilt is definitely an antique.

Thistle Dew is especially delightful to gardeners and gourmands. Larry is the gardener. In addition to the cactus garden, he also tends a grape arbor in the breezeway between the two houses and the roses along the driveway. But as beautiful as his plants are, Larry becomes a true artist in the kitchen. He's the one in charge of hors d'oeuvres every evening and breakfast every morning. Now, you must understand that "hors d'oeuvres" is a relative term. The evening I was there we were treated to what could have passed as a gourmet meal: home-made — and I mean everything from scratch — gnocchi (the real potato dumpling kind) cooked with Swiss chard and roasted garlic in a cream sauce.

If you dare, follow this with a walk down the block to the Plaza, where "food...looms large," as one local travel writer puts it. Here you can sample the cheeses at the Sonoma Cheese Factory, and dine on the cuisines of northern Italy at Piatti, Mexico at La Casa, Thailand at Rin's (a block off the Plaza on Broadway), or one of a dozen or more other equally enticing establishments.

Then, get up in the morning and start all over again with one of Larry's breakfasts. I began with a beautifully sliced stewed pear garnished with plum sauce and a single, perfectly sweet strawberry. Then came a Dutch Baby, an individual souffle topped with ricotta cheese and stewed fruit in a sweet sauce (yes, it's in the recipe section!).

Through all this cooking and eating at Thistle Dew, the tone is laid back California casual. As Larry and Norma put it in "The Thistle Dew Inn Story," their little message to guests, "We like to hang around the house, but we also like people. Now everyone comes to visit us while we hang around the house!"

BIKING FROM THISTLE DEW INN

Terrain Flat to rolling roads await you in the Sonoma Valley, although you'll have to climb to get to Jack London State Historic Park in Glen Ellen. There's also something of a climber's option on the ride through the Carneros wine region, a little side tour through the ranches of Lovall Valley.

Road Conditions The shoulder on Highway 12/121 is quite good, especially on the descent back to Sonoma from Napa County. However, Napa Road and Eighth Street East are shoulderless with lots of traffic.

Traffic Sonoma Plaza is a bottleneck of the first order, but most of the side streets are surprisingly quiet. Motorists tend to speed along the state highways and some main arteries like Arnold Road.

Nearest Bike Shop
Goodtime Bicycles
18503 Sonoma Highway
Sonoma, CA 95476
707-938-2909

Best Time To Ride September-October ("crush" time)

Mountain Biking Opportunities Annadel State Park, where once pioneering off-road racers met for competitions like the Rockhopper and Rumpstopper, lies about 11 miles north of Glen Ellen; you can ride in on a dirt road from Lawndale Road to the Marsh Ridge Trail. Sugarloaf Ridge State Park, at the end of Adobe Canyon Road off Highway 12, is a bit more remote, and a lot more vertical!

CARNEROS WINE DISTRICT (33.4 OR 39.9 MILES)

This is the heart of California's earliest wine-growing region, steeped in agricultural and economic history. Cuttings Wharf harbors the ghosts of sailors and farmers who shipped dairy products and wheat down the Napa River in the last century.

The Buena Vista Winery was the first to produce wine for profit, the cornerstone of the Carneros land grant and still its mighty anchor today. You'll see signs identifying Buena Vista's vineyards throughout this ride. Closer in town is Sebastiani Winery, no less a historical monument to Sonoma's dominance of the early California wine industry, and its resurgence in the last 20 years or so.

Since this ride is flat to rolling, those who relish climbing may want to take the short side option into Lovall Valley, where vineyards give way to open rangeland.

GLEN ELLEN HISTORICAL RIDE (17.7 MILES)

This ride starts from the Plaza, the heart of the Sonoma State Historic Park. Here, at the northern terminus of the Spanish Colonial "mission trail," you can tour Vallejo's headquarters and the Sonoma Barracks, where the Bear Flag was first raised. The park

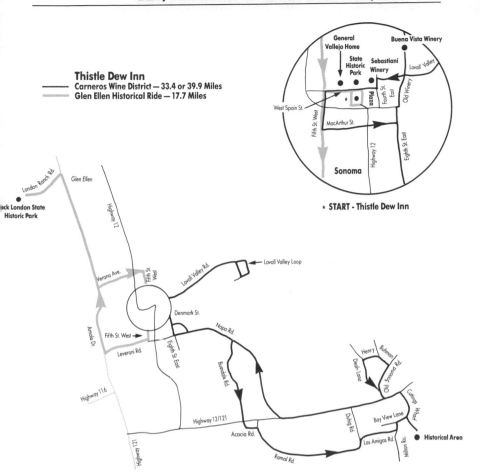

Thistle Dew Inn
Carneros Wine District — 33.4 or 39.9 Miles
Glen Ellen Historical Ride — 17.7 Miles

General Vallejo Home
Buena Vista Winery
State Historic Park
Sebastiani Winery
Lovall Valley
West Spain St.
Plaza
Fifth St. West
Fifth St. East
Fourth St. East
MacArthur St.
Old Winery
Eighth St. East
Highway 12
Sonoma

★ START - Thistle Dew Inn

London Ranch Rd.
Glen Ellen
ack London State Historic Park
Highway 12
Lovall Valley Loop
Lovall Valley Rd.
Verano Ave.
Fifth St. West
Denmark St.
Napa Rd.
Henry
Buhman Rd.
Amelo Dr.
Fifth St. West
Eighth St. East
Deer Lane
Old Sonoma Rd.
Leveroni Rd.
Burndale Rd.
Cutting
Watmaugh
Highway 116
Highway 12/121
Duhig Rd.
Bay View Lane
Highway 121
Acacia Rd.
Ramal Rd.
Las Amigas Rd.
Millon Rd.
● **Historical Area**

includes the Sonoma Mission on the corner of First Street East and East Spain, and General Vallejo's home, just north and east of Thistle Dew Inn on West Spain between Second and Third Streets West.

Your turnaround point will be Jack London State Historic Park in Glen Ellen. Here you can tour the remains of London's Wolf House and the House of Happy Walls Museum. You can buy lunch at the country store in Glen Ellen for a picnic in the park.

CARNEROS WINE DISTRICT

PT.-PT.	CUME	DIRECTION	STREET/LANDMARK
			From Thistle Dew Inn
0.0	0.0	L	**West Spain Street**
0.2	0.2		**General Vallejo Home** on right
0.4	0.4	L	**Fifth Street West**
0.6	1.0	L	**MacArthur Street**
1.8	2.8	R	**Eighth Street East**
0.7	3.5	L	**Napa Road**
0.9	4.4	R	**Burndale Road**
2.3	6.7	X	Highway 12
0.2	6.9	L	**Acacia Road**
0.5	7.4	R	**Ramal Road**
4.6	12.0	L	**Duhig Road** (no sign)
0.4	12.4	R	**Las Amigas Road**
1.9	14.3	L	**Las Amigas Road** at Milton Road
0.3	14.6	R	**Bay View Lane**
0.3	14.9	R	**Cuttings Wharf Road**
0.7	15.6		**Cuttings Wharf Historical Area**
0.0	15.6	U	**Cuttings Wharf Road**
0.7	16.3	R	**Cuttings Wharf Road**
1.8	18.1	L	**Highway 12/121**. *Caution! Heavy traffic!*
0.8	18.9	R	**Old Sonoma Road**
1.2	20.1	L	**Buhman Avenue**
0.3	20.4	L	**Henry Road**
0.8	21.2	L	**Dealy Lane** at T
1.1	22.3	R	**Old Sonoma Road**
0.3	22.6	R	**Highway 12/121**
3.0	25.6	R	**Napa Road**
2.2	27.8	R	**Denmark St.**

CARNEROS WINE DISTRICT (CONT.)

PT.-PT.	CUME	DIRECTION	STREET/LANDMARK
1.1	28.9	R	**Eighth Street East**
0.7	29.6	R	**East Napa Street**
		IL	**Old Winery Road**
1.0	30.6		**Buena Vista Winery** — Tasting room, restrooms, picnic area
0.0	30.6	U	**Old Winery Road**
0.7	31.3	R	**Lovall Valley Road**

Climbers Option (adds 6.5 miles):

0.7	31.3	L	**Lovall Valley Road**
3.6	34.9	L	**Lovall Valley Loop** at T
0.7	35.6	R	**Lovall Valley Road**
2.2	37.8	X	**Old Winery Road**

0.8	32.1	L	**Lovall Valley Road** at Seventh Street East
0.6	32.7	L	**Fourth Street East;** Sebastiani Winery on right
0.1	32.8	R	**East Spain Street**
0.4	33.2		**Sonoma Plaza. Sonoma State Historic Park** on right Cheese Factory, ice cream, restaurants, delis
0.1	33.3	C	**West Spain Street**
0.1	34.4	L	**Thistle Dew Inn**

GLEN ELLEN HISTORICAL RIDE

PT.-PT.	CUME	DIRECTION	STREET/LANDMARK
			From Thistle Dew Inn
0.0	0.0	R	**West Spain Street**, to Sonoma Plaza
0.1	0.1	C	**East Spain Street**. Circle Plaza for historic points of interest as well as stores, delis, restaurants.
		IR	**First Street East**
0.2	0.3	R	**West Napa Street**
0.2	0.5	R	**First Street West**

GLEN ELLEN HISTORICAL RIDE (CONT.)

PT.-PT.	CUME	DIRECTION	STREET/LANDMARK
0.1	0.6	L	**West Spain Street**
0.5	1.1	L	**Fifth Street West**
1.3	2.4	R	**Leveroni Road**
1.2	3.6	R	**Arnold Drive**
1.7	5.3		Deli/market on right
1.3	6.6		**London Ranch Road** in **Glen Ellen**. Country store on right
0.8	7.4		**Glen Ellen Winery** on right
1.3	8.7		**Jack London State Historic Park**
0.0	8.7	U	**London Ranch Road**
1.3	10.0	R	**Arnold Drive**
5.0	15.0	L	**Verano Avenue**
1.0	16.0	X	Highway 12
0.5	16.5	R	**Fifth Street West**
0.8	17.3	L	**West Spain Street**
0.4	17.7	L	**Thistle Dew Inn**

THE WEBBER PLACE

Diane Bartholomew
6610 Webber Street
Yountville, CA 94599
800-647-7177; 707-944-8384
Ambience: Down Home Americana

Rates: $69-$119
Bed & Breakfast
Full breakfast
No Smoking

The town of Yountville may be one of the best-kept secrets of the Napa Valley. Except for a couple of gourmet restaurants and exclusive shops, it rarely gets mentioned in the tourist brochures. What they don't tell you is that Yountville represents a remnant of a dying way of life in the Valley...a place where everyone knows everyone else, kids can roam free to play, and the hottest topics of conversation are the weather and how it affects the crops (in this case, the vines).

It's also a perfect place to take off on — or take a break during — a bicycle tour of the Napa Valley. That's why the Eagle Cycling Club always chooses the local park as a rest stop or lunch stop on the Napa Valley Century.

Slip away from the shops and (relatively subdued) bustle of Washington Street and you enter hometown America. Walk up Webber Street and, kitty-corner from the fire station, you'll find The Webber Place, built in 1850 by the family the street is named for. Walk on in and meet the present owner, artist Diane Bartholomew, and you'll discover a truly unique bed-and-breakfast.

Just how unique is apparent in the backyard, which is filled with plywood cutouts of romping children. They are self-portraits of the members of an art class Diane taught last summer.

Inside, The Webber Place has much of the original construction still in evidence, including the redwood plank floors and the redwood paneling in the dining room. Diane has painted the common room walls a watermelon red as a background for displaying her paintings, including several "portraits" of The Webber Place itself.

Above an oak secretary in the corner of the parlor hang photographs of the Webber family taken in 1910. A gilt and wood framed three-section mirror hangs above the marble mantel. Antique brass lamps, one with a fringed pink brocade shade, provide lighting.

The dining room looks out through oak French doors to a breezeway between the house and Diane's studio in a separate building. On the opposite wall is a red-and-white log cabin quilt, and another wall holds a woven tapestry showing yet another aspect of The Webber Place. Breakfast is served on the oak table, surrounded by four lovingly restored oak Queen Anne chairs. An ancient pump organ sits in the corner under a photo of the house on Halloween (more about this later).

The kitchen too maintains the flavor of the old turn-of-the-century farmhouse, with an old gas stove on legs, an oak cupboard with a roll-down bread nook, a pair of ancient spectacles in a tiny basket on a battered old work table, and on the wall a "corn tree" made of dried ears of different varieties of corn strung on wire.

From this kitchen every morning emanate delicious aromas, wafting up through the upstairs hallway and waking guests to the prospect of an ample American country breakfast, from home-made biscuits and preserves to baked apples, bacon and eggs, and fresh-ground coffee.

It takes such a breakfast to lure guests from The Webber's charming rooms. I stayed in the Redwood Room, with its one wall entirely paneled in the same redwood as downstairs. The wrought-iron double bed was covered with an eyelet spread, and an absolutely gorgeous Tiffany shade adorned the lamp next to the bed. The windows looked out over the roof of Diane's studio to a view of the mountains.

The Sun Room down the hall is large and airy, with another iron double bed, a walnut shaving stand with mirror and a carved oak dresser with beveled mirror, plus a daybed for extra guests. The Sun Room and Redwood Room share a bath with oak paneled walls and oak framed windows. The huge bathtub is painted blue, and the old-fashioned commode toilet has an oak-encased basin above it.

The East Room has a private bath with the same sort of toilet and tub. It's furnished with oak antiques, including a rocker, dresser and double bed. The Veranda Suite on the first floor has a private entrance, private latticed porch, a private bath with clawfoot tub, and a queen-size bed.

Once lured from these homey environments, there's plenty to explore off your bike in Yountville. Food is one of the town's claims to fame, particularly at Mustard's Grill and the Yountville Market, which is reputed to serve the best coffee in the Valley, not to mention delicious made-to-order sandwiches. Or you can actually dine at one of the Valley's most elegant wineries, Domaine Chandon.

If you're looking to buy some of the wines you've tasted on your Valley tours, Groezinger's Wine Shop is probably a better bet than buying directly from the wineries, according to Diane.

Walking seems to be almost as popular as cycling in the area; many guests take walking tours of the village and into the local cemetery, where founder George Yount and his neighbors are buried.

Finally, if you're visiting Yountville around Halloween, you'll soon be drawn into the festivities at The Webber Place. Diane goes all out, with Jack o'Lanterns filling up the porch, the front yard, the sidewalk and across the street to "Boot Hill" (come to "life" especially for the occasion).

BIKING FROM THE WEBBER PLACE

Terrain The Napa Valley is as flat as anyone could wish, and the crossroads keep it that way, except for the small bumps when they cross the river (no more than a rivulet in most places). The Silverado Trail follows the base of the eastern foothills, rolling gently from Napa all the way up to Calistoga.

Road Conditions Some of the side roads may be a bit potholey (particularly Rutherford Cross Road/Route 128 connecting Rutherford with Silverado Trail). The Silverado itself, however, "is a joy to ride," *Rides in and around Napa Valley* puts it, "with its wide shoulders, slightly rolling hills, and beautiful views of the vineyards and valley."

Traffic Except for early in the day, well before wine tasting buffs rise and roll out, Highway 29 is extremely congested; the best strategy is to avoid it if at all possible. Once you turn on any of the cross roads or onto the Silverado Trail, the congestion magically disappears and the riding is a pleasure.

Nearest Bike Shop
Napa Valley Cyclery
4080 Byway East
Napa, CA
707-255-3377

The author also highly recommends:
The Bicycle Works
3335 Solano (in the Redwood Plaza)
Napa, CA
707-253-7000

Best Time To Ride Mid-October to mid-November when the vines have turned to brilliant fall colors

Second Best Time To Ride Mid-March to early May when the mustard is in bloom in the vineyards and, as Diane Bartholomew says, "it's cadmium yellow from one end of the Valley to another."

Mountain Biking Opportunities Although Napa County boasts one of the most challenging sections of the Bay Area Ridge Trail in Sugarloaf Ridge State Park, you'll have to drive to Sonoma County to reach it. The nearest access is over Oakville Grade, down Dry Creek Road, over Trinity Road, then north on Highway 12 to a right on Adobe Canyon Road. Do not attempt this route on your bike, then expect to ride the trails — it's more than 20 miles, over one of the most difficult climbs in Northern California!

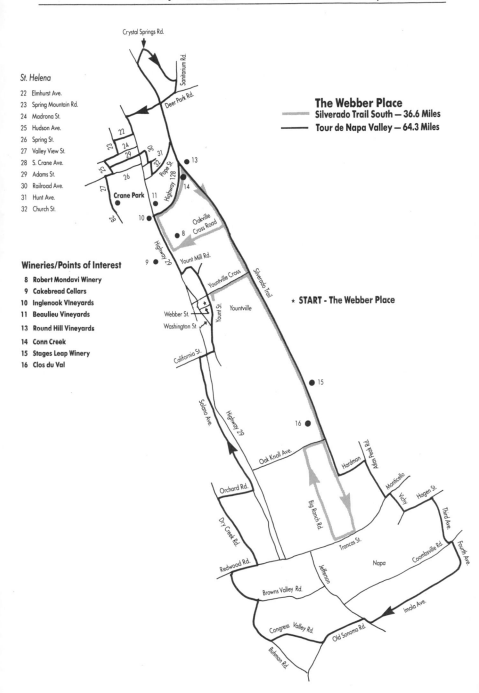

St. Helena

22 Elmhurst Ave.
23 Spring Mountain Rd.
24 Madrona St.
25 Hudson Ave.
26 Spring St.
27 Valley View St.
28 S. Crane Ave.
29 Adams St.
30 Railroad Ave.
31 Hunt Ave.
32 Church St.

The Webber Place
Silverado Trail South — 36.6 Miles
Tour de Napa Valley — 64.3 Miles

Wineries/Points of Interest

8 Robert Mondavi Winery
9 Cakebread Cellars
10 Inglenook Vineyards
11 Beaulieu Vineyards
13 Round Hill Vineyards
14 Conn Creek
15 Stages Leap Winery
16 Clos du Val

★ START - The Webber Place

SILVERADO TRAIL SOUTH (36.6 MILES)

This is the ideal wine tasting ride; a tour of the cross roads and Silverado Trail, with more wineries along the way than you ever thought possible. I've pointed out a few along the route, but feel free to stop and explore as the fancy takes you. You may discover a wine you'll call favorite for years to come!

TOUR DE NAPA VALLEY (64.3 MILES)

This ride is adapted from the 65-mile option on the Napa Valley Century, put on every August by Eagle Cycling Club and The Bicycle Works in Napa. It will take you up to St. Helena, into the east foothills, down the Silverado Trail to Napa, and back to Yountville through just about every landscape the Valley has to offer.

SILVERADO TRAIL SOUTH

PT.-PT.	CUME	DIRECTION	STREET/LANDMARK
			From The Webber Place
0.0	0.0	L	**Webber Street**
		IL	**Yount Street**
0.3	0.3	R	**Yountville Cross Road**
1.9	2.2	L	**Silverado Trail**
2.3	4.5	L	**Oakville Cross Road**
2.5	7.0	R	**Highway 29** — cafe, grocery on right
0.4	7.4		**Robert Mondavi Winery** on left
0.5	7.9		**Cakebread Cellars** on right
1.0	8.9	R	**Highway 128/Rutherford Cross Road. Inglenook Vineyards** on left **Beaulieu Vineyards** on right on Highway 29 just beyond intersection
0.1	9.0		Market on right
1.4	10.4	L	**Highway 128** at Conn Creek Road
1.3	11.7	R	**Silverado Trail; Round Hill Vineyards** directly across Silverado
0.1	11.8		**Conn Creek** on right
7.8	19.6		**Stags Leap** on left

SILVERADO TRAIL SOUTH (CONT.)

PT.-PT.	CUME	DIRECTION	STREET/LANDMARK
0.3	19.9		Chimney Rock Golf Club on left — coffee shop
3.3	23.2		Soda Canyon Store on left
2.3	25.5	R	**Trancas Street;** Silverado Plaza on left — market, drugstore, etc.
0.6	26.1	R	**Big Ranch Road**
2.9	29.0	R	**Oak Knoll Avenue**
0.8	29.8	L	**Silverado Trail**
1.4	31.2		**Clos du Val** on right
3.2	34.4	L	**Yountville Cross Road**
1.9	36.3	L	**Yount Street**
0.3	36.6	R	**Webber Street** **The Webber Place** on right

TOUR DE NAPA VALLEY

PT.-PT.	CUME	DIRECTION	STREET/LANDMARK
			From The Webber Place
0.0	0.0	L	**Webber Street**
		IL	**Yount Street**
1.2	1.2	L	**Yount Mill Road**
1.2	2.4	R	**Highway 29**
3.0	5.4	R	**Highway 128/Rutherford Cross Road**
0.1	5.5		Market on right
2.0	7.4	L	**Highway 128** at Conn Creek Road
0.8	8.2	L	**Silverado Trail**
7.4	15.6	R	**Crystal Springs Road**
2.1	17.7	R	**Sanitarium Road**
0.6	18.3	C	**Deer Park Road**
0.4	18.7	X	Silverado Trail
0.6	19.3	L	**Highway 29** into St. Helena
0.9	20.2	R	**Elmhurst Avenue**
0.2	20.4	L	**Spring Mountain Road**
0.2	20.6	R	**Madrona Street**

TOUR DE NAPA VALLEY (CONT.)

PT.-PT.	CUME	DIRECTION	STREET/LANDMARK
0.3	20.9	L	**Hudson Avenue**
0.3	21.2	R	**Spring Street**
0.1	21.3	L	**Valley View Street.** Becomes **South Crane Avenue**
1.0	22.3	R	**Into Crane Park** — restrooms, picnic tables
0.2	22.5	R	**South Crane Avenue**
0.5	23.0	R	**Spring Street**
0.1	23.1	L	**Hudson Avenue**
0.2	23.3	R	**Adams Street.** Napa Valley Coffee Roasting Co. on left
0.5	23.8	X	Main Street/Highway 29. Bakery to right on Main Street, on right. St. Helena Cyclery to right, on left
		IR	**Railroad Avenue**
0.2	24.0	L	**Hunt Avenue**
		IR	**Church Street**
0.1	24.1	L	**Pope Street**
0.8	24.9	R	**Silverado Trail**
15.5	40.4	L	**Hardman**
1.0	41.4	R	**Atlas Peak Road**
0.9	42.3	L	**Monticello**
0.1	42.4	R	**Vichy**
1.2	43.6	L	**Hagen Street**
0.9	44.5	R	**Third Avenue**
1.8	46.3	L	**Third Avenue**
0.7	47.0	L	**Coombsville Road**
0.1	47.1	R	**Fourth Avenue**
1.3	48.4	C	**Imola Avenue**
3.2	51.6	R	**Jefferson**
0.4	52.0	L	**Old Sonoma Road**
1.7	53.7	R	**Congress Valley Road**
0.9	54.6	C	**Buhman Road**
1.4	56.0	L	**Browns Valley Road**
0.7	56.7	R	**Redwood Road**
0.9	57.6	L	**Dry Creek Road**
2.1	59.7	R	**Orchard Road**

TOUR DE NAPA VALLEY (CONT.)

PT.-PT.	CUME	DIRECTION	STREET/LANDMARK
1.3	61.0	L	**Solano Avenue**
3.9	63.9	R	**California Street**
0.1	64.0	L	**Washington Street**
0.1	64.1	BR	**Yount Street**
0.2	64.3	L	**Webber Street**
			The Webber Place on right

RECIPES FROM NORTHERN CALIFORNIA INNS

Bicycling has a habit of generating tremendous appetites. Not only are we out in the open air (often gulping huge drafts of it as we labor uphill and/or against the wind), but at the same time we're also expending vast amounts of aerobic energy, requiring equally vast amounts of refueling. Thankfully, country inns are notorious for whipping up some of the most scrumptious loads of carbohydrates any cyclist could hope to encounter.

These recipes are much-requested favorites at inns I visited. (There are also a couple of great things to do with cheese, from the Marin French Cheese Company.) For a touch of country inn at home, try them in your own kitchen. Bon appetit!

BEAR VALLEY INN — JOANNE'S APPLE WALNUT BUTTERMILK CAKE

2-1/2 cups flour
1 tsp baking soda
1 tsp baking powder
1/2 tsp salt
2 tsp cinnamon
1 cup chopped walnuts
5 tbsp butter or margarine
2 cups chopped apples
1 egg
1/2 cup oil
1 cup buttermilk

Mix flour, baking soda, baking powder, salt, cinnamon and walnuts. Cut in butter and add chopped apples. In a separate bowl, combine egg, oil and buttermilk. Turn into dry mix. Pour batter into a 9"x12" greased baking dish. Bake at 350 degrees for 30 minutes. Serve with a topping of fresh fruit and honeyed yogurt.

BLUE SPRUCE INN — BRUNCH ENCHILADAS

2 cups (12 oz.) ground, fully cooked ham, turkey or chicken
1/2 cup sliced green onions
1/2 cup finely chopped green bell pepper
2-1/2 cups shredded cheddar cheese
8 7" flour tortillas
4 eggs, beaten

2 cups light cream or milk
1 tbsp flour
1/4 tsp salt (optional)
1/4 tsp garlic powder
A few drops of hot liquid pepper sauce
Combine ground meat, onion and green pepper in a bowl. Place 1/3 cup of the mixture and 3 tbsp cheese at one end of each tortilla. Roll up. Place seam side down in a greased 12"x7-1/2"x2" ovenproof casserole. Combine eggs, cream, flour, salt, garlic powder and hot pepper sauce. Pour over tortillas. Cover and refrigerate several hours or overnight. Bake uncovered at 350 degrees for 45 to 50 minutes, or until set. Sprinkle with remaining cheese. Bake 3 minutes more until cheese melts. Let stand 10 minutes. Serve with garnish of avocado slices, fresh salsa and sour cream. Serves 8.

"For a wonderful mixture of textures and temperatures, I serve this entree with spicy corn muffins and chilled shrimp gazpacho." — Pat O'Brien, Blue Spruce Inn.

CHANEY HOUSE — SWAHILI PIE

6 tbsp butter or margarine
6 eggs
3 cups milk
1/4 cup honey
1-1/2 cups flour
Melt butter in 9"x13" dish in oven, until it sizzles. Mix other four ingredients with an electric mixer and pour over butter while still very hot. Bake at 450 degrees for 15 minutes, then at 350 degrees for 25 minutes. Top with hot apples. Serves 8.

HOT APPLES

6 apples, cored and cut into chunks
3/4 cup raisins
1/2 cup brown sugar
1/2 cup water
1 tbsp butter
1/2 tsp cinnamon
1/2 tsp nutmeg
1 tsp arrowroot (to thicken)
Cook all ingredients on stovetop until apple chunks are tender.

HIGH COUNTRY INN — SPICED PUMPKIN PANCAKES

1/2 cup yellow cornmeal
1/2 cup unbleached flour
1/4 cup brown sugar
1 tsp baking powder
1/2 cup pumpkin, pureed
1/4 tsp salt
1/2 to 1/3 tsp pumpkin pie spice
1/2 tsp dried orange peel, or 1 tsp fresh grated orange peel
1 extra-large, or 2 small eggs
1 tbsp vegetable oil
3/4 cup milk

Combine pumpkin with dry ingredients. Mix egg, oil and milk together and add to batter. Beat until smooth. Cook on lightly oiled hot griddle or skillet. Turn when bubbles appear at edges. Remove when golden and firm to the touch. Serve with hot maple syrup, apple cider syrup, chopped pecans or thinly sliced sweet apples sauteed in butter, served hot on the side. Makes 12 3" pancakes.

CHICHESTER-MCKEE HOUSE — CHOCOLATE CHIP OATMEAL CAKE

1-3/4 cups boiling water
1 cup uncooked oatmeal (quick or old-fashioned)
1 cup lightly packed brown sugar
1 cup granulated sugar
1 stick (1/2 cup) margarine
2 large eggs
1-2/3 cups flour
1-1/2 tsp soda
1/2 tsp salt
1 tbsp cocoa
1 package (12 oz.) chocolate chips
3/4 cup chopped walnuts

Pour boiling water over oatmeal. Let stand at room temperature 10 minutes. Add both sugars and margarine and stir until melted. Add eggs. Mix well. Sift together flour, soda, salt and cocoa. Add flour mixture to sugar mixture. Mix well. Add about half of the chocolate chips. Pour batter into greased and floured 9"x13" pan. Sprinkle walnuts and remaining chocolate chips on top. Bake at 335 degrees about 40 minutes.

FAIRVIEW MANOR — EGGS FOR A GANG

12 beaten eggs
1 tsp salt
1/2 tsp pepper
2 17-oz cans of cream-style corn
1 tbsp Worcestershire sauce
8 oz chopped green chiles
1 lb grated sharp cheddar cheese
Combine all ingredients and mix well. Bake in a 9"x13" dish at 325 degrees for 1-1/4 hours.

NANCY'S QUICHE

1 egg
1 tbsp flour
1/2 cup milk
1/2 cup mayonnaise
1 tbsp chopped onion
1 frozen deep pie shell
8 oz grated Swiss cheese
8 oz flaked crab, or 3 medium-size zucchini
Beat egg. Add flour, mayonnaise and milk. Mix well. Add cheese, onion and crab or zucchini. Prebake pie shell at 350 degrees for 10 to 15 minutes. Add filling and bake at 350 degrees for 45 minutes.

GINGERBREAD MANSION INN — LEMON BREAD

1/2 cup shortening
1-1/8 cups sugar
2 eggs, slightly beaten
1-1/4 cups flour, sifted before measuring
1 tsp baking powder
1/2 tsp salt
1/2 cup milk
1/2 cup nuts, finely chopped
Grated peel of 1 lemon
Juice of 1 lemon
Cream shortening and 1 cup sugar. Mix in eggs. Sift flour again with baking powder and salt. Alternately add flour mixture and milk to shortening mixture, stirring constantly. Mix in nuts and lemon peel. Bake in greased 5"x9" loaf pan at 350 degrees for about 50 minutes. Remove from oven and immediately poke holes

in top with fork, and spoon over topping of 1/8 cup sugar and lemon juice. (Mix topping just before use so it will be smooth.)

GOSBY HOUSE INN — BUTTERMILK ALMOND SCONES

1 egg
1-1/4 cups buttermilk
2 tsp almond extract
4 cups flour
4 tsp baking powder
1 tsp baking soda
1 tsp salt
1/2 cup sugar
1-1/2 sticks butter
2 cups toasted sliced almonds, chopped
Whisk together egg, buttermilk and almond extract. Combine flour, baking powder, soda, salt, sugar. Cut in butter until mixture is coarse crumbs. Add almonds. Add liquids to dry mixture. Mix lightly with fork until mixture clings together and forms a soft dough. Turn dough onto lightly floured surface and knead gently 5 or 6 times. Divide in quarters and roll out 1/2" thick. Cut into 6 wedges. Brush with cream and sprinkle with sugar and a few sliced almonds. Bake on greased sheet at 425 degrees for 12 to 15 minutes. Makes 2 dozen.

HOPE-MERRILL HOUSE — PEAR PIE

1 deep dish pie shell, unbaked
3 pears, any variety (or more, depending on size)
3 eggs
1/3 cup melted butter
2/3 cup sugar
1 tsp almond extract
1/3 cup flour
Peel and core pears and cut in quarters, or slice thin and place pinwheel fashion in the pie shell. Mix remaining ingredients in a large bowl and pour over the pears. Bake at 350 degrees for 45 minutes, or until the mixture is set. Serve hot.

Suggestion: When slicing pears thin, prepare individually as tarts instead of a pie.

THE INK HOUSE — HASH BROWN QUICHE

1 24-oz package frozen shredded hash browns, thawed
1/3 cup butter, melted
1 cup shredded jalapeno cheese
1 cup shredded jack cheese
1 cup diced cooked ham
1/2 cup milk
2 or 3 large eggs
1/4 tsp seasoned salt
Preheat oven to 425 degrees. Grease a 9" pie pan. Press hash browns into pan to form a crust. Brush with melted butter. Bake 25 minutes. Reduce oven temperature to 350 degrees. Fill crust with cheeses and ham.
Whisk together milk, eggs and seasoned salt. Pour into pan and bake 30 to 40 minutes, or until knife inserted in center comes out clean. Serves 8.

MARIN FRENCH CHEESE COMPANY — CAMEMBERT SHORTBREAD

1/4 cup butter
4 oz ripe Camembert cheese
1/4 cup shredded Swiss cheese
3 eggs
2 cups sifted flour
1 tsp salt
Cream butter until soft. Blend in ripe Camembert, rind included, and Swiss cheese. Add eggs one at a time, beating well after each addition. Stir in flour and salt. Mix until a soft dough is formed. Pat out on lightly floured board into a 10" circle. Place on greased baking sheet and bake at 400 degrees for 25 to 30 minutes, or until golden brown on top. Cut into small squares. Spread on a thin layer of your favorite jam before serving.

BRIE WITH SUN-DRIED TOMATOES BELDEN

1 lb Brie cheese, chilled
2 tbsp minced fresh parsley leaves
2 tbsp freshly grated Parmesan cheese
4 sun-dried tomatoes packed in oil, drained (reserve 1 tbsp oil) and minced
6 cloves garlic, minced and mashed to a paste
1 tsp dried basil

Place Brie on a serving plate. In a small bowl combine the parsley, Parmesan, sun-dried tomatoes, garlic and basil. Add the reserved oil. Combine mixture well. Spread mixture over Brie and let stand for 1 hour before serving. Serve with crackers. Serves 6.

RANCHO SAN GREGORIO — ZUCCHINI WAFFLES

1-1/2 cups flour
1 tsp baking powder
3/4 tsp baking soda
3/4 tsp salt
1/4 cup nuts
2 eggs, beaten
1 cup sour cream
1/2 cup milk
1/4 cup oil
1/2 cup shredded zucchini

Beat eggs. Add sour cream, milk, oil and zucchini. In separate bowl mix flour, baking powder, baking soda, salt and nuts. Pour wet ingredients into dry ingredients. Stir to blend. Bake in greased waffle iron. Top with syrup. Serve with sausage or ham slices and fresh fruit. Makes about six 6" waffles.

ARTICHOKE MUSHROOM FRITATA

3 eggs
3/4 cup mayonnaise
3/4 cup milk
3 tbsp flour
2 cups Swiss cheese
2 cups jack cheese
16 small artichokes, steamed
1/2 lb mushrooms
1/3 cube butter
2-5 tbsp green onions, chopped

Beat the eggs, mayonnaise and milk. Add flour and set aside. Shred cheese and set aside. Peel and slice artichokes and layer in two shallow 1"x9"x6" pans greased with 1 tbsp olive oil. Saute sliced mushrooms and onions in butter. Layer over the artichokes. Mix cheese and milk mixture and divide, pouring half over mixture in each pan. Bake at 400 degrees for 10 minutes, then at 350 degrees for 30 minutes. Slice and serve warm. Serves 6 to 8.

THE RED CASTLE INN — FAUX CHEESE SOUFFLE

10 to 12 slices bread, buttered and torn into pieces
3/4 to 1 lb sharp cheddar cheese, grated
6 eggs, slightly beaten
3 cups milk
1/2 tsp dry mustard
1/2 tsp salt
1/8 tsp cayenne pepper
In a buttered casserole with deep sides, layer cheese and torn buttered bread pieces. Mix liquids and spices and cover layers. Bake in a pan of hot water for about 1 hour. Can be refrigerated overnight. Top with Miracle Mushroom Sauce or a chunky tomato-basil sauce.

MIRACLE MUSHROOM SAUCE

2 lbs sliced mushrooms
2 cups whipping cream
2 tbsp lemon juice
Saute mushroom slices in cream and lemon juice until sauce is slightly thickened.

THE COUNTRY CAFE AT SORENSON'S RESORT — BASIL VINAIGRETTE

1 bunch fresh basil
5 cloves garlic
1/2 tsp salt, or to taste
1/4 tsp fresh ground pepper, or to taste
3-1/2 cups olive oil
1 cup red wine vinegar
3 dashes Worcestershire sauce
2 tbsp stone-ground mustard
3 tbsp honey
Combine basil, garlic, vinegar and spices in a blender. Add olive oil slowly, while continuing to mix ingredients. Finish by adding the Worcestershire, mustard and honey. Mix thoroughly, chill and serve.

HOPE VALLEY AUTUMN PIE

Your favorite unbaked pie shell
3/4 cup sugar
1 cup corn syrup
2 tbsp flour
2 tbsp melted butter
3 eggs
1 tsp cinnamon
1 tsp vinegar
1 tsp vanilla
1 tsp almond flavoring
1/2 cup each: chopped pecans; chopped walnuts; chopped peanuts; chopped cashews

Combine sugar, cinnamon, flour, corn syrup and butter. Cream well. Beat in eggs, one at a time. Add vinegar, vanilla and almond flavoring and mix well. Add chopped nuts and pour into pie shell. Bake at 300 degrees for 20 minutes, then increase temperature to 350 degrees and bake an additional 20 minutes, or until set. Filling should be set slightly less in center than around edges.

WEDGEWOOD INN — SIMPLE PEACH DELIGHT

8 cups (12 medium) fresh peaches, peeled, pitted and sliced
Ground cinnamon and/or nutmeg
1-1/2 cups all-purpose flour
1 cup granulated sugar
1/2 cup brown sugar
1/4 tsp salt
1-1/2 tsp baking powder
2 eggs
1/4 cup butter or margarine

Arrange peach slices on bottom of greased 8"x8"x2" glass baking dish. Sprinkle with cinnamon and/or nutmeg. Set aside. Blend flour, sugars, salt and baking powder. Add eggs and mix with pastry blender or fork until fine and crumbly. Sprinkle mixture over fruit. Melt butter and drizzle over all. Bake at 350 degrees for 30 minutes or until top is browned. Serves 9.

WE NEED YOUR HELP!

The information contained in this book was as accurate as could be determined at the time of publication. But roads change: housing developments spring up, towns decide to make through roads dead end, or new roads are built. And even occasionally, an error by a researcher, writer, author or publisher manages to make it to print.

That's why we at White Meadow Press rely on you, our readers, to help us keep our guidebooks up to date. If you see something on your bicycle that does not correspond to what's in this book, whether it be a cue sheet turn, description, a line on a map, or text, please do not hesitate. When you get home from your ride, jot it down and send it off to us in a letter (be sure to pedal to the post office!). We will acknowledge your efforts with a return letter and a coupon good for one free book at your next purchase directly from the publisher.

Send your comments and notes to:

Publisher
White Meadow Press
P.O. Box 56
Boonton, NJ 07005
Thank you very much!

ALSO:

If you enjoy writing and researching bicycle routes, we want to hear from you at the above address. We are always looking for new authors to expand our line of guidebooks, both local *RIDE GUIDE*s and our *Bed, Breakfast and Bike* series. Thanks!

ORDER THESE WHITE MEADOW PRESS BICYCLE GUIDES!

Bed, Breakfast & Bike/New England, by Alex and Nancy May ($12.95). Come join the Mays as they visit 30 bike-friendly inns from Maine to Connecticut, and sample the best holiday bike riding in the region — as well as each inn's food and amenities! Two or more routes from each inn described in detail.

Bed, Breakfast & Bike/Mid-Atlantic, by Alex and Nancy May ($12.95). The Mays take you from the Finger Lakes and Adirondacks of New York, through Pennsylvania's Amish Country and Bucks County, "down the shore" in New Jersey, Delaware, Maryland and Virginia and into the hills of West Virginia.

RIDE GUIDE/North Jersey/2nd Edition, by Dan Goldfischer ($10.95). Cycle past the hills, farm valleys, lakes and rivers of the northwest part of New Jersey, as well as quiet suburban streets and large mansions closer to the metropolis. The new edition includes off-road rides as well.

RIDE GUIDE/Central Jersey, by Dan Goldfischer ($9.95). Explore the horse country of Far Hills and Somerset County, the Princeton area, along the Delaware near New Hope and Lambertville, hilly Hunterdon County and the Jersey Shore from Sandy Hook to Island Beach.

RIDE GUIDE/South Jersey, by Alex and Nancy May ($9.95). Pedal the flat end of the state, including the Pine Barrens, Shore areas from Long Beach Island to Cape May, pretty riverside jaunts along the Maurice River and old-time oyster villages of the Delaware Bay.

RIDE GUIDE/Hudson Valley and Sound Shore, by Dan Goldfischer and Melissa Heffernan ($7.95). Features Westchester County, back-country Greenwich, views of Long Island Sound and the Greenwich Rivers, and the pretty (but hilly) Hudson Highlands by West Point and Bear Mountain.

Please send me these books:

Qty.	Title	Amount
___	_____	___
___	_____	___
___	_____	___
	Shipping	$2.00
	N.J. residents please add current sales tax	___
	Total	___

Send books to:
Name: _____

Address: _____

City/State/Zip/Country: _____

(If this is a gift, please note your name and address as well). Make checks payable to White Meadow Press (out of U.S., please pay with U.S. funds drawn on U.S. bank). Send coupon and payment to: **White Meadow Press, P.O. Box 56, Boonton, NJ 07005.** Sorry, no C.O.D. credit card or billed orders.